The Cardinal O'Hara Series
*Studies and Research in Christian Theology
at Notre Dame*

Volume IV

The Cardinal O'Hara Series

STUDIES

AND RESEARCH

IN CHRISTIAN

THEOLOGY

AT NOTRE DAME

VOLUME FOUR

A TRILOGY ON WISDOM
AND CELIBACY

J. Massingberd Ford

UNIVERSITY OF NOTRE DAME PRESS · 1967
NOTRE DAME · LONDON

NIHIL OBSTAT: Joseph Hoffman, C.S.C.,
    Censor Deputatus
IMPRIMATUR: ✠ Leo A. Pursley, D.D., LL.D.,
    Bishop of Fort Wayne-South Bend

    May 31, 1967

DILECTISSIMO SPONSO

HOC PIGNUS AMORIS

AMORE

DEDI

ACKNOWLEDGEMENTS

The author is grateful to the editors of the following journals for allowing her to use material which appeared in the following articles:

New Testament Studies:

"Levirate Marriage in St. Paul," 10 (April, 1964), pp. 361–365.
"St. Paul, the Philogamist (1 Cor. vii. in Early Patristic Exegesis)," 11 (July, 1965), pp. 326–348.
"The Meaning of Virgin," 12 (July, 1966) pp. 293–299.

Journal of Theological Studies:

"Hast Thou Tithed Thy Meal and Is Thy Child *Kosher?* (1 Cor. x. 27ff. and 1 Cor. vii. 14)."

Journal of Ecclesiastical History:

"Was Montanism a Jewish-Christian Heresy?" 17, No. 2 (October, 1966) pp. 145–158.

Novum Testamentum:

"The Parable of the Foolish Scholars (Matt. 25:1-13)" (April, 1967).

Journal of Jewish Study:

"Rabbinic Background to St. Paul's Use of *Hyperakmos"* (Scheduled to appear in a future issue).

PREFACE

Cicero has said "*Nullum enim officium referenda gratia magis necessarium est*" (*De Officiis*, 1, 15, 47) and yet perhaps there is nothing more difficult than the giving of adequate appreciation. My debt to many scholars in diverse fields and of diverse religious persuasions cannot be expressed in a short preface, but I wish to mention particularly the following persons who have helped me. Prof. M. Black has continued his interest in and has accepted my articles for publication in *New Testament Studies*. Dr. J. Crehan, S.J. has given unstintingly of his time and of his encyclopaedic knowledge both while I was a student in London and in my position at Makerere University College. But it is to Prof. David Daube that I owe my present position and my love of Torah and to Prof. W. D. Davies that I owe my appreciation for first recommending "Levirate Marriage in St. Paul" for publication; both have continued to give me encouragement and help. While Prof.

A Trilogy on Wisdom and Celibacy

R. P. C. Hanson guided my first extremely unsure steps in research and gave me the benefit of his precise scholarship and teaching, Mrs. P. Hitchman has taken a continued interest in my thesis and has consulted many and various references for me which were unobtainable in East Africa. Mr. Horton-Smith gave generously of his time to teach me German with constant patience and humor. By taking the bold step of appointing a woman and a Catholic as Lecturer in Religious Studies, Prof. N. Q. King not only enabled me to enter the world of Theology, but he also gave me marvellous encouragement and followed each stage of my work with sound advice and enlightening references; both he and my colleagues in the Department of Religious Studies took upon themselves extra departmental burdens, even to the extent of depriving themselves of opportunity for research, to allow me time to complete this thesis. For my last two years, Dr. A. R. C. Leaney supervised my work and studied my preliminary drafts with meticulous care; in addition he gave me every conceivable help and benefit from his scholarship. The librarians and photographers of Nottingham University gave me express service in microfilming texts. To the members of the Makerere Research Grants Committee who voted me three handsome sums of money to finance my research goes my sincere gratitude. Prof. E. A. Thompson and my former tutors in the Department of Classics accepted a most unlikely student and gave her every attention: without them she would never have entered academic life. Finally I wish to thank the University of Notre Dame Press for accepting this manuscript and for the editorial services of Anne Kozak and Sharon Willy.

Last but not least my mother has followed with unfailing understanding and patience the strange career of her daughter, and as well as giving her financial assistance to continue her work has constantly and tirelessly relieved her of those domestic duties normally incumbent upon an only daughter, which so often stifle creative activity and leave no time or energy for scholarship.

Rosh Ha-Shanah, 1966 (5727)   J. Massingberd Ford

ABBREVIATIONS TO SINGLE TEXTS

Athanasius	*Adv. Arian.*	*Adversus Arianos*
Athenagoras	*Supp.*	*Supplications for Christians*
Barnabas	*Ep. Barn.*	*Epistle of Barnabas*
Clement of Alexandria	*Strom.*	*Stromata*
Diogenes	*D.L.*	*Diogenes Laertes*
Epiphanius	*Pan.*	*Panarion* (Haereses)
Eusebius	*H.E.*	*Ecclesiastical History*
Hermas	*Mand.*	*Commandments*
	Sim.	*Similitudes*
Hippolytus	*Phil.*	*Philosophoumena*
Josephus	*Ant.*	*Antiquities*
Justin	*Apol.*	*Defence* (apologia)
	Dial.	*Dialogue with Trypho*
Juvenal	*Sat.*	*Satire*
Origen	*Ad Rom.*	*On the Epistle to the Romans*
	In Num. Hom.	*Homily on Numbers*
	Lev. Hom.	*Homily on Leviticus*
Philo	*All. Leg.*	*Allegorical Interpretation*
	Cher.	*The Cherubim*
	Hypo.	*Apologia pro Iudaeis*
	Post.	*On the Posterity and Exile of Cain*
	Quod omn.	*Every Good Man is Free*
	Spec. Leg.	*On the Special Laws*
	Vita Cont.	*The Contemplative Life*
Pliny	*N.H.*	*Natural History*

ABBREVIATIONS TO SINGLE TEXTS

Ps. Justin	*De Resurr.*	*Concerning the Resurrection*
St. Ignatius	*Ad Phil.*	*To Philadelphians*
	Ad Poly.	*To Polycarp*
	Smyrn.	*Smyrnians*
Sozomen	*H.E.*	*Ecclesiastical History*
Tertullian	*Ad Ux.*	*To my Wife*
	Adv. Jud.	*Against the Jews*
	Adv. Marc.	*Against Marcion*
	De An.	*Concerning the Soul*
	De Cult. Fem.	*Concerning the Dress of Women*
	De Jejun.	*Concerning Fasting*
	De Mon.	*Concerning Monogamy*
	De Orat.	*Concerning Prayer*
	De Pud.	*Concerning Modesty*
	De Virg. Vel.	*Concerning the Veiling of the Virgins*
	Exhort. Cast.	*Exhortation to Chastity*

ABBREVIATIONS TO BOOKS OF REFERENCE

Arndt and Gingrich	*A Greek-English Lexicon of the New Testament and other Early Christian Literature*, trans. and ed. by W. F. Arndt and F. W. Gingrich from W. Bauer's *Griechisch-deutsches Wörterbuch zu den Schriften des Neuen Testaments und der übrigen Urchristlichen Literatur*, 4th ed., 1949–1952.
BDB	*A Hebrew and English Lexicon of the Old Testament*, ed. by F. Brown, S. R. Driver and C. A. Briggs, Oxford, 1952.
Jastrow, Marcus	*Dictionary of Talmud Babli, Yerushalmi, Midrashic Literature and Targumim*, New York, 1950.
JE	*Jewish Encyclopedia*, ed. by I. Singer and others, 12 vols., New York, 1901–1906.
ODCC	*Oxford Dictionary of the Christian Church*
PGL	*A Patristic Greek Lexicon*, ed. by G. W. Lampe, Cambridge, 1961ff.
S-B	Strack, H. L. and Billerbeck, P., *Kommentar zum Neuen Testament aus Talmud und Midrasch*, Murchen, 1961.
SJE	*Standard Jewish Encyclopedia*, ed. by C. Roth, London, 1959.
LXX	*Septuagint*.

ABBREVIATIONS TO TEXT

ANF	*Ante Nicene Fathers*
GCS	*Griechische Christliche Schriftsteller*
ICC	*International Critical Commentary*
NEB	New English Bible
PG	*Migne Patrologia Graeca*
PL	*Migne Patrologia Latina*
MP Syriaca	*Migne Patrologia Syriaca*
PRE	*Pirke Rabbi Eleazer*
RSV	Revised Standard Version
TB	Babylonian Talmud
TJ	Jerusalem Talmud

ABBREVIATIONS: JOURNALS

BA	*Biblical Archaeologist*
BJRL	*Bulletin of John Ryland's Library*
CBQ	*Catholic Biblical Quarterly*
HTR	*Harvard Theological Review*
JBL	*Journal of Biblical Literature*
JJS	*Journal of Jewish Studies*
JSS	*Journal of Semitic Studies*
JTS	*Journal of Theological Studies*
NTS	*New Testament Studies*
Nov. Test.	*Novum Testamentum*
RB	*Revue Biblique*
Rev. de Q.	*Revue de Qumran*
Rev. d'Hist.Eccles.	*Revue d'Historie Ecclésiastique*
Rev. des Etud. Juives	*Revue des Etudes Juives*
Sci. Eccl.	*Science Ecclésiastique*
Stud. Theol.	*Studia Theologica*
Theol. Lit. Zeit.	*Theologische Literatur Zeitschrift*
VT	*Vetus Testamentum*
Verb. Dom.	*Verbum Domini*

TABLE OF CONTENTS

CHAPTER 1

Prologue

The title "A Trilogy on Wisdom and Celibacy" has been chosen for this monograph to indicate both the scope and limitation of the thesis presented.

The book stands essentially as a thesis and deals with only one aspect of its subject which is divided into three areas. The author's intention is twofold. Firstly, the material was collected and composed while she was pursuing pioneer work in the new Department of Religious Studies in Makerere University College, University of East Africa, under the inspiring and energetic leadership of Professor Noel King. Scholarship in the rapidly developing countries is often restricted by the resources available and in the present case it was decided that the work should take the form of independent criticism of a certain number of original texts and that the material should be channelled in one particular direction. The specific aspect chosen was the "Jewish Influence on Christian Virginity and Continence"; in addition the work was confined to literature normally dated before the death of Tertullian. It was impossible under these circumstances to examine the voluminous literature which now surrounds the discoveries at Nag Hammadi, to read the different theories of "Protean" Gnosticism or to enter into a discussion of the psychology or mysticism of consecrated celibacy. Similarly from the thesis has been omitted any discussion of the Virgin Mary on whom so many notable scholars have written and are still writing with better textual sources at their disposal than could be obtained in East Africa.

Yet the omission of these aspects of celibacy, however important they may be, has caused one to concentrate upon and to isolate the very beginnings of celibacy and hence to see it unembellished by either orthodox or unorthodox developments. Therefore, in this thesis four basic assumptions, by which the study of celibacy in the first three centuries of the Christian Era has been governed, will be challenged. These are as follows:

(a) that the words *bethulah*, *parthenos* and *virgo* denote *virginitas intacta*;[1]

(b) that from earliest times these terms in the Latin and Greek tongue were used as frequently, or more frequently, in reference to women than to men;[2]

(c) that the earliest written record of Christian teaching on celibacy is found in I Cor. 7 and that the recipients of this epistle included a group of women (and possibly men) celibates who had already established themselves in the newly founded Christian community at Corinth;

---

[1] It is regretted that the fascicle of the *Patristic Greek Lexicon*, ed. by Prof. G. W. H. Lampe, Oxford, 1961 ff., which contains the entry *parthenos* has not appeared yet.

[2] I shall discuss the use of *eunouchos* below p. 130.

(d) that numerous Christians contemporary with Jesus (for example, St. Paul and some of the disciples) and also those of the subapostolic age embraced lives of consecrated celibacy.[3]

These assumptions have had far-reaching consequences. Scholars, who have found that celibacy was apparently embraced with such alacrity and fervor by the early Christians, have naturally sought to find the origin of such a practice in the contemporary environment. Because they realized that voluntary celibacy was wholly repugnant to the non-sectarian Jew and that there is no definite allusion to ascetic virginity in the Old Testament,[4] they have turned to study the influence arising not only from sectarian Judaism but also from pagan ascetic practices and the mysteries and taboos concerning sexual life which cling to so many shades and varieties of religion.[5] Such is the view expressed unreservedly by Fehrle[6] and with greater discrimination by the *auctores diversae* (–i) in *Mystique et Continence*.[7] It is in this way that Christian celibacy be-

[3] For example, St. John the Evangelist is supposed to have left his bride at the marriage feast of Cana! Cf. G. B. Gartner, *The Theology of the Gospel of Thomas*, London, 1961, pp. 251 f.

[4] The story of Jephthah's daughter (Jud. 15:29–40) is the most outstanding example of the repugnance toward childlessness and virginity; see Lucien Legrand, *The Biblical Doctrine of Virginity*, London, 1963, pp. 19 f., 27. I cannot agree, however, with the same author who seems convinced about the celibacy of Jeremiah (*op cit.* pp. 22, 25–30, 35, 37, 151), *vide infra*, p. 24.

[5] See, for example, Ottakar Nemeck, *Virginity, Pre-Nuptial Rites and Rituals*, New York, 1958. This book, while accumulating much evidence from a wide range of periods and geographical areas, lacks much critical discrimination and is completely innocent of any reference to texts used or sources of information obtained in ways other than reading. In addition the Rabbinic and Christian references are unreliable.

[6] Eugen Fehrle, *Kultische Keuscheit in Altertum*, Giessen, 1910.

[7] *Mystique et Continence, Les Etudes Carmelitaines*, Paris, n. d.

came associated in the minds of many with the Gnostic
movement and its aberrations concerning marriage and
procreation; thus Christianity was accused of a misogyny
which is wholly inconsistent with Jesus' attitude toward
women. Yet it must be borne in mind that the early
Fathers unanimously contrast pagan celibacy, which they
attribute to the demons, and Christian celibacy; moreover
they repudiate without hesitation all Gnostic errors with
regard to sex. One must take their assertions as they stand
and impute neither arbitrariness, delusion nor dishonesty
to these early Christian writers:[8] it is not reasonable to
suppose that they were concealing facts of which they
were ashamed.

A more healthy attitude has arisen since the "rediscovery"
of the Rabbinic background of the New Testament.
Studies in this direction encourage one to assume with
greater confidence that the influence of Judaism on the
Church extended until at least the mid-second century and
in some areas very much later than this.[9] The maintenance
of Jewish influence with regard to celibacy means that
from the very beginning of the study, one must assume
the absolute sanctity of marriage and the sacredness of
the *copula carnalis.* Fehrle[10] makes the error of imputing
to the Jews the thought that legitimate coition between
husband and wife was polluting whereas in actual fact,
coition for the Jews was "unclean" in the sense of "holy"
rather than "unclean" in the sense of "polluted."[11]

---

[8] See, for example, St. Clement of Alexandria, *Stromata*, Book III.
[9] It must have existed until the revolt under Bar Cochba in 132 A.D.
[10] Fehrle, *op. cit.*, p. 33.
[11] In T.B. Yeb 16a, one reads that the menstrual blood of an Israelite
woman is unclean, that of a heathen woman is clean, that is the
Israelite blood is holy, not polluted.

Celibacy among the Jews cannot be proven before the time of R. Akiba and Simeon ben Azzai,[12] and the history of both these men evidences a balanced view of "celibacy" —a "celibacy" perfectly in accord with that of Christianity, completely alien to that of paganism, wholly abhorrent of any taint of superstition or idea of pollution of sex.[13] It is from this period and milieu that the author wishes to challenge the assumptions cited above [14] and from which she believes that the origins of Christian celibacy can be traced.

This essay, therefore, will study first the meaning of "virgin" and will question whether the people of the first three centuries A.D. denoted by this epithet were necessarily unmarried. When the meaning of "virgin" is determined, it will be necessary to examine the concepts "virginity" and "continence" in the Old Testament, in the Jewish sectarians and among the second-century Rabbis. This examination of biblical and extra-biblical material will form the necessary background for a fresh exegisis of the New Testament material with particular reference to I Cor. 7. It may be that this chapter is wholly devoted to a discussion of certain Jewish legal controversies concerning marriage and widowhood and that it does not refer to celibacy at all.

The sifting of the evidence in this sphere suggests that it would be fruitful to investigate the Greek Fathers: firstly, to see the use they make of I Cor. 7 and secondly, to discover whether there is any evidence that there existed a

[12] They were both Third Generation Rabbis i.e., from A.D. c. 120–140 (see Mishna, trans. by H. Danby, reprint, London, 1958, Appendix III, p. 799).
[13] *Vide infra*, p. 49f.
[14] P. 2f.

class or community of "virgins" as a recognized body in the Church.

The only Latin Fathers treated are Minucius Felix and Tertullian. It has been necessary to prepare research into Tertullian's attitude toward chastity by a rather long digression on the Jewish background of the Phrygian New Prophecy and also of Tertullian's Montanist work. However the purpose of this digression is to explain the peculiarity of Tertullian's views on purity and to demonstrate that they are isolated from the traditional Jewish and Christian views.

In the last chapter the author attempts to answer two questions. Firstly, why celibacy became practical and popular in the mid-third century. This question anticipates the objection of those who may complain that the author makes it arise much later than the time ordinarily assigned to it. She argues that the lapse of time between the fragmentary teaching of Jesus on this subject in Matt. 19:11, 12 and the time in which it was put into practice allows an interval in which pagan and heretical ideas can recede, Christian doctrine and practice can be formulated and the necessary social and political adjustments come into being. Secondly, it is necessary to give some account of the relationship between wisdom and continence. The question which must arise is "What connection is there between Philo's Platonic allegorization of marriage and virginity as education in wisdom and between the practical tenets of the Rabbinic scholars who were regarded as "bridegrooms of Torah" and who embraced long periods of continence?" I shall discuss whether it is necessary to seek for a mutual relationship or to regard them as separate entities — mutually opposed like the Alexandrian and Antiochene schools of philosophy and theology.

The restriction of this book to one aspect of celibacy does not mean that the author denies all Gentile influence or that she overlooks the valuable work of scholars who have presented exactly the opposite view, especially of those who have stressed Hellenistic influence on consecrated virginity. In the author's view this latter influence is undeniable in every aspect of Christianity even if one glances but momentarily at, for example, the Pseudepigraphal literature, the fragments of mystical nature found at Qumran or Samaritan literature or at the artistic motifs found in Jewish synogogues and burial places both within Palestine and in the diaspora.[15]

It is hoped, therefore, not that this interpretation of celibacy will supercede others, but rather that to some extent it will modify them and lead readers to consider that the pedigree of consecrated celibacy has a purer strain than misogamous gnosticism.

[15] E. g. The Synagogue of Capernaum and the necropolis of Beth Shearim.

CHAPTER 2

The Meaning of Bethulah, Parthenos *and* Virgo

Wh+++en one approaches the study of celibacy in the early Church, it is important to discover whether the term "virgin" was used in the modern sense of *virginitas intacta* or whether a more ambiguous sense prevailed. Cruden,[1] Young,[2] A. Richardson,[3] Kittel,[4] Hastings,[5] Lewis and Short,[6] and Arndt and Gingrich[7] all refer to the sense of

[1] Alexander Cruden, *Concordance of the Old and New Testaments*, rev. ed., London, 1863.

[2] R. Young, *Analytical Concordance to the Holy Bible*, London, 1953.

[3] Alan Richardson, *A Theological Word Book of the Bible*, London, 1957.

[4] Gerhard Kittel, *Theologisches Wörterbuch zum Neuen Testament*, Stuttgart, 1957.

[5] J. Hastings, ed., *Dictionary of the Bible*, 5 vols., Edinburgh, 1898–1902.

[6] Charlton T. Lewis and Charles Short, *A Latin Dictionary*, Oxford, 1890.

[7] W. F. Arndt and R. W. Gingrich, *A Greek-English Lexicon of the New Testament and other early Christian Literature*, translated from W. Bauer's *Griechisch-deutsches Wörterbuch zu den Schriften des*

virginitas intacta and to the spiritual and metaphorical application of the word. For this reason one should examine certain texts in Hebrew, Greek and Latin which suggest that "virgin" does not always denote a man or woman who has abstained from coition.

A. BETHULAH

One may cite three texts from the Hebrew Canon where *bethulah* appears to be used ambiguously.

(1.) Gen. 24:16 "The maiden was very fair to look upon, a virgin, whom no man had known . . .".

והנער טבת מראה מאד בתולה ואיש לא ידעה

The LXX reads:

ἡ δε παρθένος ἦν καλὴ . . . παρθένος ἦν, ἀνὴρ οὐκ ἔγνω αὐτὴν

(Some authorities omit παρθ. ἦν. This may indicate that they were exercised about the apparent tautology.)

(2.) Lev. 21:3 " . . . or his virgin sister (who is near to him because she had no husband; for her he may defile himself)."

ולאחתו הבתולה הקרובה אליו אשר לא היתה לאיש לה יטמא:

The LXX reads:

καὶ ἐπ' (ἀδελφῇ) παρθένῳ τῇ ἐγγιζούσῃ αὐτῷ τῇ μὴ ἐκδεδομένῃ ἀνδρί . . . .

These two texts may contain mere repetitions which are introduced for the sake of emphasis, but the third text cannot be explained away in this manner.

Neuen Testaments und der übrigen Urchristlichen Literatur, 4th edition, Chicago, 1949–1952.

(3.) Joel 1:8 "Lament like a virgin girded with sackcloth for the bridegroom of her youth."

אלי כבתולה הגרת שק על–בעל נעוריה

The LXX reads (significantly):

θρήνησον πρὸς με ὑπὲρ νύμφην . . . ἐπὶ τὸν ἄνδρα αὐτῆς τὸν παρθενικόν . . . .

Here one must note the following points:

(a.) the virgin must be married, for the word בעל means lord or husband and the verb means "marry, rule over" [8] in Biblical Hebrew; this is confirmed in Midrashic Hebrew where the verb is frequently used for engaging in coition; [9]

(b.) the LXX translates "husband of her youth" τὸν ἄνδρα . . . τὸν παρθενικόν;

(c.) the LXX also clearly indicates that *bethulah* is a married woman by translating this word as νύμφη;

(d.) Joel describes a theme which is common in Rabbinic literature, namely the great sorrow felt over the loss of one's first wife: such sorrow does not seem to have been customary after the loss of a fiancée;

(e.) an unconsummated marriage would be extremely rare among the Jews; I can trace only one reference to such a marriage, namely the case where the *kethubah* [10] was not able to be paid and therefore the husband refrained from coition. [11]

It would seem, therefore, that *bethulah* points to the age of the girl rather than to the fact that she is unmarried.

---

[8] See BDB under בעל.

[9] See M. Jastrow, *Dictionary of Talmud Babli, Jerusahalmi. Midrashic Literature and Targumin* (New York, 1950) under בעל.

[10] *Kethubah* means the wife's marriage settlement or the marriage contract determining the mutual obligations between the two parties.

[11] In the circumstance the wife praised her spouse for his continence.

This interpretation is strengthened if one turns to the Mishna where there is found a definition of *bethulah*:

> Who is accounted a *bethulah*, she who has never yet suffered a flow, even though she was married . . . (Nidd. 1:4.)

אירו היא בתולה כל שלא ראתה דם מימיה אעפ שנשואה . . . . .

The criterion of virginity lies in the age of the girl rather than in the fact that she has abstained from coition. This is further attested in Nidd. 5:7–9:

> "What are the tokens in her that she has past her girl-hood?" (כיו שבגרה) R. Jose, the Galilean says, "when the wrinkle appears beneath the breast. . . ."[12]

This sense of *bethulah* lies behind the Rabbis' discussion of Lev. 21:14 in Yeb. 59a, 60a and 60b:

> *And he shall take a wife in her virginity* excludes one who is adolescent, whose virginity is ended; so R. Meir, R. Eleazar and R. Simeon permit the marriage of one who is adolescent. On what principle do they differ? — R. Meir is of the opinion that *virgin* (בתולה) implies even one who retains some of her virginity; *her virginity* (בתולה) implies only one who retains all her virginity; *in her virginity* implies only [when previous intercourse with her took place] in the natural manner, but not when in an unnatural manner. R. Eleazar and R. Simeon, how-ever, are of the opinion that *virgin* would have implied a perfect virgin; *her virginity* implies even [one who re-tains] only part of her virginity; *in her virginity* implies only one whose entire virginity is intact, irrespective of whether [previous intercourse with her was] of a natural or unnatural character (Yeb. 59a).
>
> . . . R. Meir stated *virgin* implies even [one who retains]

[12] Cf. Jastrow, *Dict. Tal.* under בתולה.

some of her virginity.[13] . . .—It was required, because
it might have been assumed that the expression of *virgin*
shall be deduced from virgin elsewhere (Deut. 22:28
dealing with a case of outrage); as there it refers to a
na'arah only, so here also it refers to a *na'arah* only . . .
(Yeb. 60a).[14]

The most compelling reference to a "married virgin" is
found in Hag. 14b which reads:

Ben Zoma was [further] asked: May a high priest marry
a maiden who has become pregnant? Do we [in such a
case] take into consideration Samuel's statement, for
Samuel said, (15a) I can have repeated sexual connections without [causing] bleeding; or is perhaps the case
of Samuel rare? He replied: the case of Samuel is rare,
but we do consider [the possibility] that she may have
conceived in a bath [in which male seed had been cast].

The point under discussion here was whether a high priest,
who should marry a virgin only, could marry a girl who
claims that despite her pregnant condition she is still a
virgin, or, if he married her without knowing of her pregnancy and actually found her to have signs of virginity,
but subsequently learned that she was pregnant before the
marriage, may she remain his wife? The result of the discussion was to pronounce that exceptional cases could not
be taken into account and that the marriage would be
illegal.

These texts illustrate again that virginity is lost at adolescence; that it is possible to be a "partial virgin" or a
"perfect virgin" and that the manner of coition effects the

[13] Virgin includes one who is adolescent (*Yeb.* 60a p. 401, note 1).
Cf. L. Epstein, *Marriage Laws in the Bible and Talmud*, New York,
1942, p. 332.
[14] *Na'arah* is a girl of the age of twelve to twelve and one-half.

state of virginity. These facts show that the criterion of virginity did not lie entirely in the unbroken hymen.

The text from Deut. 22:28 is interesting in that *na'arah* and *bethulah* occur in apposition:

> If a man meets a virgin who is not betrothed and seizes her . . .

כי–ימצא איש נער בתולה אשר לא ארשה ותפשה. . .

The LXX reads:

> *Ἐὰν δέ τις εὕρῃ τὴν παῖδα τὴν παρθένον ἥτις οὐ μεμνήστευται . . . .*

But it would seem that the translation "who is not betrothed . . ." is not sufficient. The Hebrew reads *na'arah* which the LXX translates *παῖς*. A *na'arah* is a girl of the age of twelve to twelve and one-half; after that she became a *bogoreth* and gained her majority with the legal privileges and consequences which this entailed.

The discussion of virginity was not only of academic interest. This is seen in the regulations in the Talmud concerning minors, who, even though they have had *coitus*, were regarded as virgins when it involved settling dowry questions or giving exception to the levirate obligation, cf., for example, Keth. 10b:

> A maiden—her *ketubah* is two hundred zuz and a widow—a *maneh*. *A maiden who is a widow*, or divorced, or a *haluzah*[15] from betrothal her *kethubah* is two hundred zuz and there lies against them the charge of non-virginity,

and Keth. 11b

> . . . A virgin, who was a widow (בתולה אלמנה), a divorcee,

[15] *Haluzah*, a woman who performed the ceremony of *halizah*, that is taking off the shoe of the brother of a husband who has died childless and is not going to take her to wife. For a description of the ceremony, see Epstein, pp. 122–130.

or a haluzah from marriage — her *kethubah* is a *maneh* and there is with regard to them no charge of non-virginity.

Here one sees clearly that there can be such a state as "virgin-widowhood" and such a person as a "virgin-widow."

A girl was also regarded as a virgin if she had been a proselyte, a captive or a slave and coition had taken place at an early age (three years and one day) when the hymen might grow again (Keth. 11b) or if a small boy, a minor, came in unto her (Keth. 11b). Again this is not a case of *virgo intacta*.

Further a girl might be accounted both a widow and *virgo intacta* when she was betrothed rather than married and her spouse either died or divorced her. This is evident both from the fact that a bill of divorce was necessary to break off a betrothal (Kidd. iii.8) and that a girl could be betrothed *in utero*:

> So, too, if a man said to his fellow, "If thy wife bears a female child let it be betrothed to me", her betrothal is not valid. But if his fellow's wife was with child and her pregnancy was manifest, his words hold good, and if she bore a female child her betrothal is valid.

In view of the above quotations it seems, therefore, that the phrase "virgin-widow" is not a contradiction in terms but denotes a special class of widow. The general conclusion of the above discussion appears to be that *bethulah* is not confined to an unmarried girl.

B. PARTHENOS

The Jewish writers had at least three words to describe young girls:

bethulah,   one who had not reached adolescence;
na'arah,   one whose age was between twelve and twelve
             and one-half years;
bogoreth, one whose age was twelve and one-half years
            plus one day and onwards.

The Greek *parthenos* possibly covered all these meanings. This is indicated in Liddel and Scott's latest edition of the *Greek Lexicon*[16] where they supply two references where the noun *parthenos* refers to women generally.[17] An even more interesting reference is given with regard to the adjective παρθένιος. For ὁ παρθένιος means "the son of an unmarried girl" and παρθένιος ἀνήρ means "the husband of maidenhood, the first husband" (Plu., *Pom.* 74). There is a similar use of παρθένικος which is found on sepulchral inscriptions quoted by Leon.[18] Agentia is said to have lived with her virgin husband (μετὰ παρθενικου) for nine years; the same is said of Rebecca who died at the age of forty-four. A woman called Irene is recorded as having been the "virgin wife" of a certain Clodius. These tombs are certainly Jewish, for both Hebrew and Greek are inscribed on them and it would seem that *"parthenos"* and its cognates here are used in the same sense as the Hebrew *bethulah,* that is it does not refer to *virginites intacta.* Indeed, it renders the same meaning as the phrase τὸν ἄνδρα . . . τὸν παρθενικόν translating בעל נעורית in Joel 1:8.

---

[16] Henry George Liddell and Robert Scott, *A Greek-English Lexicon,* a new edition revised and augmented throughout by Henry Stuart Jones, reprint, Oxford, 1953.

[17] *Il.* ii. 514; *Pi. P.* iii. *S. Tr.* 1219, *Ar Nu.* 530. (The references in Sophocles appear a little ambiguous.)

[18] H. Leon, *The Jews of Ancient Rome,* Philadelphia, 1960, p. 230. Prof. Leon comments that it is interesting that the words *parthenikos* and *virginius* are apparently used of a spouse who had not been married before.

It is possible that the same meaning can be assigned to the masculine noun *parthenoi* in Rev. 14:4: these may refer to men who have only been married once, that is only had the wife of their youth.[19]

The verb παρθενεύω is found in this sense in Pseudo-Justin (*De Resurrection* 3):

καὶ τοὺς ἄρρενας δὲ τοὺς μὲν ἀπ᾿ ἀρχῆς παρθενεύοντας ὁρῶμεν τοὺς δὲ ἀπὸ χρόνου.

One could not be *virgo intacta* except "from the beginning." These must be people who embrace virginity from the beginning or continence after a certain time.

The passages quoted from the Mishna and Gemara could explain St. Ignatius' strange phrase παρθένους λεγόμενας χήρας (*Smyrn.* 13).[20] Lightfoot[21] writes an interesting note on the phrase in which he carefully distinguishes the widows from both deaconesses and virgins and states that it is improbable that virgins were admitted into the order of widows. Lightfoot himself offers a "wholly different interpretation." Quoting Clement of Alexandria (*Strom.* vii.12):

[19] Daube has observed in a conversation with me that the evil impulse is not used with reference to legitimate relationships between husband and wife. He remarks that "one passage in Genesis Rabba ix. might seem to tend that way, where Samuel bar Nehman says that even the evil impulse is in a way good since, but for it, man would neither build a house, nor marry nor beget children nor trade." But the Rabbi (Prof. Daube thinks) is here referring not to the sexual aspect but to possessiveness, greed, competition. This is clear from the various activities listed, and it is confirmed by the quotation of Ecc. 4:4, "The jealousy between man and his fellow." Cf. Epstein, *Sex Laws and Customs in Judaism,* New York, 1948, p. 14.

Indeed, the present author would add that the abundant evidence that marriage was regarded as a divine ordinance (for example, see Keth. 62b) and *coitus* a sacred act would argue against the use of μολύνω with reference to marriage, especially in a book as patently Jewish as the Revelation of St. John.

[20] J. B. Lightfoot, *The Apostolic Fathers*, vol. II, London, 1889.

[21] *Ibid.*, pp. 322–324.

"...For he who has felt desire and has gained mastery over himself, like the widow also, becomes virgin again through chastity... they are virgins who abstain from evil..."[22] and Tertullian (*De Virg. Vel.* 10) who says of widows: "...*malunt enim Deo nubere; Deo speciosae, Deo sunt puellae*," Lightfoot suggests that the meaning is "I salute those women whom, though by name and in outward condition they are widows, I prefer to call virgins, for such they are in God's sight by their purity and devotion." Lightfoot then cites Jahn and Renan with reference to a similar idea about virgin-widows.[23]

It would seem, however, that a less complicated explanation can be offered if one takes the phrase παρθένους λεγόμενας χήρας in the same sense as the "virgin-widow, virgin who is divorced, virgin who is a *haluzah*" quoted on page 13f. (*supra*). St. Ignatius would then be referring to a girl who was widowed before puberty, or who was divorced before puberty, or a widow from betrothal, not from marriage. Perhaps he would designate her a "so-called widow." In this case she forms a contrast to the ἡ δὲ ὄντως χήρα (genuine widow) to whom three references are made in I Tim. 5:13–16 and who there is contrasted with "young widows." The criterion of a genuine widow seems to be that the woman

(1.) has no relatives to care for her (*v.* 5);
(2.) gives herself to prayer (*v.* 5 cf. Luke 2:37f);
(3.) has reached a certain age (*v.* 9 cf. Nidd. 1:5);
(4.) has become known for her good works and has brought up children (*v.* 10).

The "virgin-widow" could hardly qualify on any of these

[22] Trans. by H. Chadwick, *Alexandrian Christianity*, vol. II, London, 1954.
[23] Lightfoot, *op. cit.*, p. 324.

points and certainly not the last. The regulations found in
I Tim. are close to those discussed in the Talmud, where
the children by the widow's deceased husband's other wife
are required to give her maintenance (Keth. 103a). Here
the *kethubah* ceases to be incumbent on the "heirs" if the
widow has lived in her husband's house for twenty-five
years (Keth. 104a) during which time she "has sufficient
opportunities of rendering favours" and in Keth. 96a
where it is required of her that "All manner of work
which a wife must render to her husband, a widow must
render to the orphans, with the exception of serving one's
drinks...." The "orphans" are those "who are legally
bound to maintain her."[24]

The above examination of the Greek *parthenos* suggests
that like *bethulah*, it does not always refer to *virginitas
intacta.* Indeed, perhaps in many contexts a less misleading
translation of both the Hebrew and the Greek might be
"youth" or "youthfulness" with no reference to marriage.
The LXX uses παρθενεία, παρθενία for בתולים in Deut.
22:14, 15, 17, 20 and Jud. 11:37, 38, where this is a clear
case of *virginitas intacta.*

But παρθενία is also used to translate נעורים which in Si.
15:12 ὡς γυνὴ παρθενίας προσδέξεται αὐτόν... in Jer. 3:4
οὐχ ὡς οἶκόν με ἐκάλεσας καὶ πατέρα καὶ ἀρχηγὸν τῆς παρθενίας σου and in the Hebrew

‎... הלוא מעתה קראתי לי אבי אלוף נערי אתה:

can be simply translated "husband of her youth," i.e.,
taken when she was young.[25] (Cf. Joel 1:8 cited above
p. 10).

Parthenos is also used to translate עלמה in Gen. 24:43 and
Is. 7:14. In the latter case it is worth commenting that

[24] Keth. 96b, p. 612, note 8.
[25] Whether she was adolescent or not.

little is gained by arguing from the text of Is. 7:14 and the fact whether he used בתולה or עלמה with reference to the birth of the Messiah. Whether he used בתולה or עלמה casts no light on the *virginitas intacta* of the Mother of Jesus: this could only become clear from the historic event of the virgin conception and birth of the Savior.

C. THE LATIN *"VIRGO"*

The ambiguity of "virgin" also exists in the Latin. That Tertullian uses the term "*virginitas*" in the sense of "continence" is clearly seen from the following passage in *Exhort. Cast.* 1:4:

> "*Prima species est virginitas a nativitate; secunda virginitas a secunda nativitate, id est a lavacro, quae aut in matrimonio purificat⟨o⟩ ex compacto aut in viduitate persereverat ex arbitrio: tertius gradus superest monogamia, cum post matrimonium unum interceptum exinde sexui renuntiatur.*"

It is noticeable that throughout Tertullian's works on chastity, he rarely alludes to *virginitas intacta* and when he does so he uses the word "eunuch," for example, with reference to Christ: "... *ipso Domino spadonibus aperiente regna caelorum, ut et ipso spadone, ad quem spectans et apostolus propterea et ipse castratus continentiam mavult*" (*De Mon.* 3:1)
and
"... *se spadonatui obsignant...*" (2 *De Cultu Fem.* 9:7). In other instances Tertullian qualifies "*virginitas*" with some emphatic epithet, for example, "... *etiamsi totam et solidam virginitatem sive continentiam Paracletus hodie determinasset...*" (*De Mon* 3:2).
Tertullian also uses "*virgo*" (feminine) in the same sense

as *bethulah* as defined in Nidd. 1:4 (see p. 11). In *De Virg. Vel.* 9:2–4[26] he says:

> ... Ex illo enim virgo desinit ex quo potest non esse. Et ideo penes Israel illicitum est ad virum tradere nisi post contestatam sanguine maturitatem; ita ante hunc indicem acerba res est. Igitur si tam·diu virgo quamdiu acerba est, desinit virginem cum matura cognoscitur, et ut non virgo iam legi applicatur, sicut et nuptiis .... Si congressio viri mulierem facit, non tegantur nisi post ipsam nuptiarum passionem.

The translators of this passage[27] have pointed to Deut. 22:13–21 as the background of Tertullian's statements here, but Nidd. 1:4, 5, 7 and 8 appear to give a much better understanding of this text, for it refers to the puberty of the girl, not to the shedding of blood when the hymen is broken.

Another passage from Tertullian seems to be a direct commentary on the situation depicted by I Timothy and Ignatius and to be explained by the legal phrase "a virgin who is a widow" occurring in the Talmud (see p. 13f. *supra*). Here Tertullian fulminates against a "virgin" who has insinuated herself into the rank of widows, but the phrase "*virgo vidua*" suggests that she is not unmarried, not *virgo intacta*:

> Plane scio alicubi virginem in viduatu ab annis nondum

[26] This treatise deals with the question whether unmarried women should cover their heads. Among the Jews a woman covered her head when she married, but there does not seem to be any regulation about unmarried women. Under these circumstances it seems that Tertullian may well be dealing with people who were influenced by Judaism and he rebuts them by appealing to Jewish law. *Vide infra*, pp. 165 ff. on the Jewish communities at Carthage. cf. Epstein, *Sex Laws... Judaism*, pp. 36–52.

[27] A. Roberts and J. Donaldson, *Ante-Nicene Fathers*, New York, 1890.

viginti collocatam (cf. Nidd. 5:9). Cui si quid refrigerii debuerat episcopus, aliter utique salvo respectu disciplinae praestare potuisset, ne tale nunc miraculum, ne dixerim monstrum, in ecclesia denotaretur, virgo vidua, hoc quidem portentuosior, quod nec qua vidua caput texit, utrumque se negans, et virginem, quae vidua deputetur, et viduam, quae virgo dicatur (*De Virg. Vel.* 9:2).

Then Tertullian alludes to I Tim: 5 and the qualifications for introduction into the rank of widows:

> ...*ad quam sedem praeter annos sexaginta non tantum univirae, id est nuptae, aliquando eliguntur, sed et matres, et quidem educatrices filiorum, scilicet ut* ... (*ibid* 9:3).

Here then is the בתולה אלמנה translated into Latin. Lightfoot[28] quotes Seneca *Agam* 196 which has the same phrase as Tertullian but in the plural:

> *An te morantur virgines viduae domi?*

The above study of the terms *bethulah, parthenos* and *virgo* suggests that these terms are not confined to people who have never been married but, on the other hand, can be used of minors who have married and been widowed and, on the other, of people who have only taken one spouse during their lifetime. It is, therefore, with this double meaning of "virgin" that we should approach the study of "celibacy" among the Jewish sectarians, in the New Testament and the early Christian Communities.

A Note on ἀεὶ παρθένος

It is interesting to note that Philo distinguishes between "virgin" and "ever-virgin." He speaks of Sarah changing

[28] Lightfoot, *op. cit.*, p. 324.

from womanhood to virginity "after the custom of women had ceased" and he says that this means that her passions were perfectly controlled then.[29] But he prefers Rebecca to Sarah and calls her "ever-virgin."[30] One cannot build up a linguistic argument from the use of these terms, but they do suggest that he could think in terms of "partial" virginity and "perfect" virginity. In *Cher.* 50, Philo says that God makes the soul turn from being a woman to become a virgin again, "for He takes away the degenerate and emasculate passions which unmanned it and plants instead the native growth of unpolluted virtues. Thus He will not talk with Sarah till she has ceased from all that is after the manner of women (Gen. 18:11), and is ranked once more as a pure virgin." His thought seems to be that this type of wisdom and spirituality is a return to the innocence and unemotionalism of childhood.

However, a more concrete use of ἀεὶ παρθένος is found with reference to the Virgin Mary. The use of this epithet for her suggests that the writers (cited in the notes) did not feel that *parthenos* alone was an adequate term for her. The *Patristic Greek Lexicon* only refers this term to Mary.[31]

[29] *Cher.* 49 f.

[30] *Post.* 134.

[31] Peter of Alexandria, a fragment of his *Chronicon Paschale PG* 18:517; Athanasius, *Adv. Arianos* 2:70; *PG* 26:296 and on Ps. 84:11 *PG* 27:373. Epiphanius, *Haer.* 39:10 G.C.S. 31:79. Didymus Alex. *De Trin.* I:27, *PG* 39:404. One awaits eagerly the fascicle containing *pas* and *parthenos* to seek the use of *panparthenos* for Mary. One must also take account of the numerous references to αεἴ παρθένος in the early liturgies; again this epithet is usually confined to the Virgin Mary (see, for example, *Liturgy of St. James*; F. E. Brightman, *Liturgies Eastern and Western.* Oxford 1896, p. 35) but cf. p. 141 *infra*).

CHAPTER 3

Celibacy in the Old Testament

I

Both the story of Jephthah's vow and the consequent sacrifice of his unmarried daughter[1] and the mourning over her virginity and the anxiety of Sarah,[2] Rachel[3] and Hannah[4] over their childlessness and the regulations concerning levirate marriage[5] in order to secure progeny indicate clearly enough the attitude of the people of the Old Testament toward marriage and fertility. In the Old Testament itself, in the early Midrashim[6] and in the Pseud-

[1] Judges 11:29–40.

[2] Gen. 16:1–2.

[3] Gen. 30:1. "... and she (Rachel) said to Jacob, 'Give me children, or I shall *die*!'"

[4] 1 Sam. 1.

[5] Deut. 25:5–10.; L. M. Epstein, *Marriage Laws in the Bible and Talmud* (Camb., Mass., 1942) gives a fuller account and discussion of the Levirate, pp. 77–144. He discusses the difference between Deut. and Leviticus and Numbers on this point (see esp. pp. 81 ff. on Lev. 22:13; Num. 27:8–11; Lev. 18:16 and 20:21.)

[6] *Vide infra*, pp. 130–136 for a fuller discussion of the Midrashim.

epigrapha there is no reference to anyone's embracing a life of voluntary celibacy.[7] While some scholars[8] have suggested that Jeremiah remained unmarried, it seems unlikely that this was so. Even if one considers that the prophet was called at a very early age[9] this would not preclude marriage, for boys were probably married between the ages of twelve and eighteen. The text which has led scholars to presume that Jeremiah was a celibate is found in chapter 16:1–4 לא-תקה לך אשה ולא-יהיו לך בנות... במקום הזה. But the command from Yahweh here is qualified three times, twice with the phrase במקום הזה and once with the phrase בארץ הזאת. The command seems to require only a temporary continence;[10] this may be further corroborated by Jeremiah's later purchase of the plot of land[11] which suggests that he intended to settle down to a normal life. For the Hebrew, this would be a married life with children. It seems to the present writer that the injunction

---

[7] Although, for example, *Test. Naph.* 8:8 advises temporary abstinence.

[8] For example, Lucien Legrand, *The Biblical Doctrine of Virginity*, London, 1963, pp. 22, 25–30, 35, 37, 151.

[9] As implied in Jer. 1, esp. *v.* 5.

[10] In Jer. 16:2 the Hebrew "take" may be used in the sense of "cohabit." I should not wish to press this point, but the Hebrew for "marry" and "have legitimate coition" is often synonymous (for example, the verb בעל). "Take" in the sense of "select" a wife would be "to betroth." As a prophet (*vide infra*, p. 54), it is more likely that Jeremiah abstained from coition after marriage than abstained from marriage altogether. One finds no reference in Jewish or early (i.e., of the first three centuries) Christian literature which suggests that he remained a celibate, not even in the *Apocryphon of Jeremiah*, (Woodbrooke Studies, *Editions and Translations of Christian Documents in Syriac and Garshuni* by A. Mingana. With Introductions by Rendel Harris, Fasc. 2 (i) *A New Jeremiah Apocryphon*, p. 329–395). Cf. Kidd. 9a. Contrast p. 141, *infra*.

[11] Jer. 32:6–15.

in c. 16 is merely a prophetic *ôth* of temporary duration as was the wearing of the yoke.[12]

However, there seems to be a case of voluntary continence[13] where Judith is concerned. In Judith c. 8 she is described as a widow; moreover the text implies that her husband died a sudden death and that she was left a young and beautiful widow. Her mourning was conducted with severe asceticism, but *v.* 4 informs one—almost with a touch of surprise—that " . . . Judith his relict was a widow now three years and six months"[14] and later in *v.* 8 one is assured that no one "spoke an ill word of her." Judith's case seems to be an exception for normally a brother would inherit his sister-in-law on the death of her husband and raise up children to him: the reader is not told that Judith had children although one learns (*v.* 7) that "her husband had left her great riches, and very many servants, and large possessions of herds of oxen, and flocks of sheep." Even if a widow had children, it is probable that, if she were young, she would remarry for the sake of her reputation (cf. *v.* 8). Judith is not mentioned in the Midrash Rabbah, the Mishna or the Gemara.[15] Thus Judith's case seems to be an exception; in view of the doubtful historicity of the

[12] Jer. 28:10.

[13] The writer uses the term "continence" to denote abstinence of a married person or widow and "celibacy" and "virginity" to denote a *virgo intactat(–us)*

[14] Judith 8:4. A widow was normally required to wait three months before remarriage in case she was pregnant, (L. M. Epstein, *Marriage Laws... Talmud*, pp. 303–305). It seems that Judith might have been subject to levirate marriage for the reasons for levirate were not only to "raise up seed" but also for the purposes of dealing with the estate as well as for protection of the widow; Epstein, *ibid.*, pp. 77–93.

[15] The Judith mentioned in Talmud is Judith the wife of R. Hiyya (Kidd. 12 b).

book, one cannot build any strong argument from her conduct to assert that voluntary widowhood for young women was regarded as a meritorious state.[16]

The only specific requirement for continence in the Old Testament is found in the event of the Holy War. This is mentioned 1 Sam. 21:5 and David's answer indicates that this was a customary[17] discipline along with fasting[18] and a state of ritual holiness.[19] These rules apparently apply only to the combatants, for it would appear that the noncombatants were sorted out before the approach of the enemy.[20] Certain people were exempt for economic and social reasons—the betrothing of a wife,[21] the building of a house,[22] the planting of a vineyard: the fainthearted[23] and young men and women did not approach the battlefield lest they should distract the warriors.[24] Yet, perhaps one cannot say that these rules about continence, whether from women, prostitutes or boys, were anything but temporary and expedient measures and one would hesitate to class them with continence embraced for a purely spiritual motive, although the secular and the religious in Israel

[16] Cf. the attitude in 1 Cor. 7 and in 1 Tim. 5:9–16.

[17] The RSV translates: "of a truth women have been kept from us *as always* when I go on an expedition...." *V.* 5b indicates that abstinence was also observed on a journey.

[18] Cf. Max Weber, *Ancient Judaism*, London, 1952, p. 91; De Vaux, *Ancient Israel*, London, 1961, p. 258 f., p. 262.

[19] Jos. 3:5; De Vaux *op. cit.*, p. 258.

[20] Y. Yadin, *The Scroll of the War of the Sons of Light*, Oxford, 1962, pp. 63–79. This gives a detailed discussion of the rules concerning conscription. He distinguishes between those who were eliminated before the battle and those who might be eliminated at the last moment because of certain unfitness. See also pp. 290–291.

[21] Deut. 24:5; Deut. 20:7.

[22] Deut. 20:5.

[23] Deut. 20:6 and 8. Cf. 1 Macc. 3:56.

[24] Yadin, *op. cit.*, pp. 71–72 and pp. 290–291.

were so closely interwoven that it is difficult to separate the one from the other except in thought. The fact that a newly married man was given exemption from war service for a whole year indicates that the duty of marriage had priority over the duty of fighting.[25]

There is one more point to be considered before embarking upon a discussion of the practices of the Jewish sectarians: this is the matter of the Nazarite vow. One must ask whether wartime continence was in any way connected with the Nazariteship. M. Weber[26] states:

> Midway between such individual heroes appearing as ecstatic berserk and the acute collective ecstasy of the war dance stands the ascetic training of a body of professional warriors for war ecstasy. Such is, in vestige indeed to be found in the "Nazarites", the "separated ones". Originally they were ascetically trained warrior ecstatics who—in the single certain tradition—left their hair unshorn and abstained from alcohol and originally, also, from sexual intercourse.

Weber[27] suggests that Samson may have perished because he allowed himself to break the sexual taboo: it would seem, however, that he did not take the sexual taboo very seriously and the prohibition of coition for the Nazarite does not occur in the regulations concerning this vow, for example, in Numbers 6. Therefore the continence of the warriors must be incumbent on them because of their fighting, not because of their Nazariteship. When the

[25] Cf. Luke 14:20 "And another said, 'I have married a wife and therefore I cannot come'" (to the great banquet).

[25] Weber, *op. cit.*, pp. 94–95.

[27] *Ibid.*, p. 95.

[28] That is by perpetuation of the family, see De Vaux *op. cit.*, pp. 41–42.

Nazarites cease to fight, there is no trace of abstinence from coition.

To conclude, one must admit that the Old Testament does not give any clear indication of virginity or continence embraced for its intrinsic value and this is entirely consonant with the idea that children were perhaps the greatest gift from God, not only procuring for man a type of immortality but also in the hope of gaining for the Israelite people a human Messiah born of woman.[29]

II SECTARIAN MOVEMENTS

The Essenes

The whole question of Essene celibacy is complex. Philo speaks of one group of Essenes[30] who were celibate,[31] but Josephus[32] distinctly says that some were married.[33] He informs one that Essenes married in order to preserve the race[34] and that some of them regarded the renunciation

[29] In Jewish belief there does not seem to be any belief in a Messiah born from a virgin. For the most useful book on the Jewish beliefs concerning the Messiah, see J. Klausner, *The Messianic Idea in Israel*, London, 1956. Klausner is careful to distinguish between a personal Messiah and general Messianic expectation, e.g., p. 9.

[30] Besides noting the different groups of Essenes, one must consider the different periods and developments of Essenism; see J. T. Milik, "Esseni et historia populi Judaici," *Verb Dom.* 35 (2/1957) pp. 65–74. One cannot lightly disregard scholars, e.g., John Bowman, "Contact between the Samaritan Sects and Qumran," *VT*, VII (1957) pp. 188–189, who suggest that the Essenes may be a branch of the Samaritans.

[31] Philo, *Hypo.* 11, 14 (Loeb edition).

[32] Josephus, *B.J.* II, 121, 160. Para. 121 refers to the "unmarried Essenes" and para. 160 to the "marrying Essenes."

[33] Cf. Hipp., *Phil.* 11, 28.

[34] Cf. G. Vermes, "Essenes, Therapeutae, Qumran," *The Durham*

of marriage as equivalent to murder.[35] Yet this stress on marriage is also accompanied by an intensification of the sanctity of marriage and an emphasis on discipline in legitimate sexual relationships by restricting them to the primary object of marriage, that is the procreation of children. Hippolytus[36] notes that they subjected their wives to three years probation and required them to bathe and wear linen garments;[37] Josephus[38] says that they abstained from their wives during pregnancy: this is supported by Philo's statement that they only cohabited for the purpose of procreation, which purpose could not be present if the woman was known to be pregnant.[39]

Univeristy Journal, vol. 52, no. 3; New Series, vol. 21, no. 3 (1960) p. 101 who refers to Dupont-Somers' suggestion that *genos* might be translated "mankind" rather than "race" (Josephus, *B.J.*, II, para. 121 and 160).
[35] Cf. the Rabbinic expression, "the man who does not marry is like one who sheds blood" Yeb. 63 b.
[36] Hipp., *Phil.*, c. 23; cf. also Hipp., *Ref. Haer.*, 9:18–28.
[37] Josephus, *B.J.*, 2:161 tells us that they abstain while their wives are pregnant, but he also gives us a very interesting sideline on "purification" after coition. "Even after the legitimate relations of husband and wife ablutions are required. For the Law regards this act as involving a partition of the soul [part of it going] into another place, for it suffers both when being implanted into bodies and again when severed from them by death. That is why the Law has enjoined purifications in all such cases"; (note c [*ibid.*] reads "There is transference of part of the soul or life-principle from the father," *Contra Apion* 2, p. 374, Loeb edition). This means that coition was regarded as "unclean" in the sense of "holy." The menstrual blood of an Israelite was regarded as unclean, that of a Gentile was clean. Cf. *Tobit*, c. 8 and also Ned. 11 (vows against taking baths). Cf. Num. Rabb., 10:14 where the king's wives abstain from the king when they are pregnant but Bathsheba forced her way in (p. 353, n. 1, *ibid.*) because "cohabitation in the last three months is beneficial to the embryo."
[38] Josephus, *B.J.*, 2:161.
[39] Cf. note 37 *supra*.

In view of this evidence with regard to marriage, one must approach Philo's statement[40] about celibacy with some reservation. He states:

> Furthermore they eschew marriage (γάμον παρητήσαντο) because they clearly discern it to be the sole or the principal danger to the maintenance of the communal life, as well as because they particularly practise continence (ἐγκράτειαν). For no Essene takes a wife ('Εσσαίων γὰρ οὐδεὶς ἄγεται) because a wife is a selfish creature....[41]

However, immediately before this statement one reads:

> The old men, too, even if they are childless (οἱ δὲ δὴ πρεσβῦται, κἄν εἰ τύχοιεν ἄτεκνοι) are treated as parents of a not merely numerous but very filial family....

If we consider this statement in the light of another in ibid. 11, 3:

> ...no Essenes are mere children nor even a stripling or newly bearded... ('Εσσαίων γοῦν κομιδῇ νήπιος οὐδείς, ἀλλ' οὐδὲ πρωτογένειος ἢ μειράκιον) but full grown and already verging on old age... nor led by the passions..., τέλειου δ' ἄνδρες καὶ πρὸς γῆρας ἀποκλινόντες ἤδη ... μηδ' ὑπὸ τῶν παθῶν ἀγόμενοι...

one is led to the supposition that the Essenes probably married and produced children according to the Jewish law either before they joined the community or at

[40] Philo, *Hypo.*, 11, 14.

[41] It is important to note the tense of παρητήσαντο perhaps denoting "punctiliar" instantaneous action in past time. That they rejected marriage is not to say that they never married and this is further supported by the fact that Plutarch (2. 206a) speaks of παρ. γυναῖκα meaning "divorce a wife" (trans. by Liddell and Scott) Cf. παρ. οἰκέτην "dismiss him," *D. L.* viii. 82 and παρ. τινὰ τῆς οἰκίας *Luc. Abd.* 19. I suggest that one should translate "the Essenes have given up their married life."

an early stage in their membership of the community.[42] Josephus' evidence for celibacy among the Essenes is equally open to question and seems to be consonant with Philo's ideas and the interpretation of them. Josephus states[43] that "they disdain marriage but they do not, indeed, on principle, condemn wedlock or the propagation of the race . . .

(καὶ γάμου μὲν παρ᾽ αὐτοῖς ὑπεροψία . . . τὸν μὲν γάμον καὶ τὴν ἐξ αὐτοῦ διαδοχὴν οὐκ ἀναιροῦντες . . .)".

One notes that both the word παρήτησαντο used by Philo and the word ὑπεροψία used by Josephus are mild words especially when they are contrasted with καταφρονηταὶ which is used with reference to riches.[44] Josephus gives the same reason as Philo for the Essene "disinclination" for marriage, namely a prejudice against women. Smith[45]

[42] Cf. the useful information which Black gives in chapters III and IV of his work, *The Scrolls and Jewish Origins*, Edinburgh, 1961.

[43] Josephus, *B. J.*, 2:120, 121.

[44] *Ibid.*, para. 122.

[45] Kevin Smyth, "The Dead Sea Scrolls and Christianity: Ten Years After," *Studies*, 50 (1961) p. 37. Brownlee (*The Meaning of the Qumran Scrolls for the Bible*, New York, 1964, pp. 80–81) gives a further, yet similar, reason for Jewish asceticism. "The real reason for Essene asceticism, I believe, is related to the idea that sexual intercourse is defiling. . . . A few Essenes, according to Josephus, married, doing so out of this sense of duty" (sc. to propagate the human race). "Nevertheless, according to the Old Testament, he who would be cultically clean for participation in rites and festivals or for close contact with the numinous or holy must be free from this defilement. Purifying baths and refraining from the conjugal relationship were necessary preparation on the part of the men of Israel at the foot of the Mount of God (Ex. 19:10–15). Similarly David's men were given the sacred bread at the sanctuary of Nob only on condition they had kept aloof from women (1 Sam. 21:4–6). Pharisaic tradition explains that the complaint of Miriam and Aaron against Moses concerning his Cushite wife (Num. 12:1–2) was that he had not been fulfilling the obligation of a husband to her. The reason for such strange asceticism on the part of Moses was that he

suggests that these misogynist commonplaces about the infidelity of women may perhaps be explained "by the way the writers (that is, Josephus and Philo) coloured their Essene history with Greek philosophy: anything which the Greek could dream of, the Jew did much better."

One difficulty which one must face, however, is Josephus' statement [46] that the Essenes adopted other people's children and Pliny's statement that no one is born in the Essene communities.[47] Light is thrown on these statements by a passage in St. Augustine's *De Haer.* 87 (*PL* 42, 47)[48] concerning two Jewish-Christian sects, the Abelonians and the Caelicoles.

---

had to maintain ritual purity in the presence of God with Whom he was in daily communication. Non-marrying Essenes probably believed that in their daily assemblies and sacred repasts their association with the holy was so great that marriage would interfere with their ceremonial fitness." (Midrash Rabba, Ex. Rab. 19:3; Deut. Rab. 11:10; also the Babylonian Talmud, Shabbath 87a, Yebamah 62).

While there is a great deal of truth in this, it is not consistent with the Jewish idea of the sacredness of coition. The crux of the question rests on the definition of "defilement." For the Jews "defilement" would include marrying out of one's class or associating with such people of either sex. Defilement, of course, is ceremonial, not moral. A woman is "defiled" automatically if she is captured and she is not allowed to return to a priest-husband even though she is quite innocent (Epstein, *Marriage Laws... Talmud*, pp. 326 f.). Hebrew terms denoting "defilement" or "uncleanness" must be treated with caution, for one often finds the use of euphemisms or, which is more important, the exact opposite of the word required, e.g., the use of "enemies of Israel" instead of "Israel" is found not infrequently throughout Rabbinic literature. This "uncleanness" may be used for "cleanness"; cf. "the books which 'defile' the hands."

[46] Josephus, *B.J.*, 2:120.

[47] Pliny, *N. H.*, 5:17.

[48] Quoted in M. Simon. "Le Judaise berbere dans l'Afrique ancienne," *Revue d'Histoire et de Philosophie Religieuses*, Tome 26 (1946) pp. 106–107.

These sects imposed on their adepts rigorous chastity:

mais condemnait en même temps le célibat: c'est dans le mariage que les Abélonians observaient la continence. Le groupement se perpétuait par des adoptions: chaque couple recueillait un garçon et une fille, étrangers par naissance à la secte, issue de deux familles différentes et qui, une fois mariés, s'abstenaient comme leurs parents adoptifs de toutes relations charnelles, et adoptaient à leur tour deux enfants.[49]

Thus in this Jewish sect in Africa, one sees ideas similar to those of the Essenes. One must not overlook the fact that the divergent information which is extant about the Essenes may be due to the description of different groups; however the Essenes are said to have been numerous and to have spread over various countries,[50] and, as shall be seen below,[51] Judaistic influence was very strong in Africa. Therefore, it is not wholly improbable that there might be some similarity between the Essenes and the Abelonians; and it would not be temerarious to say that the statements of Josephus, Pliny and Philo are all compatible if the Essenes, like the Abelonians, married, produced two children, entered the community and then bestowed parental care upon children (not their own) adopted by them, just as, according to Philo, the old men "even if they are childless are treated as parents of a numerous but very

[49] Cf. also p. 108 (*ibid.*) where it is remarked that, like the Essenes, they practiced total continence and also adoption, "*à cette seule différence pres-elle n'a pas capitale—qu'ils condemnait le mariage en même temps que la procreation, 'gens in qua nemo nascitur', ainsi les qualifie Pliny* (*Hist. Nat.* V. 17:73, cf. Jose. *B.J.* 2:8, 2)." If one denies absolute celibacy to the Essenes then their similarity with the Abelonians is striking.
[50] See e.g., J. Daniélou, "Eglise primitive et communauté de Qumran." *Etudes* (May '57) pp. 216–235.
[51] *Vide infra*, pp. 165 ff.

34   A Trilogy on Wisdom and Celibacy

filial family." If women were rejected because they broke
up community life perhaps natural children were replaced
by adopted children for the same reason.

Thus one concludes that it cannot be asserted with confidence that any Essenes practiced absolute celibacy although
there is a strong stress on continence and some of them
may have abstained from their wives after a certain age.

The Therapeutae

The other Jewish[52] community which appears to have
practiced celibacy is the Therapeutae. Here one finds men
and women forming one community. They are contem-
platives and they "flee without backward glance and leave
their brothers, their *children*, their *wives*, their parents, the
wide circle of their kinsfolk:[53] . . . φεύγουσιν ἀμεταστρεπτὶ
καταλιπόντες ἀδελφούς, τέκνα, γυναῖκας, γονεῖς, πολυανθρ-
ώπους συγγενείας, φιλικὰς ἑταιρέιας, τὰς πατρίδας, ἐν αἷς
ἐγεννήθησαν καὶ ἐτραφησαν. . . ."[54]

Conybeare[55] suggests that ἐπιμιξία may carry with it the
idea of contagion; and this approximates the idea in the
Essene community where a senior must bathe if touched
by a junior.[56] This may suggest a kind of hierarchy such
as one finds among the Pharisees who formed groups resembling "castes."[57] Both the stress on study and this
separation from "uncleanness" may indicate a Pharisaic

[52] It is generally accepted that this is a Jewish community although
Eusebius, *H.E.*, 2:17 says that they are Christian.

[53] The italics are mine.

[54] Philo, *Vit. Cont.*, para. 18 ff. (Loeb edition). Cf. Luke 14:26.

[55] *Ibid.*, p. 124, note (a).

[56] Josephus, *B.J.*, 3:150, (2:150). Cf. also the grades of *haberim*
among the Pharisees, *infra* pp. 64 f.

[57] See e.g., Max Weber, *op. cit.*, pp. 387, 390, 411, 417.

origin: indeed this might have been the common background of both this community and that of the Essenes,
namely the Diaspora Pharisaic brotherhoods. However,
επιμιξια may be used more in the sense of "forbidden relationships" both inside and apart from marriage. These
people are to "keep *kosher*" within their "caste," (compare
the flight of the Jewish sectarians to the wilderness of
Judaea for similar reasons).

The statement which has led most scholars to conjecture
celibacy for the Therapeutae is Philo's affirmation that
most of the women were "aged virgins" (*γηραιαì παρθένοι*) [58]
who have kept their chastity (*άγνείαν*) "not under compulsion, like some of the Greek priestesses, but of their own
free will in their ardent yearning for wisdom . . ." and for
this reason they have "spurned the pleasures of the body
and desire no mortal offspring."

In view of the above discussion concerning the meaning of
parthenos [59] in general and more particularly of Philo's use
of the same word,[60] one would hesitate to accept the literal
meaning of *parthenos* here. The juxtaposition of *γηραιaì*
and *παρθένοι* and their use in the context of seeking wisdom and discipline over the emotions reminds one forcibly
of Philo's picture of Sarah.[61] Have these ladies, like Sarah
and Rachel, grown young again when they are already old
(i.e., post menopausal) through their pursuit and attainment of wisdom and does Philo argue that they have "no
mortal offspring" in the same way that he argues that
Abraham and Issac did not really have wives but were

[58] Philo, *Vit. Cont.*, para. 68.

[59] *Vide supra*, pp. 14–19 and 21–22.

[60] *Vide supra*, pp. 21 f.

[61] *Cher.*, 49–50 "Thus He (God) will not talk to Sarah till she has
ceased from all that is after the manner of women (Gen. 18:11), and
is ranked once more as a pure virgin."

wedded to virtues?[62] This interpretation is not untenable especially because the word *parthenos* is not used in any description of the Essenes and in this account of the Therapeutae is not used of the men, who are said *to have left their wives*. If the men left their wives, then possibly the women left their husbands and embraced not παρθενία in the modern sense of the word but ἐγκράτεια or continence. Added to this the Therapeutae, like the Essenes and the Abelonians, seem to have had spiritual, adopted relationships as one conjectures from *Vit. Cont.* paragraph 71 which states that services are rendered "by free men who try to serve as to real fathers and mothers." Thus one may conclude that the Therapeutae seem akin to the Essenes in their practice of continence, rather than celibacy.

Qumran

The matter of celibacy among the members of the Qumran community is as complex[63] as that which exists among the Essenes; moreover the question is further complicated

---

[62] *Cher.*, 40 f., the partiarchs have nothing to do with women, for they reject sense; their wives are virtues.

[63] But cf. E. F. Sutcliffe, *The Monks of Qumran* (London, 1960) who finds similarities between Christian monasticism and the Qumran virtues of Poverty, Obedience and Celibacy.

Leaney has placed this idea in a more historical context and expressed it in less Christian terms. In his *Rule of the Community*, London, 1966, pp. 164 f. he says:

> The sharing of property arises naturally from the act of separation from unreformed Israel. As Hengel (*Die Zeloten*, pp. 255 ff.) convincingly explains, the motives are both practical and religious: in 1 Macc. 2:28, Mattathias and his sons have to leave all they possess in order to take to the mountains.... Again 1 Macc. 3:56 gives Judas' venture the character of a holy war (Deut. 20:5–8) implying that all who will follow him must abandon all personal ties with normal life—including wives and possessions....

because the parts of the Qumran literature which are devoted to a discussion of marriage or abstinence may belong to different stages in the development of the sect or may be of a composite nature whose component parts may have differing dates; thus one part may be directed to a certain section of the community while another to one under different discipline and regulations.

Bearing in mind the above considerations one can, nevertheless, make the following observations about celibacy at Qumran.

Firstly there is no formal statement that celibacy should be practiced but there is substantial evidence for the presence of married people: [64]

(a.) boys are enjoined to marry at the age of twenty, not before; [65]

(b.) bone remains indicate that women lived in the camp; women appear to have attended meetings [66] and there

[64] I should note here the precaution expressed by G. H. Hunzinger, "Aus der Arbeit an den unveroffentlichten Texten von Qumran," *Theo. Lit. Zeit*, 85, no. 2 (1960) pp. 151–152 that much of the Qumran material is unpublished and one should not form too simple a view of the sect and its teaching, for example, the eschatology differs in the various scrolls. It seems to the present writer that, if one discovered a library today containing a few books on virginity, one should not immediately conclude that the library was staffed by celibates. Therefore, one should exercise every caution in making dogmatic statements about the practices of the whole community without leaving scope for individual piety and asceticism. Cf. also L. E. Tombs, "Barcosiba and Qumran" *NTS* 4, 1 (1957) pp. 65–17 who suggests that the Dead Sea Scrolls may not be the distinctive teachings of a small community but ideas generally current in the second century. It is for this reason that the author will attempt to compare Montanism and Qumran *infra*, pp. 168 ff.

[65] *Damascus Document*, 1, 9–10 cf. G. Vermes, "Essenes-Therapeutae-Qumran," *The Durham University Journal*, vol. 52, no. 3, New Series, vol. 21, 3 (June 1960) pp. 97–114, esp. p. 110.

[66] J. M. Baumgarten, "On the Testimony of Women in 1 Q S a,"

seems to have been a fund for unmarried women and orphans (*C.D.C.* 14, 13);

(c.) *C.D.C.* 7:6 ff. possibly polemicizes against some who thought that life in the camp should be celibate: "if members of the community happen to be living in encampments, in accordance with a usage which obtains in this country, and if they marry and beget children, they are (in such matters) to follow the precepts of the Law and the disciplinary regulations therein prescribed for the relationship of husband and wife and of *father to child*." Sutcliffe[67] thinks there is an implicit reference to celibacy here, but I would tend to agree with Smith[68] who observes that the camps are contrasted with "cities" and the implication need only be that the Essenes who left the cities should still observe the marriage laws of the sect. Yet it must also be observed that the "disciplinary regulations," especially since they affect the *child* as well as the parents, may suggest similar regulations for the Essenes, Therapeutae and Abelonians concerning adoption for the sake of the community; that is the regulations may concern abstinence from one's wife and exchange of children. The arguments in favor of celibacy for the members of Qumran range round the following facts:

(a.) There is complete silence with regard to women and children in the *Rule of the Community*;

(b.) the *copula carnalis* is forbidden in the "city" of the sanctuary (*C.D.C.* 11:18–12:2);

JBL. no. 76, fasc 4 (1957) pp. 266–269. But see the discussion on the translation and compare P. Borgen, "At the Age of Twenty in I Q S a," *Rev. de Q*. no. 10, Tome 3, fasc. 2 (Mai, 1961) pp. 267–275.
[67] Sutcliffe, *op. cit.*, p. 98.
[68] K. Smyth, *art. cit.*, p. 37.

(c.) women and males under twenty-five are excluded from the camp (*C.D.C.* 25:3–6);

(d.) in *C.D.C.* 4:12–17 there is a possible prohibition against successive polygamy;

(e.) the righteous in the Holy War are associated with angels.

Cross[69] thinks that this is one reason for the continence of members of Qumran: "this is the situation which prompts counsels against marriage, at least for some. In the new age he will live eternally in the presence of the holy ones, the angels of God, and even in the very presence of the Holy God. In this new age the righteous live like angels without need of procreation, and preserve themselves in perpetual 'purity' before the throne of God." Cross also compares Luke 20:34–36; Matt. 22:30 and 19:10–12; Mark 12:25 and 1 Cor. 7.

Leaney has suggested to me that the angels are not only associated with the Holy War and with the future life. Commenting on the sect's connection with the Temple and its desire to replace the defiled Temple and its priesthood with their own priesthood and the service in their "sanctuary," he remarks:

If the whole represents the Temple, the laity represent the sanctuary and the priests of the sect the holy of holies. Further, the priests believed themselves to serve among the angels, and this fellowship with the heavenly company helped to explain the divine character of the knowledge of the cosmos and calendar which they held and which ruled their practice, a practice shared with the angels (see especially 1 Q H 3. 22; 11. 11). The association of angels with priests arises from the convic-

[69] F. M. Cross, *The Ancient Library of Qumran*, the Haskell Lectures, 1956–1957, London, 1958, p. 72 ff. See also pp. 56 ff., pp. 74 f.

tion that the priests are like the angels of the presence in serving "before God...."

Leaney then cites the instance of Gabriel and Zacharias in Luke 1:8–20; both serve "before God," Zacharias (verse 8) (ἔναντι τοῦ θεοῦ) and Gabriel (verse 19) (ἐνώπιον τοῦ θεοῦ).[70]

However, none of this evidence is decisive. One does not know for whom the *Rule of The Community* was written; furthermore the omission of reference to women may be due to the fact that the Jewish law did not impose on a woman any religious obligation which had to be fulfilled at a definite point of time.[71] The *Rule of The Community* may be written only for priests and levites in the community. In this case, the women would not be eligible for this section of the community, and the priests would follow their courses during which time they would be separated from the wives.

Gartner[72] stresses the point that the community at Qumran was founded on the notion that the members were the true Temple and that its nucleus was formed of priests from the Old Temple. Hence "priestly marriage was 'hedged about' by a multitude of restrictions..." (*ibid.* p. 1).

The exclusion of women and men under twenty-five may

---

[70] Leaney, *op. cit.*, pp. 94 f.

[71] Kidd. 29 a "... The observance of all the positive ordinances that depend on the time of year is incumbent on men but not on women.... The observance of all the negative ordinances, whether they depend on the time of year or not, is incumbent both on men and on women, excepting the ordinances 'Thou shalt not mar [the corners of thy beard]' and 'Ye shall not round [the corners of your heads]', and 'Thou shalt not become unclean because of the dead'".

[72] Bertil Gartner, *The Temple and the Community in Qumran and the New Testament*, Cambridge, 1965.

only be an application of the martial discipline which eliminated the less suitable for battle.[73] The age of twenty-five gives the young men time to fulfil their obligation of marriage (from the age of twenty) and then to be ready for battle. As young married people they would be exempt from military service.[74] The five years between twenty and twenty-five gives time for at least two pregnancies and therefore the men would fulfil the injunction that they should procreate two children.

The prohibition of *copula carnalis* in the City of Holiness appears to be a provision against *niddah* for priest and warrior. Kosmala[75] thinks that the "City of Holiness" is the community itself, but on the other hand it may only be a section of the community. This continence is probably temporary like that imposed on the priests in Jerusalem during their courses or the same type of regulation which one finds among the Therapeutae for their holy room.[76] One does not know the extent of the prohibition regarding the persons to whom it applied or the area or time to which it was restricted. Indeed, the statement might only be directed toward a prohibition of temple prostitution.[77] The above considerations lead one to endorse Black's conclusions, namely that Qumran monasticism very possibly has its roots not only in the priestly character of the whole movement but also in the Hasidaean warrior's abstention

[73] See Y. Yadin, *op. cit.*, pp. 65–79 and pp. 290–291.

[74] Cf. Deut. 20:7 and also Luke 14:20.

[75] *Hans Kosmala, Hebraer – Essener – Christen – studien vorgeschichte der fruhchristlichen verkundgung*, Leiden, 1959, p. 369 ff.

[76] Philo, *Vit. Cont.*, 3:25 (Loeb edition).

[77] It is known that the official priesthood in Jerusalem was criticized for its Hellenistic and perverted practices (see M. Black, *op. cit.*, p. 32). The statement could, therefore, be merely a regulation for holiness and cleanness before God.

from sexual relations—the revival or perpetuation of ancient Israelite custom.[78]

But neither the priestly or warrior continence was permanent and not even of very long duration. As Smith concludes,[79] celibacy itself, "surprisingly, in the view of Josephus, naturally, in the view of the Old Testament and rabbinic Judaism" is never praised, imposed or stated directly in the Scrolls.

One would conclude, then, that, if abstinence from marriage existed at all at Qumran, it was confined to warriors and priests and was of a temporary nature; it was not embraced for its intrinsic value. It would seem that priestly continence may have been confined to those for whom the *Rule of the Community* was written whereas the *Damascus Document* appears to regulate for men and women who lived a less strict and less *kosher* life and pursued the ordinary affairs of life, such as marriage, commerce, travelling and mingling to some extent with Gentiles. Neither the *Rule of the Community* or the *Damascus Document* appears to envisage "poverty" in the ascetic sense. The "poverty" of the *Rule of the Community* comprises abstinence from other peoples' property as an extension of their personality in order to maintain the purity of the more select community which observed the Rule. The adherents to the *Damascus Document* may well have been a prosperous community, e.g., thriving on the salt trade or agricultural prosperity of the Salt Sea area and it may have been the riches thus accumulated which enabled the schol-

---

[78] M. Black, *op. cit.*, p. 29 f. and p. 83 f. Cf. 1 Sam. 21:4 ff.; Deut. 22 and 24. Cf. also E. Nielsen, "La Guerre considerée comme une religion et la Religion comme une guerre. Du chant de Debora au Rouleau de la Guerre de Qumran?" *Stud. Theol.*, 15 (1961) pp. 93–112.

[79] K. Smyth, *art. cit.*, p. 37.

ars to pursue their studies and writing and which permitted the warriors to entertain thoughts of a large scale
and grandiose war such as is depicted in the War Scroll,
if, indeed, this war is not merely allegorical. The present
writer can see little affinity between the supposed Qumran
"poverty, chastity and obedience" and that of the Christian
monks of the third century C.E.[80]

III CONTINENCE AMONG THE ACADEMICS

It would seem necessary to preface this discussion of
scholastic continence to which one finds references in the
Talmud with a brief outline of the idea of marriage as it
is presented here and elsewhere in the Rabbinic literature.
Celibacy was almost unheard of for the Jew. A word for
"bachelor" does not exist in the Hebrew language and, as
has been seen in the examination of *bethulah*, this word
did not necessarily denote an unmarried woman. In fact
the Hebrew had little use for such words.[81] The first precept of the Pentateuch[82] bade men "Be fruitful and multiply"[83] and the Rabbis[84] laid down the injunction that
men should marry by the age of about eighteen,[85] although

[80] The section on celibacy among the Essenes and at Qumran should
be compared with Abel Isaksson, *Marriage and Ministry in the New
Temple*, Lund, 1965. Dr. Isaksson in pp. 45–65 has come to similar
conclusions, although independently of the present writer's.

[81] For the reason that marriages were contracted at an early age and
betrothals could be arranged before the birth of the child. Kidd. 3:5.
[82] Gen. 1. 28.

[83] Yeb. 6:6; cf. also G. F. Moore, *Judaism in the First Centuries of
the Christian Era*, 3 vols., Cambridge, Mass., 1932, vol. 2, pp. 119 f.
[84] It is striking that the subject of continence rarely occurs in the
Midrashim (except the case of Moses [Ex. R. 19:3, Deut. R. 9:10]).
[85] Kidd. 29b–30a "Raba said, and the School of R. Ishmael taught
likewise: Until the age of twenty, the Holy One, blessed be He, sits

approximately two years grace was allowed for the purpose of study.[86] Yet marriage could be preferred to study;
this is illustrated by such stories as that of the son of
Rabbi:

> It was agreed that he should spend twelve years at the
> academy. When the girl was led before him he said to
> them, "Let it be six years". When they made her pass
> before him [a second time] he said, "I would rather
> marry [her first] and then proceed [to the academy]."
> He felt abashed before his father, but the latter said to
> him, "My son, you have the mind of your creator; for
> in Scripture it is written first, 'Thou bringest them in
> and plantest them' and later it is written, 'And let them
> make Me a sanctuary, that I may dwell among them'."
> The son had the "mind of his creator" because he was
> influenced by affection to shorten the courting interval
> and to hasten the marriage day just as the Holy One
> hastened the day of His union with Israel.[87]

One can compile an impressive collection of Rabbinical
sayings about the man who does not marry: (1.) "R. Jacob:
One who has no wife remains without good, and without a
helper and without joy, and without a blessing, and without atonement";[88] (2.) "He is not a whole man";[89] (3.)

---

and waits. When will he take a wife? As soon as one attains twenty
and has not married; he exclaims, 'Blasted be his bones' (29a). 'This
is disputed by the Tannaim,' 'Train up a youth in the way he should
go', (Prov. 22:6 i.e. marry him). R. Judah and R. Nehemiah (differ
thereon). One maintains (Youth means) between sixteen and twenty-
two; the other affirms, between eighteen and twenty-four" (Kidd.
30a).

[86] See Keth. 61b and also the stories related in Keth. 62b.
[87] Keth. 62b.
[88] Gen. R. 17:2.
[89] *Ibid.*

"He is like one who sheds blood";[90] (4.) "He diminishes the likeness of God in him";[91] (5.) "He withdraws the *Shekinah* from Israel."[92] Additionally bachelors were even precluded from certain occupations, such as elementary teaching and tending cattle,[93] and the court could compel a man to marry.[94]

It is disputed whether a woman was under an obligation to marry[95] but one can find no example of a woman who embraced voluntary celibacy or even postponed marriage for the purposes of study.[96] The sayings of the Rabbis

[90] Yeb. 63b.

[91] *Ibid...* and diminishes the Divine image.'

[92] *Ibid.* 64a "Our Rabbis taught: And when it (the Ark) rested he said: 'Return, O Lord, unto the ten thousands and thousands of Israel', (Num. 10:36), teaches that the Divine Presence does not rest on less than two thousand and two myriads of Israelites. Should the number of Israelites happen to be two thousands and two myriads less one, and any particular person has not engaged in the propagation of the race, does he not thereby cause the Divine Presence to depart from Israel. Abba Hanan said in the name of R. Eliezer: He deserves the penalty of death; for it is said, *And they had no children,* but if they had children they would not have died. Others say: He causes the Divine Presence to depart from Israel; for it is said, *To be God unto thee and to thy seed after thee*; where there exists 'seed after thee' the Divine Presence dwells [among them]; but where no *seed after thee* exists, among whom should it dwell! 'Among the trees or among the stones?'."

[93] Kidd. 82a.

[94] *JE* under 'marriage.'

[95] See the discussion in Yeb. 65b and 66a where the question is not decided.

[96] One must not forget the great women scholars among the Jews, for example, Beruriah, the wife of R. Meir, whose interpretation of a point in Torah was accepted even though all the male scholars had originally thought differently, (G. F. Moore, *op. cit.*, vol. 2, p. 128 f.). Even so some seem to have been commended for their generosity in allowing their husbands to absent themselves for the honor of the Torah, Keth. 62b; cf. also Hag. 129 (n.s.) On scholarship for women, cf. Epstein, *Sex Laws and Customs in Judaism*, New York, 1948, pp. 81–98.

point to the desirability in all things that a woman should marry and have children[97] and a man was advised to marry his daughter to his slave rather than leave her single[98] and to sell a scroll of the Torah rather than allow want of a dowry to prevent the marriage of his daughter.[99] There was also a special fund for orphan girls that they might be assisted with their trousseaux; in the matter of alms giving girl orphans were given priority over boys.[100] Furthermore the sacred and obligatory character of coition is obvious from Rabbinic writings. Coition was as sacred a duty as unchastity was the work of Satan.[101] Some teachers required scholars to perform their marital duty every Friday night.[102] The story is told of Judah, the son of R. Hiyya, who was accompanied by a pillar of light (probably an allusion to the *Shekinah*) when he returned from the school to fulfil this duty. On one occasion, engrossed in his study he forgot. "Not seeing that sign R. Jannai said to those [around him] 'Lower his bed, for had Judah been alive he would not have neglected the performance of his marital duties'." The same passage suggests that Rabbis who neglected this duty died before their time. Indeed, on the whole, the Rabbis did not approve of as-

[97] Cf. Keth. 64a, "I wish to have a staff in my hand and a spade for my burial" (i.e., a son to provide for her when alive and when dead). Cf. for example, the proverb, "A women prefers one *kab* with frivolity to ten *kab* with abstinence" (cf. Sotah 20a, 21b). The meaning of this is that a woman prefers a poor living in the enjoyment of the company of her husband to a more luxurious one in his absence.

[98] See pp. 97 f., *infra* for the question of marrying a slave.

[99] A. Cohen, *Everyman's Talmud*, London, 1961, p. 162.

[100] *Ibid.*, p. 172.

[101] Cf. Kidd. 81b.

[102] Keth. 62b. This section also mentions the belief that early death was due (sometimes) to neglect of this duty.

ceticism[103] and the character of vows taken by Jews is very different from those prevailing among the Christians in later times.[104] Very often they were taken in anger, for example when a man vowed not "to benefit from the object of his displeasure, or forbade the latter to benefit from him."[105] Some Rabbis completely condemned vows.[106] Furthermore vows taken with a good intention of honoring God were normally akin to the Nazirite vow which is treated at length in the tractate *Nazir*. By this vow a man, woman or slave undertook three things:

  (a.) not to cut any hair;

  (b.) not to drink wine or eat the fruit of the vine;

  (c.) not to become defiled by contact with the dead.

But these vows were rarely perpetual and they contained no reference whatsoever to abstinence from cohabitation.[107] Further, Nazarite vows—with rare exceptions—

[103] See the Introduction to TB, vol. III, *Nedarim*, p. 11. and also G. F. Moore, *op. cit.*, p. 263 ff., especially the quotations on p. 265, "A vow of abstinence is an iron *collar* (such as is worn by prisoners) about a man's neck; and one who imposes on himself a vow is like one who should find such a *collar* lying loose and stick his own head into it"; TB Ned. 9., para, 1 f.; 41b, line 62. This is very close to 1 Cor. 7:35... οὐχ ἵνα βρόχον ὑμῖν ἐπιβαλω...). Cf. also C. G. Montefiore and H. Loewe, eds., *A Rabbinic Anthology*, London, 1938, p. li. and chapter 25, and Lewis Browne, *The Wisdom of Israel*, London, 1960, p. 192 f.

[104] To say that there were "vows" of virginity from earliest times and to quote 1 Cor. 7, seems to be an anachronism, see "Vows" ODCC.

[105] Introduction to TB, vol. III, Ned., p. 11.

[106] See Ned. 9a.

[107] The vows of marital abstinence seem to be among those taken in anger and the regulations about the frequency of coition militate against such vows of abstinence taken for the honor of God. Further one reads in Ned. 14a, "He who says to his wife, 'Behold! Thou art unto me as my mother' etc.—Said Abaye: His words are of no effect by Biblical Law, yet absolution is required by Rabbinical

disappeared after the second Temple period possibly because of the difficulty of fulfilling the sacrificial obligations
after breaking the requirements of the vow and at the
termination of the period.[108]

Not only are these points very important for the study of
celibacy among the Jewish sectarians and the Pharisaic
scholars, but also they are significant in treating early
Christian celibacy.

Yet, even if one cannot trace a practice of "vows" of continence, it cannot be denied that the Talmud witnesses the
priority of study over marriage—the only reason for which
the Talmud allows delay in marriage. Usually the marriage was postponed to the age of twenty,[109] but at times
there seems to have been an even longer postponement.[110]

Laws...." A fuller opinion on the subject is given in Ned. 15b,
p. 41, "If one say to his wife, '*Konam* if I cohabit with you', he is
liable to [the injunction] he shall not break his word. But he is obli-
gated to her by Biblical law, as it is written, 'her food, her raiment
and her marriage rights he shall not diminish' (Exod. 21:10). How
then can he free himself by a vow? It means that he vows, 'The pleasure of cohabitation with you be forbidden me': thus he surely denies
himself the enjoyment of cohabitation," (note 8 *ibid.*: hence his vow is
valid, since it falls primarily upon himself). "For R. Kahana said
[If a woman says to her husband] 'Cohabitation with me be forbidden to you', she is compelled to grant it, since she is under an
obligation to him. [But if she say] 'The pleasure of cohabitation with
you be forbidden me' he is forbidden [to cohabit] since one may not
be fed with what is prohibited to him."
[108] SJE under "Nazarite." Compare also Isaksson, *op. cit.*, pp.
155–201 where there is some convincing exegesis concerning Christian Nazarites and prophets and prophetesses.
[109] Cf. p. 37 f., *supra* on Qumran and delay of marriage until the age
of twenty.
[110] Cf. also the regulations about the interruptions of study on
account of works of mercy, e.g., a funeral or wedding; it should not
be interrupted unless there are insufficient numbers of people in
attendance, (*Ab. R.N.*, II, 8, 11b).

This dispensation for the sake of the Torah was also
granted with reference to the duty of coition incumbent
on married people. The Mishnah and Gemara lay down
precise rules concerning the frequency of coition, " . . .
every day for them that are unoccupied; twice a week for
labourers; once a week for ass drivers; once every thirty
days for camel drivers; and once every six months for
sailors. So, R. Eliezer."[111] Abstinence was only permitted
(apart from that caused by a particular occupation) for
one to two weeks; thus "If a man vowed to have no intercourse with his wife, the School of Shammai says: [She
may consent] for two weeks, and the School of Hillel says:
For one week [only]."[112] Yet in spite of this a more gen-
erous dispensation was given to scholars—"The Disciples
[of the Sages] may continue absent for thirty days against
the will [of their wives] while they occupy themselves in
the study of the Law; and labourers for one week."[113]
It would seem that this type of dispensation for scholars
was gradually extended subject to permission being granted
from their wives. By the second century C.E. three notable
examples exist of Rabbis who absented themselves from
their wives for a number of years in order to give more
time and energy to the Torah. The first example is the
famous Rabbi Akiba[114] who gained permission from his
wife to be away for twelve years but on his return he heard
the good woman remark that she would grant him another
twelve years if necessary and he immediately departed for
another twelve years. R. Akiba, of course, would require

[111] Keth 61b to 62b may be compared with this where the details of
these points are disputed.
[112] Keth. 5:6.
[113] *Ibid.*
[114] Keth. 62b.

this long period for his extensive travelling necessitated by his collecting material for Mishna. His wife's generosity was rewarded by the number of disciples who were attracted to her husband.[115]

The daughter of R. Akiba "acted in a similar way [as her mother had done towards R. Akiba] towards Ben Azzai," her husband. "This is an illustration of the proverb: 'Ewe follows ewe; a daughter's acts are like those of her mother'." This text suggests that Ben Azzai was married but spent years away from his wife in order to devote himself to study and teaching. However, in Sotah 4b there is a suggestion that he was a celibate: "Each of the teachers defined the duration [of coition] from his own experience. But they included Ben Azzai who was unmarried:—If you wish I can say that he had married and separated [from his wife]. . . ." Another text also seems to reprimand the Rabbi for celibacy: "They said to Ben Azzai: Some preach well and act well, others act well but do not preach well; you, however, preach well but do not act well: Ben Azzai replied: But what shall I do, seeing that my soul is in love with the Torah; the world can be carried on by others."[116] It is conjectured that Ben Azzai was married but had no child,[117] for it is highly unlikely that a Rabbi should be unmarried.

Hananiah ben Hakinai also separated from his wife for twelve or thirteen years while he studied with R. Akiba and when he returned home he did not recognize his

[115] Yeb. 62b, "It was said that R. Akiba had twelve thousand pairs of disciples. . . ." Both R. Akiba and Simeon ben Azzai belong to the third generation of Rabbinical teachers (C.E. 120–140).

[116] Yeb. 63b.

[117] Consideration of all these texts convinces me that one cannot assert that Ben Azzai was a celibate (in the sense of *virginitas intacta*). Cf. Tos. Yeb. 8:4 n.s.

daughter who had grown to maturity.[118] Rabin quotes
Baron[119] who asserts that Ben Zoma was not married but
no precise reference for this is given. All these men belonged to the Holy Congregation who entered the garden
of mysticism and they seem to have embraced continence
solely for the love of Torah. Yet in all these stories and
references about the continent Rabbis, the faithfulness
and devotion of the wife is mentioned. There is not a trace
of misogyny or misogamy and the husbands show tender-
ness toward their wives and recognize the duty of procreation. Permission from the Rabbi's wife is always sought
before the Rabbi departs to the academy and procreation
is attended to when he returns.

The Rabbis' attitude to their families is best expressed in
Lev. R. 19:1:

> R. Samuel b. Ammi [further] said: Seeing that the words
> of the Torah require to be attended to early at dawn and
> late in the evening, whence will one's livelihood come,
> [even as it is said]. "Who shall provide for the raven his
> food," when his young ones cry unto God, and wander
> for lack of food? This implies: If a man does not show
> himself as cruel towards himself, his children and his
> household as a raven [to its young], he does not succeed
> in acquiring Torah.

This is explained (*ibid.* note 4 p. 235) because the "rigid
regimentation of oneself and one's family, even to the
point of apparent cruelty, may be indispensible for the
acquisition of a knowledge of the Torah."

---

[118] Keth. 62b. He received a message that she had reached maturity
and left his studies in order to provide a husband for her.
[119] C. Rabin, *The Zadokite Documents*, Oxford, 1958, p. 46. He
quotes Baron (*Social and Religious History of the Jews*, 2nd ed.) but
states that he cannot trace the source.

One may compare this passage with Luke 14:26 (cf. Matt. 10:37–38):

> If any one comes to me and does not *hate* ($\mu\iota\sigma\epsilon\tilde{\iota}$) his own father and mother and wife and children and brothers and sisters, yes, and even his own life, he cannot be my disciple.

The word "hate"[120] is the corollary of "cruelty" in the Midrash quoted above. However, both in the Jewish and Christian practice of "hating" the family, one sees the wives and widows co-operating in the "missionary" work. Some rabbis' wives are reported to have supported their husbands by their own earnings (Tos. Ket. 4:6; Ket. 58b; Pes. 50b) and the early Christian wives seem to have administered to husbands in a similar way.

Motives for Continence

In examining the Old Testament, the Essene community, the Therapeutae and the Qumran communities with reference to the practice of celibacy, one may generally conclude that while absolute celibacy does not seem to be probable, there was a great stress on continence both within marriage and after a period of marriage. One must now examine the motive behind this practice of continence.

The Old Testament motive is sufficiently clear. Continence was an exceptional practice embraced as a military discipline and at least by one prophet, Jeremiah, as a symbolic *ôth*.

On the other hand Essene continence is more complex. It does not seem to be either military or sacerdotal in char-

---

120 "Hate" is probably in the sense of love less.

acter (*vide infra* p. 55). The tenets of the Essenes and their insistence on the purity laws suggest that it might arise from this motive but would not arise from any thought that the *copula carnalis* were intrinsically evil but from the fact that, apparently, the Essenes feared contamination from unfaithful wives[121] and, as has been observed above, this may be due either to a Hellenistic misogyny, or to "keeping *kosher*." There are, however, two other motives which may have influenced Essene continence. The first is their devotion to philosophy which may well have led to continence and disdain of marriage if one is to judge from the views of Philo.[122] Secondly, their ideas on continence may have arisen from their interest in and practice of prophecy. One knows that the Essenes foretold the future from the story of the Essene, Menahem, in Josephus[123] and from this extract one also learns that the friends and disciples who accompanied him were there to learn about foretelling the future.[124] Therefore the Essene continence was possibly a combination of scholastic and prophetic continence which Josephus and Philo misunderstood as misogyny.[125] Nonbiblical Jewish

[121] For the strict rules of conduct between the sexes see Epstein, *op. cit. Sex Laws*, pp. 104–131: any slight infringement would be counted as "unfaithfulness."

[122] *Cher.* 40 f, 47, cf. *Post.* 62 "... Isaac and the other lovers of wisdom and those of like spirit did not know women, but rather rejected sense. Their wives are called women, but are really virtues...."

[123] Josephus, *B.J.*, 15:10 (para. 373 ff.); *B.J.*, 2:159.

[124] The gift of prophecy is attributed to other Essenes, e.g., Judas, a contemporary of Aristobulus I (*Ant.* 13:311). Cf. also *B.J.*, 15, para. 379 where, after saying that Herod held the Essenes in honor, Josephus says, "... many of these men have indeed been vouchsafed a knowledge of divine things because of their virtue."

[125] Although the Pseudepigrapha do not expressly state that continence was necessary for visions and revelations it may be included

tradition is rich in references to continence required or practiced by prophets. Sifre Num. 99 records Zipporah's exclamation when she heard Eldael and Medad had become prophets, "Wo to the wives of these men!" (for this meant cessation from conjugal intercourse). There are also various references to Moses[126] who is said to have separated from his wife for all time after the Revelation on Sinai[127] and the Essenes who had a devotion to the Law would possibly have a deep veneration for Moses. But Moses was not a celibate prior to the Revelation.

Similarly, Therapeutic continence may be due to both prophetic and scholastic continence. Philo states clearly that the women embraced chastity "in their ardent yearning for *wisdom*"[128] and one also knows that the Therapeutae in general were interested in philosophy[129] and in prophecy.[130]

When one considers the Qumran community, many of these motives seem to be present, but the situation in which they are practiced appears to be different. While the question whether the men of Qumran were Essenes or not depends partly on matters outside the scope of this essay, as far as its celibate ideals are concerned the sect of Qumran cannot be too closely approximated to Essene celibacy. The points of difference which are germane to the present study are:

---

under the term "fasting" or the term "affliction." "To afflict the soul" meant to practice abstinence; see, for example, Daube's interesting argument concerning Deut. 26:7, *op. cit.*, pp. 5 ff.

[126] E.g. Exod. R. 19:5.

[127] See further the section on Tertullian *infra*, pp. 197 ff.

[128] Philo, *Vit. Cont.*, para. 68 f.

[129] *Ibid.*, para. 28.

[130] *Ibid.*, para. 84 and 86; cf. para. 25.

(a) The Essenes seem to be philosophers[131] who keep the Mosaic law but tend to be more Hellenistic than Palestinian: there is little stress on either philosophy or Hellenistic Judaism at Qumran.

(b) Philo[132] lays great stress on the Essenes' peacefulness and cheerfulness. This is very different from the martial spirit and fever of urgent expectation found at Qumran.[133] In fact this is a point in favor of Roth's thesis[134] that the Qumran community is a Zealot company whereas Philo especially notes that the Essenes did not make weapons[135] and probably cut themselves off from the means of procuring them by their abstention from commerce through which they could have obtained the necessary materials.

(c) The Essene community does not seem to be essentially sacerdotal in character; indeed, Josephus[136] only once mentions a priest, who merely says grace and Philo[137] informs one that they were "holy, not by offering animal sacrifices, but by sanctifying their minds." At Qumran the relics of animal bones and documents of liturgical character suggest that sacrifices might have been offered. Apparently the Essenes did

[131] Philo, *Quod omn.*, para. 80 says that they abandon the quibbles of philosophy but one feels that their general deportment is rather like an Epicurean community.

[132] Philo *ibid.*, para. 78.

[133] It is, of course, possible that the War Scroll is purely allegorical, but Yadin, *op. cit., passim* shows the accuracy of the details of the military campaign. See also the same author's *The Art of Warfare in Biblical Lands*, London, 1964.

[134] C. Roth, *The Historical Background of the Dead Sea Scrolls*, Oxford, 1958.

[135] Philo, *Quod omn.*, para. 76–78.

[136] Josephus, *B.J.*, 2:131.

[137] Philo, *Quod omn.*, para. 76.

send offerings to the Temple (unlike Qumran); this implies that they themselves did not offer and therefore did not need to prepare for sacrifice by the regulations concerning *niddah* for priests.[138]

(d) The Essenes did not seem to re-enact the Mosaic camp and the second Exodus with quite as much exclusiveness as Qumran although their purity rules were only relaxed when charity demanded.

(e) The information which is possessed about the Essenes only contains one reference to angels[139] and there is no reference to continence with regard to association with them.

(f) The eschatological aspect is almost nonexistent among the Essenes and there does not appear to be an expectation of a Messiah in whose time one might expect the practice of continence.[140]

All these omissions may be due to differences between Hellenistic Judaism and Palestinian Judaism, but they enable one to place Qumran continence in a situation different from that of the Essenes and the Therapeutae. Qumran continence is essentially military, sacerdotal, eschatological and intimately connected with the regulations concerning *niddah*. Further, whereas Essene continence seems to be adopted as a state of life, Qumran continence appears to be a temporary affair.

[138] See G. W. Buchanan, "The Role of Purity in the Essene Sect," *Rev. de Qumran*, 15. vol., 4 fasc. (Oct. 3, 1963) pp. 379–406.

[139] Josephus, *B.J.*, 2:134. p. 142–3.

[140] Cf. e.g., Yeb. 62a, p. 415; Yeb. 63b, p. 426 and Nidd. 13b, p. 89— all of which refer to the belief that the Son of David will not come until all "the souls in *Guf* (*Guf* is the region uninhabited by unborn souls) are disposed of. . . ." Also cf. W. Zimmerli and J. Jeremias, *The Servant of God*, London, 1957, pp. 52–53 where reference is made to the Hellenistic-Judaistic belief in a "collective 'Messianic' expectation"; cf. also K. Klausner, *op. cit.*, p. 9.

It is questionable whether Qumran can be called a prophetic community in the sense that they themselves were
prophets although their interest in prophetic writings is
phenomenal when compared with Philo's and Josephus'.[141] Therefore perhaps prophetic continence did not
affect them personally. However, one passage suggests
that they might have been influenced by scholastic continence. This may be the point behind the strange admoni-
tion at Qumran that a man should not marry until the age
of twenty. Rabin[142] points out that he knows of no other
Jewish literature which enjoins a delay in marriage. The
only postponement of marriage which I know of is for
the purpose of study. The reason given in this passage,
namely that the men should know good and evil, implies
a period of some kind of training or study. This would be
provided by the study of Torah. Therefore, Qumran continence based itself on 1) Old Testament principles and
2) "Rabbinic" dispensations for study.

IV   CONCLUSION

From the above considerations it does not appear that one
can assert that any of these communities practiced absolute celibacy.[143]. The word εὐχνοῦχος and its cognates are
not used and παρθένος only appears once. The words denoting continence are ἐγκράτεια and ἁγνεία both of which

[141] One can readily see this by comparing the biblical references
referred to in the respective authors.
[142] C. Rabin, *Qumran Studies*, Oxford, 1957, pp. 5, 23 ff., 45 ff.,
71 ff. See especially note 8, p. 91. Cf. also P. Borgen, *art. cit.*, where
this statement is related to similar remarks in Aboth 5, 21 and Eccles.
Rabb. 1, 2, para 1.
[143] One must, however, note the present tense in Matt. 19:11, 12
unless Jesus is referring to Himself.

have a wide range of meanings and by no means make clear reference to celibacy or *virginitas intacta*.

It is singularly striking that, although the early fathers make many references to pagan celibates, they never mention Jewish celibates, not even Ben Azzai. It would seem therefore that the Christian ideal of virginity was not attained by the Jews, but as shall be seen, their ascetic principles arising from eschatology, prophetism, pursuit after wisdom, sacerdotalism and Pharisaism did influence Christianity in the direction of absolute celibacy and urge them to put into practice the teaching recorded in Matt 19:11, 12.[144]

---

[144] For further ideas on continence and pursuit after wisdom, see the unpublished dissertation of Richard Baer, *Philo's use of the Categories Male and Female*, Harvard Ph. D. Thesis, 1965, especially pages 23–34 and 84–104. The present author has not sought permission to quote or use the material.

CHAPTER 4

Celibacy in the New Testament

I

The study to this point has suggested that there is no clear reference to the practice of celibacy among peoples of the Jewish faith in the pre-Christian era. Bearing this thought in mind, one must approach the New Testament teaching on marriage and virginity fully aware of the revolutionary character of Christ's advocacy of the celibate life, (Matt. 19:10–12). First, however, it is necessary to examine the earliest written source of teaching on Christian marriage and celibacy, namely 1 Cor. 7. The present writer does not wish to repeat the various exegeses[1] of this passage but rather to attempt a fresh approach in order to try to resolve some of the apparent inconsistencies in the apostle's teaching. It would appear that many of these difficulties have arisen because, until recently, exegetes have tended to undermine the historical and

---

[1] Readers are referred to the general bibliography for the commentaries and works used.

60 A *Trilogy on Wisdom and Celibacy*

cultural background of the chapter and to read into it
ideas which do not occur until perhaps the third century
A.D.[2] It would seem more feasible to plead for the almost
exclusively Jewish background to the problems raised by
the Corinthians both in chapter 7 and in other portions
of the Epistle, for an examination of Acts 18 may show
that the Christian community at Corinth originated from
a Jewish environment and was fostered by Jewish-
Christian teachers.

When St. Paul visited Corinth, he followed his customary
practice of resorting to the Jewish community and teaching in the synagogue. One learns that he lodged with two
Jews, Priscilla and Aquila, and "argued in the synagogue
every sabbath, and persuaded Jews and Greeks." Here
the term "Greek" may refer to a proselyte Jew, for both
the "Jews" and the "Greeks" seem to be present in the
synagogue: it would be unlikely that pure pagans were
worshipping there. The first nucleus, then, of the Christian
community at Corinth appeared to consist of pure Jews
and Greek-speaking people, possibly proselytes, who were
instructed by three Jewish-Christians, Paul, Priscilla and
Aquila. St. Paul was still preaching in the synagogue when
Silas, a Jerusalem Jew, (Acts 15:22, 27, 32) and Timothy,
a Greek Jew but circumcised (Acts 16:1ff.), arrived from
Macedonia. Presumably it was at this point that some of
the Jews or the pure Jews, as opposed to the Greek Jews,

[2] But compare, for example, T. W. Manson, *Studies in the Gospels
and Epistles*, Manchester, 1962, pp. 197–198, also F. F. Bruce, *The
Spreading Flame*, London, 1961, pp. 13 ff.; S. G. F. Brandon, *The
Fall of Jerusalem and the Christian Church*, London, 1957, pp. 21 f.
who notes the thoroughly Jewish method of St. Paul's teaching. See
also Klausner, *From Jesus to Paul*, New York, 1943, pp. 455–458.
The author has discussed this further in "To the Corinthians or to
the Hebrews?" *CBQ* (October, 1966).

resisted St. Paul and he pronounced the famous words, "I will go to the Gentiles (ἔθνη)" (Acts 18:7).

Here several points are ambiguous. Firstly, is this verse genuine? Secondly, did St. Paul mean that he would go to the Greek Jews or to the Gentile-pagans? Thirdly, is the statement to be taken literally, meaning that St. Paul is going to put this intention into effect immediately, or is it a "prophetic" statement looking toward the more remote future? St. Paul's words could be a merely hasty utterance not disconsonant with his impulsive character or, seen from the point of view of St. Luke as theologian and "dramatist," the utterance might well presage St. Paul's future destiny, not his immediate work in Corinth, and be a hint of God's gradual unfolding of the plan of redemption to the Jews, the Samaritans, proselytes and then to the pagans. At least this much is clear from the text of Acts. There does not seem to have been any violent opposition from the pure Jews for about eighteen months (*v.* 2), even after St. Paul's statement, and St. Paul does not seem to have moved far from the vicinity of the Jews but to have gone to the house of Titus Justus which was adjacent to the synagogue. If this is the synagogue which is mentioned in *v.* 4, this would indicate that the Jews and Greeks (Gentiles) were living side by side: there was no Jewish ghetto. But one must ask whether St. Paul moved to the pagan Gentiles or the proselyte Jews. Titus Justus is described as a "worshipper of God" (σεβομένου τὸν θεόν v. 7). This is a technical term used for a proselyte as it is seen, for example, in Josephus *Ant.* 14, 7 para. 2, Juvenal, *Sat.* 14, 96ff. *et cetera* and used in Acts 10:2, 22 to describe Cornelius who was εὐσεβὴς καὶ φοβούμενος τὸν θεὸν (*v.* 2) and ἀνὴρ δίκαιος καὶ φοβούμενος τὸν θεόν (*v.* 22).

Philip's Ethiopian eunuch (Acts 8), Cornelius (Acts 10)

and the first Greek Christians at Corinth appear to have been proselytes and probably fell into the various classes of *ger-toshab*, the half-convert who had no formal and active participation in the Jewish congregation and consequently no restrictions on his ritualistic behavior; of *ger-sha'ar*, who was not circumcised but was bound by the Noachidic commandments and was allowed limited participation in the synagogue (into such a class Timothy may have fallen before he was circumcised); of the *ger-zadek* (or *ger-berith*) who was circumcised and had full communion with pure-bred Jews and whose descendents were regarded as fully qualified Jews in the third generation.[3] Hence it would appear that both the term "Greeks" and "Gentiles" need not necessarily denote heathens but bear a sense of religious and moral inferiority rather than lack of belief in the Jewish faith.[4] In fact in Acts 10:45, "believers from among the circumcised" were amazed that the Holy Spirit should fall even upon the Gentiles (ἔθνη): Cornelius and his household were certainly not "pagan"; rather they appear to fall more into the class of the *ger-sha'ar*, the proselyte of the gate. There may have been separate synagogues for the proselytes.

The admission of genuine pagans into the Christian Church may have been quite gradual. Missionary work seems to have been embraced first among the Jews, then the Samaritans, then the proselytes, then pagans. It is not impossible that there were Samaritans at Corinth, for the Samaritans had a large Diaspora. The Samaritans, just like the proselytes, were sometimes called heathen, sometimes Israelites. Therefore, one cannot take ἔθνη to be used exclusively for "pagan."

[3] Max Weber, *Ancient Judaism*, London, 1952, pp. 419–421.
[4] For a fuller study see D. Georgi, *Die Gegner des Paulus*, Neu-

As Peter in Acts worked with proselytes (Acts 10), so in Acts 18 St. Paul appears to be working with proselytes or Greek Jews rather than pagans. Crispus, the ruler of the synagogue, and all his household were converted and for eighteen months relationships with the Jews were fairly peaceful.

When the peace is broken and the Jews bring St. Paul before Gallio, the proconsul, the accusation against St. Paul does not concern association with pagans, but rather it is an accusation of Jew against Jew and concerns only the manner of keeping the Law: it seems to be an internal conflict. The question of circumcision is not raised. The Jews turn their wrath not against a pagan Christian, but against Sosthenes, the ruler of the synagogue (probably the Sosthenes of 1 Cor. 1:1) who still seems to hold the office even though he is a Christian. The pure Jews may well have felt that the proselytes were going beyond the privileges allowed them.

Indeed, perhaps one's picture of Corinth should comprise a large and varied Jewish community in the diaspora. Its size may be indicated by the fact that the "scandalous affair" of Acts 18:12–17 could occur in the very presence of the Roman governor. Perhaps one should not think of a homogeneous group but of Jewish communities having their own synagogues—St. Paul leaving one, for example, the "conservative", or pure Jewish, and attaching himself to another, the Greek or the proselyte. Such a situation exists in Rome[5] and in Jerusalem.[6] The synago-

---

kirchenvluyn, 1964.

[5] Harry J. Leon, *The Jews of Ancient Rome*, Philadelphia, 1960, pp. 135–166.

[6] Cf. C. Spicq, "L'Epitre aux Hebreux, Apollos, Jean-Baptiste, les Hellenistes et Qumran," *Rev. de Q.* 1 (3 1959) p. 369.

gues in Rome were named after their patrons.[7] This may provide a clue to the divisions in Corinth; the four parties may be four synagogue communities who adopt the name of their Christian patrons or they may be divided according to nationalities or language. From the few Christian-Jews known one surmises that it must have been a cosmopolitan group, for Priscilla and Aquila came from Rome, Silas from Jerusalem, Timothy from Lystra, Apollos from Alexandria and Paul from Tarsus; moreover, there may well have been influence from the Qumran community if there is, indeed, a connection between Acts 18 and 19.[8] Corinth may have been a community not unlike Damascus in which Jews and Samaritans dwelt side by side, in which Essenes resided and in which "almost all women" observed Jewish customs.[9]

Thus in this cosmopolitan city there may have been divisions of race, language, and synagogue adherence; over and above these were the "caste" system of the Pharisees and the varying grades of proselytes.[10]

It could not be expected that these divisions in society could evaporate as soon as Christianity arrived in

---

[7] Leon, *op. cit.*, pp. 135–166.

[8] Spicq, *op. cit.*, 365–390.

[9] *JE*, iv. 565.

[10] R. Travers Herford, *The Pharisees*, Boston, 1962, pp. 31 ff. Travers mentions the four grades of the *haberim* which were "ranged one above the other in accordance with the increasing strictness of their practice." These grades are enumerated in M. Hag. 2. 7: "The garments of the people of the land, *Am-ha-aretz*, are a source of uncleanness to the *Pherushim*, those of the *Pherushim* to the eaters of '*terumah*'; those of the eaters of *terumah* to the eaters of what is sacred; those of the eaters of what is sacred to those who use [the water of sprinkling] the sin offering. Joseph b. Joezer was a hasid of the priesthood and his kerchief was a source of uncleanness to the eaters of what is sacred."

Corinth. Class distinctions would still exist and St. Paul was obliged to deal with them with tact and intelligence. Yet over and above the social distinctions in a Pharisee community in the Diaspora, one might well expect to find different schools or traditions in learning. For the Pharisees were the scholars of the Jewish communities. Thus one finds the beginning of 1 Corinthians devoted to the refutation of a "false wisdom" of a Hellenistic type: possibly Appollo's wisdom fired the enthusiasm of many. On the other side there would be the more Palestinian scholars and also those of the Babylonian tradition who would emphasize law rather than allegorization. Whatever the divisions were there was at least a stress on wisdom and study and it is for this reason that one might suggest another interpretation of σχολάσητε in 1 Cor. 7:5. The words σχολάσητε and τῇ προσευχῇ may be the key to the situation discussed in vv. 1–7. In the New Testament σχολάσητε is a *hapax legomenon*, but in secular literature it appears more frequently, though not exclusively, with reference to philosophy, study and the pursuits of the liberal arts. For a Jew the "liberal arts" would comprise mainly the study of the Torah.[11] Ἦ προσευχή as well as meaning "prayer" also denotes a place of worship, especially among the Jews where it is a synonym for "synagogue."[12] Prayer and study for the Jews were two facets of one activity, and the school and the *Beth Ha-*

---

[11] This is not to deny that they also studied profane disciplines, see, for example, T. F. Glasson, *Greek Influence in Jewish Eschatology*, London, 1961, pp. 5 f. Glasson refers to a remark of Rabban Simeon b. Gamaliel, "There were a thousand young men in my father's house, five hundred of them studied the Law while the other five hundred studied Greek Wisdom." The "father" was Gamaliel II who became *Nasi* in 80 A.D.

[12] Liddel and Scott προσευχή.

Midrash were attached to the synagogue.[13] If one places this situation in the Corinthian context, one may ask whether the question which St. Paul answers here concerns both an exaggeration of the "permission" or dispensation concerning marital duties which was given to students of the law and also an overzealous enthusiasm for "Hellenistic wisdom" which might have emanated from the Apollos party. A more detailed exegesis of *vv.* 1–7 might support this suggestion.

II   I CORINTHIANS 7

Continence within Marriage (*vv.* 1–7)

v. 1   Περὶ δὲ ὧν ἐγράψατε, καλὸν ἀνθρώπῳ γυναικὸς μὴ ἅπτεσθαι

According to Origen this verse with its ascetic tendency probably belongs to the letter which St. Paul received from the Corinthians.[14] Perhaps the Corinthians were being persuaded by some "scholastic" Jewish sectarian movement, such as the Essenes.[15] St. Paul therefore, writes back in *vv.* 2–7 and reinforces Rabbinic principles, that is he refutes the statement ". . .it is good not to touch a woman," a statement which savors of Hellenistic misogyny which we found in Josephus and Philo's account of the Essenes and which Strack and Billerbeck comment

---

[13] G. F. Moore, *Judaism*, vol. 1, Cambridge, Mass., 1942, p. 314. For a description of the earliest *proseuche* discovered see the chapter, "Synagogue Architecture in the Classical Period" by Michael Avi-Yonah in *Jewish Art*, ed. by C. Roth, London, 1961, pp. 157–190.
[14] *Vide infra*, p. 158.
[15] The wide distribution of the Essenes has been noted *supra*, p. 33.

is directly opposed to the teaching of the Rabbis.[16]

v. 2 διὰ δὲ τὰς πορνείας ἕκαστος τὴν ἑαυτου γυναῖκα
ἐχέτω, καὶ ἑκάστη τὸν ἴδιον ἄνδρα ἐχέτω

supports this principle. St. Paul begins his reply with an
adversative δε, "Yes, it may be good but . . ." and then
he applies the dictum "on account of 'sin' let each one
keep[17] his own wife." This is the same dictum which is
illustrated in the story told by Rab. Namely that R. Hiyya
was constantly tormented by his wife but when Rab
commented with surprise that he still continued to bring
her gifts, he replied, "It is sufficient for us that they rear
our children and deliver us from sin."[18] R. Hiyya's
meaning of "sin" and an elucidation of the plural τάς
πορνείας, which has exercised some exegetes, may be
accounted for by reference to Kidd. 29 b: "R. Huna
turned his face from a man who was not married, for he
said, 'He who is twenty years of age and is not married
spends all his days in sin'. 'In sin'—can you really think
so?—But say, spends all his days in 'sinful thoughts.' "[19]
The strict laws about chastity which existed among the
Jews probably precluded many external acts of impurity
through the threat of the death penalty. It is, therefore,
more likely that St. Paul warns against "evil thoughts" or
"evil desires."

[16] S-B, vol. 3., p. 367 f.
[17] See the note on ἐχέτω, R. St. John Parry, The First Epistle to the
Corinthians, Cambridge, 1957, p. 109; cf. *ICC* commentary on the
same verse.
[18] Yeb. 63b, p. 422.
[19] The italics are mine. Cf. Matt. 15:19 and Mark 7:21.

vv. 3–4   τῇ γυναικὶ ὁ ἀνὴρ τὴν ὀφειλὴν ἀποδιδότω ὁμοίως δὲ καὶ ἡ γυνὴ τῷ ἀνδρί. ἡ γυνὴ τοῦ ἰδίου σώματος οὐκ ἐξουσιάζει, ἀλλὰ ὁ ἀνήρ. ὁμοίως δὲ καὶ ὁ ἀνὴρ τοῦ ἰδίου σώματος οὐκ ἐξουσιάζει, ἀλλὰ ἡ γυνή.

Strack and Billerbeck refer to the main Rabbinic texts apposite to this verse. The performance of marital duty belongs to the things which a man is bound to give to his wife; if he is bound to give clothing, food, dwelling and so on, inferring *a minori ad maius*, he has a greater obligation to cohabit. The woman, too, is not permitted to withhold herself from her husband, unless for a just cause. A woman's *kethubah* is increased if her husband refuses her and decreased if she does not consent to him.[20]

v. 5   μὴ ἀποστερεῖτε ἀλλήλους, εἰ μήτι ἂν ἐκ συμφώνου πρὸς καιρὸν, ἵνα σχολάσητε τῇ προσευχῇ καὶ πάλιν ἐπὶ τὸ αὐτὸ ἦτε, ἵνα μὴ πειράζῃ ὑμᾶς ὁ Σατανᾶς διὰ τὴν ἀκρασίαν ὑμῶν.

With some reluctance, St. Paul permits continence within marriage. The whole of verse five suggests the humanity and wisdom shown in the stories about the Rabbis who, with the permission of their wives, went to the academy for several years and then returned to their marital duties. Like the Rabbis, St. Paul stresses the necessary mutual consent.[21]

It is also possible to find a Rabbinic background for the reference to Satan in *v.* 5 b. For example, R. Hisda who felt that he was superior to his colleagues because he had married at the age of sixteen, said that if he had married

---

[20] Cf. Kidd. 29b.
[21] *Vide supra*, pp. 49 ff.

at the age of fourteen, he would have been able to meet Satan with the enjoinder, "An arrow in your eye" (i.e., "I defy you!"—being absolutely free from impure thoughts).[22]

vv. 6 and 7   τοῦτο δὲ λέγω κατὰ συγγνώμην, οὐ κατ᾽ἐπιταγήν. Θέλω δὲ πάντας ἀνθρώπους εἶναι ὡς καὶ ἐμαυτόν. ἀλλὰ᾽ ἕκαστος ἴδιον ἔχει χάρισμα ἐκ Θεοῦ, ὁ μὲν οὕτως, ὁ δὲ οὕτως.

The τοῦτο refers to the abstinence just mentioned. St. Paul means that he allows them to abstain as a concession: it would be ludicrous to read the text as if a man brought up in strict Judaism[23] regarded marriage as a concession. If one reads *v.* 6 in the sense just suggested, then the phrase ὡς καὶ ἐμαυτόν places St. Paul either in a state of temporary continence or in a married state,[24] but there is no mention of absolute celibacy until the implicit reference in *v.* 7 where the ἀλλὰ would seem to indicate a contrast and where the verse reads as if St. Paul is attributing to others, but not to himself, the *charisma* of abstinence. While *charisma* could refer to marriage,[25] it is usually reserved for special supernatural gifts and not merely duties in the natural order.[26]

[22] Kidd. 30a, p. 142.
[23] Cf. Phil. 3:4–6; S–B contrast St. Paul's idea of marriage as a voluntary state with the Jewish idea of marriage as a strict injunction, p. 373 (vol. 3).
[24] *Vide infra*, pp. 70 f where references are given to St. Paul as a married man.
[25] *Vide infra*, on Origen pp. 157 f.
[26] See B. Gerhardsson, *Memory and Manuscript*, Uppsala, Sweden, 1961, second impression; Copenhagen, 1964 pp. 306–323 for a discussion of St. Paul and Tradition and especially his treatment of

Advice to Married People (*vv.* 8–24)

vv. 8–9   *Λέγω δὲ τοῖς ἀγάμοις καὶ ταῖς χήραις, καλὸν αὐτοῖς ἐὰν μείνωσιν ὡς κἀγώ. εἰ δὲ οὐκ ἐγκρατεύονται, γαμησάτωσαν. κρεῖττον γάρ ἐστιν γαμεῖν ἢ πυροῦσθαι.*

In this section St. Paul turns to the subject of widowers[27] (*ἀγάμοις*) and widows (*χήραις*). The phrase *ὡς κἀγώ* referring to St. Paul occurs again and it is still in the context of continence, *not* virginity; but this time the passage suggests that St. Paul is widowed. One can find no explicit reference in the early fathers to St. Paul as a virgin, but there are several references to this marital status:

(a.) St. Clement of Alexandria, *Strom.* 3:52, 53 (quoted by Eusebius *H. E.* 3. 30);[28]

(b.) the longer recension of St. Ignatius' letter to the *Philadelphians* 4. col. 823 (*PG*);[29]

(c.) in Origen;[30]

(d.) in Tertullian's exegesis of 1 Cor. 7;[31]

---

halakah (sections of Rabbinic literature which deal with legal questions and decisions).

[27] It is reasonable to suppose that *ἀγάμοις* means the same as it does three verses later (*v.* 11) where it denotes one who has once been married.

[28] Clement refers to the "daughters of Philip" (probably Acts 21:9) whom he says were married. Here again one has an example of people called "virgins" but said in another place to be married. *Vide supra*, on the "Meaning of Virgin" pp. 14 ff.

[29] These references are late, but their very lateness would seem to be a point in favor of the marital status of St. Paul, for both writings come from a period when virginity was considered the ideal state and the two crowns of martyrdom and virginity were sometimes almost automatically attributed to anyone who was proclaimed a saint by the enthusiasm of the people.

[30] *Vide infra*, Origen pp. 155 f.

[31] *Vide infra*, on Tertullian pp. 210 f.

(e.) Methodius of Olympus,[32] "For holding himself (Paul) up as the greatest example, he challenged his hearers to emulation of his state of life, teaching that it is better for one who had been married to one spouse to remain single, *just as he himself did.*" (italics are mine);

(f.) the first epistle on Virginity (Pseudo-Clementine) c. 6. may refer to St. Paul as a married man but the text is not clear.[33]

V. 9 has presented a difficulty regarding the exact meaning of πυροῦσθαι which is thought to refer either to burning with passion or to burning in Gehenna. However, Kidd. 81 admirably combines both meanings: "Rab and Rab Judah were walking on a road and a woman was walking in front of them. Said Rab to Rab Judah, "Lift up your feet *before Gehenna*" (i.e., "Speed on ahead of her, lest we be tempted," [note 8 *ibid.*]).[34]

It is difficult to find Rabbinic parallels to St. Paul's advice to remain in the state of widowhood although extant are the example of Judith, discussed above[35] and the references to the sorrow felt by Jews on losing their first wives.[36] It would seem that the usual practice was to

[32] Text P.G. Methodius, *Convivium decem virginum*, 18, 27–220. Translation, St. Methodius, *The Symposium, A Treatise on Chastity*, translated and annotated by Herbert Musurillo, S.J, in *Ancient Christian Writers*, vol 27, London, 1958.

[33] The dating of the pseudo-Clementine Epistles on Virginity causes it to be outside the scope of the present study, but some consideration will be given to it in *infra*, pp. 143, 230.

[34] A man walked before, not behind, a woman in order to avoid exciting the passions. Epstein, *Sex Laws, and Customs in Judaism*, New York, 1948, pp. 114–115.

[35] Judith c. 8. *supra*, p. 25. But contrast Epstein, *ibid.*, p. 15 who points out that procreation was a biblical law and no one young or old was exempt.

[36] For example, R. Johanan said: "If a man's first wife dies, it is as

marry again after the death of the first partner, but the
eschatological context may have modified this.[37]

vv. 10 and 11   τοῖς δὲ γεγαμηκόσιν παραλλέλλω, οὐκ ἐγώ,
ἀλλ᾽ὰ ὁ Κύριος, γυναῖκα ἀπὸ ἀνδρὸς μὴ χωρισθῆναι (ἐὰν δὲ
καὶ χωρισθῇ, μενέτω ἄγαμος, ἢ τῷ ἀνδρὶ καταλλαγήτω),
καὶ ἄνδρα γυναῖκα μὴ ἀφιέναι.

These verses show that St. Paul knew of the teaching now
contained in Matt. 5:32 and its parallels. Moreover they
further indicate that St. Paul knew of no exception to the
persons marrying again after separation from a co-
religionist.[38] The fact that St. Paul appeals to the authority of the Lord indicates that Jesus' teaching probably
differed from the current Rabbinic teaching.[39]

---

if the Temple were destroyed in his day." R. Alexandri said: "If a
man's wife dies the world becomes dark for him." R. Samuel b.
Nahman said: "For everything there is a substitute except for the
wife of one's youth" (San. 22a quoted by Montefiore and Loewe, eds.,
A Rabbinic Anthology, London, 1938, p. 511, cf. also no. 1436, p. 509
and the note *ibid.* which explains that attachment to the first wife
was increased because it was believed that marriages were fore-
ordained in heaven).

[37] For example, during the Maccabean wars or for the apocalyptic
writers who believed in an imminent end of the present age.

[38] J. Bonsirven *et ceteri* have explained the meaning of πορνεία in
Matt. 5:32 as forbidden relationships. *Vide infra*, p. 82 ff. for an
explanation of 1 Cor. 7:25 where St. Paul appears to imply that he
does not know the teaching now contained in Matt. 19:11, 12. One
should now compare A. Isaksson, *Marriage and Ministry in the New
Temple*, Lund, 1965, pp. 66–152.

[39] See S-B, *op. cit.*, p. 312 on Matt. 5:32 for Rabbinic teaching on
divorce and remarriage: the teaching in Matt. 5:32 (also in Mark
10:11–12, Luke 16:18, Matt. 19:9 and 1 Cor. 7:10–11) is stricter than
the current Jewish teaching. In Deut. 24:1–4 divorce and remarriage
is allowable but a woman may not return to her former husband if
the second dies. Cf. Hermas, *Mand.* 4. 4–10.

Marriage with an *Apistos* (-ē)

vv. 12–17 τοῖς δὲ λοιποῖς λέγω ἐγώ, οὐχ ὁ Κύριος εἴ τις
ἀδελφὸς γυναῖκα ἔχει ἄπιστον, καὶ αὕτη συνευδοκεῖ οἰκεῖν
μετ᾿αὐτοῦ, μὴ ἀφιέτω αὐτήν· καὶ γυνὴ ἥτις ἔχει ἄνδρα
ἄπιστον, καὶ οὗτος συνευδοκεῖ οἰκεῖν μετ᾿αὐτῆς, μὴ ἀφιέτω
τὸν ἄνδρα. ἡγίασται γὰρ ὁ ἀνὴρ ὁ ἄπιστος ἐν τῇ γυναικί, καὶ
ἡγίασται ἡ γυνὴ ἡ ἄπιστος ἐν τῷ ἀδελφῷ· ἐπεὶ ἄρα τὰ τέκνα
ὑμῶν ἀκάθαρτά ἐστιν, νῦν δὲ ἅγιά ἐστιν. εἰ δὲ ὁ ἄπιστος
χωρίζεται, χωριζέσθω... ἐν δὲ εἰρήνῃ κέκληκεν ὑμᾶς ὁ
Θεός.

One now turns to a section of 1 Cor. 7. which possibly
centers around a legal controversy which arose from
"class distinctions" and which was probably of some
social and ritual consequence to Diaspora Jews.[40] It is
necessary to preface the discussion of this problem with an
examination of the meaning of "*apistos*" which is frequently translated "unbeliever."[41]
In secular usage the adjective ἄπιστος has predominantly
a passive sense, namely, one who is untrustworthy is to
be suspected;[42] this sense prevails in the LXX. Here

[40] Note, for example, the case of Hyrkanus (Josephus, *Ant.* 13. 10,
5–6) who was favored by the Pharisees and who desired "to be a
righteous man and to do all things whereby he might please God,
which was the profession of the Pharisees also." He was pronounced
virtuous by the Pharisees but a serious and spirited dispute began
because a man named Eleazar said: "Since thou desirest to know
the truth, if 'thou wilt be righteous in earnest, lay down the high
priesthood and content thyself with the civil government of the
people.... Because... we have heard from our elders that thy
mother had been a captive in the reign of Antiochus Epiphanes."
(Quoted by R. Travers Herford, *op. cit.*, pp. 36–44).
[41] *NEB, RSV*, Douay version, e.g., for 1 Cor. 10:27.
[42] Liddel and Scott, a New Edition, 1953.

ἄπιστος occurs only three times and one instance, Prov.
28:25, is a doubtful reading. The other two references, Prov.
17:6 and Is. 17:10, clearly appear to be passive in meaning.
At Isa. 10 both the LXX (φύτευμα ἄπιστον καὶ σπέρμα
ἄπιστον) and the Vulgate (*plantationem fidelem et germen
alienem*) imply the Hebrew reading נאמנים (לא). The same
use of אמן (without לא) is found in Mishna Peah 8:2 [43].
The Midrash [44] on Is. 17:10 interprets the verse with
reference to "degenerate Israelites," that is Israelites who
have proved untrustworthy in the sight of God. It would
appear, therefore, that the LXX does not use ἄπιστος in
the sense of "unbeliever."

When one turns to the New Testament, in the main the
same usage is found. Omitting references in the Corinthian correspondence which will be discussed below, the
passive sense comprises:

   (a.) Luke 12:46 (the servant who proves unreliable);
   (b.) Acts 26:8 (. . . thought incredible that God should
        raise the dead);
   (c.) Rev. 21:8 (where ἄπιστος occurs in a list of eight
        vices which suggests that the meaning might be
        "degenerate" or "untrustworthy" rather than "un-
        believing");
   (d.) Tit. 1:15 (" . . . to the pure all things are pure
        but to the corrupt and "degenerate" nothing is
        pure . . .").

The active sense occurs only in John 20:27 ". . do not be
faithless but believing. . . ."

An ambiguous sense is found in Matt. 17:17, "O faithless

---

[43] Jastrow, *Dict. Tal. and Midr.*, New York, 1950.
[44] Midrash Rabbah, Soncino translation, ed. by H. Freedman and
M. Simon, London, 1961. Cf. Lev. R. 18:3, p. 230; Num R. 7:4,
p. 185; 16:20, p. 687.

and perverse generation" and its parallels, Mark 9:19 as well as 1 Tim. 5:8, the latter is translated in the N.E.B. " . . . if anyone does not make provision for his relations, and especially for members of his household, he has denied the faith and is worse than an unbeliever." It might be possible, however, to render here as "bastard," that is spurious, one who does not really belong to his family. It would be curious for the author of this epistle to infer that it was usual for non-Christians to neglect their families. But the Samaritans at least taught that a daughter born of prostitution is not a proper daughter or sister (Yeb. 22 b, Sanh. 87 b). A "bastard" might not be expected to feel "*pietas*" toward his supposed relatives.

This short discussion leads one to suppose that ἄπιστος is not generally used for one who has not embraced either the Jewish and/or the Christian faith. Indeed the word for Gentile in both Testaments is not ἄπιστος but ἔθνος and when the New Testament writers wish to refer to those who have or have not converted they use relative clauses, for example, Acts 15:19; Rom. 2:14; Rom. 9:30; 1 Thess. 4:5. The word ἀδελφός is used for fellow-Christians, for example, Acts 15:23.

It is noticeable that in the whole Pauline corpus (excluding the pastorals) the adjective ἄπιστος occurs only in the correspondence with the Corinthians, eleven times in Ep. 1. and three times in Ep. 2. In the latter the meaning appears to be passive, for example, it is not conceivable that St. Paul should forbid the Corinthians to consort with non-Christians, for then they would not make converts: it is with the degenerate, untrustworthy that St. Paul forbids intercourse (2 Cor. 6:14).

However in the first Corinthian correspondence, one might suggest that there is an additional sense in which ἄπιστος might have been used. The party strifes in Corinth may well have included differences of opinion between Pharisaic brotherhoods and other Jews.[45] Those whom the Pharisees did not trust with regard to levitical rules were especially the *"am ha-aretz"* who stood as the antithesis to the *haburah*.[46] A *"am ha-aretz"* is described as "a person who through ignorance was careless in the observance of the laws of Levitical purity and of those relating to the priestly and levitical gifts."[47] A *haber* (ἀδελφός) in this context denotes an associate, especially "a member of the order for the observance of levitical laws in daily intercourse."[48] One might suggest that the Greek ἄπιστος is often used as the antithesis of ἀδελφός [49] in certain contexts and one could possibly translate it *"am ha aretz."* It is against this background that I should like to examine 1 Cor. 7:14—"Otherwise, your children would be unclean, but as it is they are holy."

Is Thy Child Kosher? (1 Cor. 7:14) [50]

In 1 Cor. 7 one is aware that marriage and continence are spoken of in an eschatological context. This is especially clear in *vv.* 29–31. To the purebred Jew the matter of the purity of one's genealogy was important for in the "last

[45] Cf. M. Weber, *op. cit.*, pp. 386 f., 396 f., 400 ff. and 417 f.

[46] Cf. *ibid.*, p. 419 for the distinction between proselytes.

[47] T. B. Soncino, trans, London, 1952; Glossary, pp. 732–747 (Index volume).

[48] *Ibid.*

[49] One might suggest that the Pharisaic words "brother" and "sister" and *"am-ha-aretz,"* if this is the translation of *apistos*, provided the vocabulary for the early Christians.

[50] Cf. C. K. Barrett, "Things Sacrificed to Idols," *NTS*, (January 1965) pp. 138–153. I have made some consideration of 1 Cor. 10. 27 ff. in a Short Study entitled "Hast Thou Tithed Thy Meal? 1 Cor.

days" Elias would come to judge between the clean and the unclean families.[51] Yet, "clean" and "unclean" did not necessarily denote Jewish marriage and Jewish-pagan marriages respectively. It denoted a blemish in the family from a previous generation, for example, by marrying a slave or an uncircumcised family.[52]

Jeremias[53] notes the "terminology of Jewish ritual," "the language of the Levitical purification ceremonies" and the "concept of holiness which deviates from the customary Pauline usage" in the passage under discussion. Yet it would seem that the passages from Talmud quoted by Jeremias and by Strack and Billerbeck are not entirely relevant to this section of 1 Corinthians, for those which they quote concern cases where the non-Jewish partner becomes a proselyte and, as a consequence of this, the children are "holy." But St. Paul, on the contrary, appears to be speaking of cases where one partner remains as he/she was before marriage and he judges that even so the children are "holy."

In addition one notes that the text reads ἄπιστος not ἔθνος ("Gentile"). One could suggest that here also ἄπιστος means "am ha-aretz", that is a marriage partner of "doubtful stock" and that behind vv. 12–24 is the type of controversy now recorded in Kidd. 70a and b. Here one reads of the ten genealogical classes that come down from Babylon and of these certain classes could intermarry but

---

10:27 ff.," *JTS*. With this section should be compared Epstein, *Marriage Laws, op. cit.*, pp. 145–219. His references show the importance of the subject in the minds of the Jews.

[51] E. g., Eduy. 8:7.

[52] See Herford, *op. cit.*, p. 33.

[53] J. Jeremias, *Infant Baptism in the First Four Centuries*, London, 1960, p. 46.

others were forbidden, that is the superior and inferior could not intermarry. The children of the forbidden unions were *mamzer* (bastard) because they were levitically unclean (cf. ἀκάθαρτα).

The germane passages in Mishna and Gemara bear close comparison with 1 Cor. 7. Perhaps either the Corinthian converts were looking upon non-Christian partners or they regarded even non-purebred Jewish-Christian partners as of "doubtful stock." (Epstein, *Marriage Laws, op. cit.* p. 175 observes that the prohibition of intermarriage was against proselytes, not idolaters).

Mishna Kidd. 4:1[54]	*Suggested interpretation of 1 Cor. 7*
"Ten family stocks came up from Babylon: the priestly, levitic and Israelitish stocks, the impaired—priestly stocks, the proselyte, freedman, bastard and *nathin* stocks, and the *shetuki* and *asufi* stocks. "The Mishna then determines who may intermarry with whom:	If a *haber* has a wife of "doubtful stock"... *v.* 12 If a woman has a husband of "doubtful stock"....

Kidd. 4:3

"They that are of assured stock may intermarry with others that are of assured stock, but they that are of assured stock may not intermarry with them that are of doubtful stock, nor they that	In the Mishna, as in 1 Cor. 7, the possibility of either the man or woman being of doubtful stock and its consequence for the child is fully discussed.

[54] Trans. of *Mishnah* by H. Danby, Oxford, 1933.

are of doubtful stock with
others that are of doubtful
stock, the *shetuki*, the *asufi*
and the Samaritan."

On the question of the bastard stock becoming clean,
there were diverse opinions among the Rabbis, for example, in Kidd. 3:13 one reads:

"R. Tarfon says: Bastard stock
can be rendered clean. Thus if
a bastard married a bonds-
woman the offspring is a
bondsman. If he is set free the
son there by becomes a free-
man. R. Eliezer said: Such a
one is a bastard slave."

1 Cor. 7. (The woman
of doubtful stock is
made holy in the man
. . .).

The Gemara is also relevant. In Kidd. 70a one reads:
  Now he [the Tanna of our Mishnah] holds that if a
  heathen or a slave has intercourse with a daughter of an
  Israelite, the issue is *mamzer* . . . but Rab Judah (Kidd.
  71b) took the opposite view, ". . . And should you
  answer, If a heathen or slave has intercourse with the
  daughter of an Israelite, the issue is fit then perhaps
  [we are descended] from those of whom it is written
  that lie upon beds of ivory . . ." (meaning that they
  themselves might be descended from good or bad
  families).
Rab Judah's thought is not dissimilar to St. Paul's but a
further similarity is found in the same tract (*ibid.*):
  "Go after the peaceful . . . ." As the Palestinians make
  a test: When two quarrel, they see which becomes silent

first and say: This one is of superior birth'. And again, (*ibid.*), 'Rab said: Silence [peaceableness] in Babylon is [the mark of] pure birth. But that is not so, for Rab visited the family of Shihla and examined them; surely that means as to their genealogy?—No, by silence. He said thus to them: Examine (them), whether they are silent [peaceable] or not. Rab Judah said in Rab's name: If you see two people continually quarreling, there is a blemish of unfitness in one of them, and they are [providentially] not allowed to cleave to each other."

This approximates the advice which St. Paul gives in *vv.* 12 and 13, namely if there is mutual agreement to dwell together, then the "certain stock" (the Christian) makes the other partner levitically clean and consequently the children are ἅγια not ἀκάθαρτα (*mamzer*). God has called the marriage partners together by the mark of peaceableness (cf. ἐν δὲ ἐιρήνῃ).[55]

Thus St. Paul satisfies the conscience of the purebred Jew or the Jewish-Christian who considers a non-Christian *apistos*. St. Paul's broadminded view on this question of "clean" and "unclean" families prepares one for his equally broad perspective involving the question of circumcision and slavery, both of which, as has been seen from the Mishna quoted above, are naturally bound up with the subject of "mixed" marriage in the eyes of

[55] Cf. D. Daube, *New Testament and Rabbinic Judaism*, London, 1956, p. 127, on this point where he remarks that Rabbinic codes contain many concessions "for the sake of peace" and that St. Paul occasionally adopts this idea. See also A. Laurentin, "We'Attah and Kai nun" *Biblica*, 45 (1964) pp. 168 and 45, 1964 pp. 413–432 where he discusses *kai nun* as a juridicial and liturgical formula. I suggest that the *nun* in 1 Cor. 7:14 may also have this technical sense; this would add to the terminology of Jewish ritual which Dr. Jeremias remarks, *vide supra*, p. 77.

the Jews and would be of major concern to a Rabbi who was consulted on such a matter but would appear superfluous if the controversy in this passage were a purely Christian one. Over circumcision St. Paul is in agreement with such liberal Rabbis as R. Joshua who thought that the bath or baptism was quite sufficient for the reception of a male proselyte (cf. 1 Cor. 7:17–24).

If this interpretation of *v.* 14b is correct, then one cannot use St. Paul's words here for or against infant baptism; the question is purely one of levitical cleanliness. The dispute which St. Paul treats is probably one which was deep rooted in every Diaspora community, especially where brotherhoods of Pharisees were present, and revolved round the "class distinction" between pure-bred Jews and Jews of mixed families. The temperament of the Corinthian community makes it feasible to suppose that the "Pharisee-Christians" regarded themselves as a "chosen race, a royal priesthood, a holy nation, God's own people" (1 Pet. 2:9) and began to adopt priestly genealogical rules because of this. It was the task of the apostle to wean them from old restrictions and to teach them that in Christ all things are new. The riot recorded in Acts 18 may well have been caused by controversies over such legal points.

The exegesis of this passage and of 1 Cor. 10:27 ff. indicates that St. Paul found the Corinthians more "bewitched" than the "foolish Galatians," but they continued to be so even until the time when St. Clement wrote his first epistle; indeed, his words might well have been a comment written by Rab or by St. Paul: ". . . Thus 'the worthless' rose up 'against those who were in honour, those of no reputation against the renowned, the foolish against the prudent, the young against the old.'"

This exegesis of 1 Cor. 7 up to *v.* 25 has suggested that almost purely Jewish problems lie behind the questions submitted by the Corinthians: the question of abstinence within marriage, probably on account of scholarship (*vv.* 1–5); the question of widowhood (*vv.* 8–11); the question of marriages between Jew and heathen, "pure Jew" and "half-bred Jew" (*vv.* 12–16). Arising out of the background discussion on these points is the question of circumcision (*vv.* 18–19) and of the status of slaves (*vv.* 20–23). St. Paul considers the last two points just as any Rabbi would be obliged to give them consideration when dealing with marriage. Therefore, the chapter so far is quite consistent, the thought developing evenly and logically. The last part of the chapter perhaps deals, as we shall see, with another question to which the Jews gave minute attention in their discussions on marriage.[56]

Widows or Virgins? (*vv.* 25–40)

The most interesting and enigmatic part of St. Paul's discourse on marriage lies in *vv.* 25–40. First of all, one might propose that the meaning of παρθένος[57] in *v.* 25 is "young

---

[56] See, for example, the lengthy list of references printed in the General Index to the TB, pp. 230–232 (Soncino translation). Cf. Epstein, *Marriage Laws, op. cit.*, pp. 77–144 for a discussion of the various aspects of the levirate.

[57] *Vide supra*, pp. 14 ff. To the material there discussed it might be of interest to readers to note 1) among some African tribes a girl upon the first menstruation is called a "bride"; 2) Mr. A. P. Ford informs me in current agricultural terminology, a filly is a filly until her fifth year irrespective of foaling; heifer remains a heifer until she has dropped her *second* calf and same applies to a ewe. I quote these examples to show the ambiguous use of terms equivalent to "virgin" in common parlance.

widows or widowers." If this is so, then the whole chapter from the beginning to the end forms a complete unity, the only subject treated being marriage:

vv. 1– 7 married people;

vv. 8– 9 widows and widowers;

vv. 10–24 "mixed" (or forbidden) marriages;

vv. 25–40 young widows and widowers (deemed in a separate class from other widows, cf. 1 Tim. 5).

The translation "widow" for παρθένος prevents (1) the abrupt change of subject[58] in the next eight verses after v. 25; Περὶ δὲ τῶν παρθένων ἐπιταγὴν Κυρίου οὐκ ἔχω γνώμην δὲ δίδωμι ὡς ἠλεημενος ὑπὸ Κυρίου πιστὸς εἶναι. (2) makes it quite understandable why St. Paul says that he has no commandment from the Lord,[59] for even if he knew the teaching concerning celibacy in Matt. 19:11–12, he could still say that he had no teaching from the Lord about remarriage after the death of the first partner. Perhaps he himself had been widowed at an early age for in v. 25 b (ὡς ἠλεημένος ὑπὸ Κυρίου πιστὸς εἶναι) pistos, used absolutely, may be an adjectival noun παρθένιος ἀνήρ and would denote "faithful to one marriage partner."[60]

[58] It has been observed that this is one of the most abrupt changes in the whole Pauline corpus.

[59] Most exegetes have argued here for a distinction between "commandment" and "counsel," for example, ICC p. 152, the one being of obligatory character, the other of advisory character. But Dibelius (From Tradition to Gospel, London, 1934, p. 242) does not make this distinction. See also W. D. Davies, Paul and Rabbinic Judaism, London, 1962, p. 195 f. But one cannot press the distinction on linguistic grounds; see Liddell and Scott (new edition) and Arndt and Gingrich. The distinction has probably been made in order to preserve the genuineness of Matt. 19:11, 12.

[60] I believe that πιστός is a term frequently found in sepulchral inscriptions. Cf. also Josephus, B.J., 2 para. 121 (Loeb edition): "... καὶ μηδεμίαν τηρεῖν πεπεισμένοι τὴν πρὸς ἕνα πίστιν." Cf. also 1 Tim. 5:12. The "first faith" probably applies to their first husband,

Thus it would have the same meaning as τὸν ἄνδρα αὐτῆς τὸν παρθένικον (Joel 1:8) and the other references quoted above,[61] where "virgin husband" means one who has only been married once. If πιστὸς does mean this, it both supports the writer's meaning of παρθένων v. 25a and is also consonant with Black's remarks on v. 25 b.[62] "These last words seem to me to imply the use of πιστὸς in the familiar sense of the Syrian *mehaimena*, the rendering of the Syriac versions of εὐνοῦχος at Matt. 19:12" (see also note 1 p. 85 *ibid.*). πιστὸς should also be considered in the light of Dr. G. W. Buchanan's note on "The Meaning of Trustworthiness":[63] he sees πιστὸς both in the sense of trustworthy and of כשר.

vv. 26 ff. Νομίζω οὖν τοῦτο καλὸν ὑπάρχειν διὰ τὴν ἐνεστῶσαν, ὅτι καλὸν ἀνθρώπῳ τὸ οὕτως εἶναι. δέδεσαι γυναικί; μὴ ζήτει λύσιν λέλυσαι ἀπὸ γυναικός; μὴ ζήτει γυναῖκα. ἐὰν δὲ καὶ γήμῃς, οὐχ ἥμαρτες καὶ ἐὰν γήμῃ ἡ παρθένος, οὐχ ἥμαρτε. θλῖψιν δὲ τῇ σαρκὶ ἕξουσιν οἱ τοιοῦτοί, ἐγὼ δὲ ὑμῶν φείδομαι.

These verses continue the subject of widows and St. Paul advises an asceticism which would be quite in keeping with Jewish law, namely one may abstain from marriage

---

not to Christ. Epstein, *Marriage Laws, op. cit.*, p. 76 remarks that a woman in a sense remained married after the death of her husband: widowhood was a married state without a husband. *Cf.* Tertullian. Cf. also note 36 *supra.*
[61] *Vide supra*, pp. 10 ff.
[62] M. Black, *The Scrolls and Christian Origins*, London, 1961, p. 85.
[63] G. W. Buchanan, "The Role of Purity in the Structure of the Essene sect" *Rev. de Q.*, 15 vol., 4 Fasc. (3 Oct. 1963) p. 403. Dr. Buchanan's note should be compared with my discussion on the meaning of *apistos, supra* pp. 73–76.

after the procreation of two children.[64] His reasons for asceticism are very similar to those prevailing after the Temple was destroyed when "the ascetics increased in Israel..." (Midr. Tehillim, 137:5), but one notes that these ascetics did not abstain from marriage[65] so that the seed of Abraham would not die out. St. Paul's teaching is also similar to that current in the time of the Maccabees (cf. Baba Bathra, 60 b)[66] which may have been a resumption of the continence belonging to the Holy War. In v. 26b the οὕτως refers to the state of widowhood and is further explained in v. 27: the tenses of δέδεσαι and λέλυσαι sufficiently indicate that St. Paul is speaking of those who had, at one time, been married. v. 28 (ἐὰν δὲ καὶ γαμήσῃς, οὐχ ἥμαρτες. καὶ ἐὰν γήμῃ ἡ παρθένος, οὐχ ἥμαρτεν...) has usually been taken as an unfulfilled condition, but one need not expect the precision of classical Greek in the New Testament. It would seem possible to

[64] See, for example, Yeb. 61b "A man shall not abstain from the performance of the duty of propagation of the race unless he already has children. (As to the number), Beth Shammai ruled: two males, and Beth Hillel ruled; male and a female, for it is stated in Scripture, male and female created He them" (Gen. 5:2).

[65] But I have no evidence that they even abstained from second marriage either, indeed, some advised marrying in old age to beget more children. If a woman had lost several husbands, it was deemed advisable for her not to remarry, Epstein, *Marriage Laws, op. cit.,* pp. 296 ff.

[66] Quoted by Montefiore, *op. cit.,* pp. 524–525; cf. p. 270 f. "R. Ishmael b. Elisha said the same, and he added: From the time that the Roman Government has power over us, and imposes hard decrees upon us, and seeks to cause the Law and Commandments to cease, and to prevent the circumcision of our sons, we ought perhaps, to ordain that no one should marry and beget children; but then the descendants of Abraham would come to an end; therefore we must allow Israel to marry, for it is better that the Israelite should *sin* unwittingly than wittingly." Cf. the reference to sin in *v.* 28b. Cf. also *v.* 26a with the quotation from Epictetus (*infra,* p. 128).

read it as a realized condition and thus to translate, "... if the widow has married, she has not sinned": [67] the definite article "the" appears to indicate a particular case rather than a class. [68] The question may have been raised whether second marriage was wrong. St. Paul replies in the negative. [69] In *vv.* 29–31, St. Paul gives general advice on being disencumbered and he seems to be placing widowhood in an eschatological situation (*vv.* 29, 31). [70] I have no new interpretation to offer for these verses.

vv. 32–34 θέλω δὲ ὑμᾶς ἀμερίμνους εἶναι. ὁ ἄγαμος μεριμνᾷ τὰ τοῦ Κυρίου, πῶς ἀρέσῃ τῷν ὁ δὲ γαμήσας μεριμνᾷ τὰ τοῦ κόσμου, πῶς ἀρέσῃ τῇ γυναικί. καὶ μεμέρισται καὶ ἡ γυνή, καὶ ἡ παρθένος. ἡ ἄγαμός μεριμνᾷ τὰ τοῦ Κυρίου, ἵνα ἡ αγία καὶ τῷ σώματι καὶ τῷ πνεύματι. ἡ δὲ γαμήσασα μεριμνῇ τὰ τοῦ κόσμου, πῶς ἀρέσῃ τῷ ανδρί.

If one is to be consistent in translation, he should again translate παρθένος as "young widow" (as in *vv.* 8, 11). However since *v.* 34 is parallel to *v.* 33, one is able to keep the better attested reading ἡ παρθένος ἡ ἄγαμος — if one understands γυνη as an older widow and παρθένος as a young widow. [71] These two verses are reminiscent of

[67] See the note above on the word "sin." For the tenses see R. W. Funk, *A Greek Grammar of the New Testament and Other Early Christian Literature* (Revision of F. ·Blass and A. Debrunner), Cambridge, 1961, p. 190.

[68] Contrast *ICC*, p. 153, and cf. the definite article in *v.* 36.

[69] I cannot trace a reference to any Rabbinic statement that second marriage was wrong but sects like the Essenes might have frowned upon it as a sign of weakness and surrender to sensual pleasures.

[70] Cf. Christ's advice about flight in Mark 13:17 and its parallels.

[71] Cf. the oft-repeated Rabbinic phrase, "a virgin, who is a widow, a divorcee or a widow who is *haluzah* from marriage..." e.g., Keth. 11b: this makes the term "unmarried virgin" comprehensible; cf. also Hag. 92 where there is reference to a "pregnant virgin."

1 Tim. 5:5 for μεριμνᾷ τὰ τοῦ Κυρίου corresponds to "setting one's hopes on God and continuing in supplications and prayers night and day." But I Tim. 5:11 seems a little skeptical of young widows. From these verses St. Paul's thought passes smoothly over to the young widow in *vv.* 36 ff.[72] Indeed, it is possible that the case of ἡ παρθένος in *v.* 28 is fully treated in *vv.* 36–40.

Levirate Marriage vv. 36–40

εἰ δέ τις ἀσχημονεῖν ἐπὶ τὴν παρθένον αὐτοῦ νομίζει, ἐὰν ᾖ ὑπέρακμος καὶ οὕτως ὀφείλει γίνεσθαι, ὃ θέλει ποιείτω οὐχ ἁμαρτάνει γαμείτωσαν. ὃς δὲ ἕστηκεν ἐν τῇ καρδίᾳ αὐτοῦ ἑδραῖος μὴ ἔχων ἀνάγκην, ἐξουσίαν δὲ ἔχει περὶ τοῦ ἰδίου θελήματος, καὶ τοῦτο κέκρικεν ἐν τῇ ἰδίᾳ καρδίᾳ, τηρεῖν τὴν ἑαυτοῦ παρθένον, καλῶς ποιήσει. ὥστε καὶ ὁ γαμίζων τὴν παρθένον ἑαυτοῦ καλῶς ποιεῖ καὶ ὁ μὴ γαμίζων κρεῖσσον ποιήσει.

These verses have been variously interpreted. The principal explanations are:

(a) a father making a decision whether to give his daughter away in marriage or to keep her as a virgin;

(b) a guardian trying to make the same decision;

(c) a man deciding whether to consummate a betrothal;

(d) a man and a woman having contracted a spiritual relationship seeking advice whether to consummate the marriage.

(a) The first suggestion is unsound on linguistic and on legal grounds. On linguistic grounds one must admit that neither the word "father" or "daughter" occur and "his

---

[72] That is, 1 Cor. 7:25–40 is a discussion on one subject. For the rest of this chapter all references to "Epstein" will refer to his first book *Marriage Laws in the Bible and Talmud.*

virgin" is peculiar usage for "daughter." On legal grounds
it is necessary to realize that a father could impose a vow
(a Nazirite vow) on a son who was a minor[73] but could
not impose a vow on a daughter, whether minor or of age.
The father and/or husband had authority to annul but not
to impose vows. Besides this, it is highly unlikely that
there was such a thing as a "vow of virginity" until about
the third century C.E.. The conjectures about Mary's
"vow of virginity" are extremely dubious.[74]

Further, a father had not absolute authority even in
marriage,[75] for in theory a girl could refuse the future husband. A girl who was orphaned and married off by her
mother or her brothers when still a minor had the privilege of *mi'"un*,[76] that is refusal to live with her husband.
Such a declaration made by her in the presence of a *Beth*

[73] Naz. 24b; Naz. 28b–29a. The *Gemara* discusses the age until
which this vow obtains.

[74] Even Roman Catholic scholars tend to feel that this terminology
is an anachronism, but this does not preclude Mary's intention to
remain a virgin after the birth of Jesus. This is not to deny that Mary
abstained from relationships from Joseph. Matt. 1:25 may perhaps
be translated, "... he did not know her even when she brought forth
her first-born...", on the analogy of οὐκ...ἕως in the sense of "not
even" in examples cited by Arndt and Gingrich: under ἕως:

  οὐκ ἔχομεν ἕ. τῆς τροφῆς τῶν κτηνῶν ἡμῶν we do not ever have
  enough to feed our cattle; οὐ... ἑνὸς νομίσματος = not a single
  coin *et cetera*.

It is possibly more likely that Joseph abstained from Mary than that
the desire of abstinence arose from Mary's side. As other Jewish
men would not return to a woman "touched" by another, so perhaps Joseph abstained for this reason from Mary who was touched
by "another."

[75] See, for example, Kidd. 51b and especially note 5, p. 259.

[76] *Mi'un*, lit. refusal, "a declaration by a fatherless girl who has been
married off by her mother or brothers under age, that she does not
wish to live with her husband. Such a declaration made by her in the
presence of *beth din* secures her freedom without the requirement of a
Get." (Glossary p. 733, TB, vol. 2 (*Kethuboth*).

din secured her freedom without the requirement of a *Get*.[77]

vv. 36–40 then do not seem to discuss the case of a father giving away his daughter or keeping her in virginity.

(b.) The same objections can be raised against the second theory, that is a guardian making provision for his ward. In both case (a.) and case (b.) the verb γαμίζων (*v.* 36) presents a difficulty because neither father nor guardian could contract marriage with the girl.

(c.) This is perhaps the most attractive theory offered and the one which Chadwick favors[78] but the verb γαμίζων poses a difficulty here, for a fiancee would hardly be in a position to give a woman away in marriage to another man.

Further the phrases: (i.) μη ἔχων ἀνάγκην and (ii.) ἐξουσίαν δὲ ἔχει περὶ τοῦ ἰδίου θελήματος are puzzling even if, as Chadwick (p. 267) suggests, there is pressure from the ascetic group at Corinth. After all it was comparatively easy to obtain a *Get* to dissolve a contract made in betrothal. A further point is that *vv.* 39–40 which speak of widowhood seem to be completely out of place if the question concerns a betrothal or a first marriage of any kind.

(d.) This "*subintroductae*" interpretation[79] has never won wide support. As Ladeuze[80] asserts one really only

---

[77] *Get*. "A deed or legal document; when used with no further specification denotes generally a writ of divorce" (*ibid.*, p. 732). A *get* was required both for dissolving betrothal and divorce.

[78] H. Chadwick, "All things to All Men" *NTS*, 1. 4 (May, 1955) pp. 261 ff.

[79] Chiefly propounded by H. Achelis, *Virgines Subintroductae, Ein Beitrag zu 1 Cor. 7*, Leipzig, 1902.

[80] P. Ladeuze, a review of H. Achelis, *Ein Beitrag zu 1 Kor. 7*, Leipzig, Hinrichs, 1902 in *Rev. d'Hist. Eccles.* 6 (1905) pp. 58–62.

finds the practice of *subintroductae* from the third century among the Montanists and the Gnostics.[81]

I should like to propose a modification of the "betrothal" theory and suggest that the question in *vv.* 36–40 concerns a couple who are awaiting levirate marriage.[82] The use of the definite article before *parthenos*, *v.* 36, and the use of τις also in *v.* 36 (denoting a definite man)[83] suggest that a particular case in Corinth was under discussion.

One knows that levirate marriage was still practiced in Talmudic times[84] although by then it was deemed objectionable (Bek. 13a) and was followed only as a matter of duty. It was still upheld by Alfasi, Maimonides and the Spanish school generally. The practice was, of course, modified by the promotion of monogamy. The Samaritans had a different practice and applied the levirate law only when a woman was "betrothed and the marriage had not been consummated" (Kidd. 65b). The *J.E.* observes that the Karaites seem to have followed the same practice. The New Testament makes both an allusion to the levirate in Mark 12:18–27 and parallels it, although one cannot exclude the possibility that the argument of the Sadducees was purely academic. Epstein (p. 135) states that the regu-

---

[81] Achelis suggests that the practice spread over Persia, Syria, Spain, Gaul: he finds references in Hermas, St. Paul and among the Therapeutae. Achelis says that it was necessary to find some place for the young virgins before monasteries were founded and suggests that they were protected by celibates. Needless to say, it was a practice disapproved of by the Church, see e.g., *De Sing Cler.* (Ps. Cyprian). The author would add that there might be a case for Achelis' theory if one changed *Virgines Subintroductae* or *Viduae subintroductae*.

[82] Either after betrothal or after marriage of the woman. But *vv.* 39 and 40 would suggest *haluzah* from marriage.

[83] See Arndt and Gingrich under *tis*.

[84] It is also practiced by the Christian today, e.g., in Africa, provided that the union is monogamous.

lations about the levirate were the same as those of Deuteronomy in postbiblical times to the end of the second commonwealth.[85]

It is important to note that a change in religion on the part of the surviving brother did not affect the obligation of the levirate, or its alternative, the *halizah*[86] (Isaac. b. Sheshet, *Responsa* 1, 2). The question of apostasy on the part of Jew was discussed, but the *halakah* agreed that he was still under the obligation of the levirate (Epstein p. 138 f). This means that a case of Christian-levirate marriage was certainly possible in Corinth.

In the passage under discussion the phrases pertinent to a case of levirate marriage are ἀσχημονεῖν, ὑπέρακμος, οὕτως ὀφείλει γίνεσθαι; μὴ ἔχων ἀνάγκην; ἐξουσίαν δὲ ἔχει περὶ τοῦ ἰδίου.

(1.) ἀσχημονεῖν. Daube has drawn my attention to the aptness of the word ἀσχημονεῖν with regard to levirate marriage and to the passage in his article[87] concerning the mode of punishment inflicted on the faithless consorts: "It is perhaps the only instance in ancient Hebrew law where the punishment consisted in nothing but a de-gradation, a loss of civic honour." The guilty party is publicly disgraced with the words, "So shall it be done unto that man that will not build up his brother's house" (Deut. 25:9). Josephus speaks of ἔχων ὄνειδος and ὑβρίζων (*Ant.* 4.256). *Halizah* was the ostracism of a brother from the estate (Epstein p. 114). Hence it seems that this *hapax*

[85] Derrett convincingly shows that St. Paul had levirate marriage in mind in Rom. 7:1–4, "Fresh Light on Rom. 7:1–4?" *JJS* vol. 15, nos. 3–4 (1965) pp. 97–108.
[86] The ceremony of taking off the shoe of the brother of a husband who has died childless according to the instructions in Deut. 25:5–9.
[87] "Consortium in Roman and Hebrew Law," *The Juridicial Rev.* 62, no. 1 (April, 1950).

legomenon may be the key to the interpretation of this passage.

(2.) ὑπέρακμος. In my Short Study,[88] I suggested that ὑπέρακμος might describe a girl who had reached the age of puberty, that is, was fully developed. I was, however, still exercised about the precise meaning of the prefix ὑπερ- and she felt that both those who advocated the translation "past one's prime," "past marriageable age," and those who suggested that ὑπερ- "expressed intensification," that is "with strong passions"[89] had many arguments in their favor.

Lately it has occurred to me that the prefix ὑπερ- need not infer ἐκτρέχουσα τὸν ἀκμαῖον. In an agricultural context ἀκμάζω means "to be just ripe" and ὑπερακμάζω "to surpass in vigour or bloom", (cf. Thuc. 4:2).[90] St. Paul may have been using ὑπέρακμος in such a context but referring to figs, not to corn. In Mishna Nidd. 5:7, the Rabbis tell this parable (משל) about a woman:[91] "[She is like] an unripe fig, (פגה), or a ripening fig (בוחל) or a fully ripe fig (צמל)—an unripe fig—while she is yet a child (עודה תנוקת); and 'a ripening fig'—these are the days of her girlhood (נעוריה אלו ימי) . . . and 'a fully ripe fig'— after she is past her girlhood (כיון שבגרה), when her father no more has rights over her" (אין לאביה רשות בה). Thus the three stages are:

analogy of fig	name given to girl at this stage	suggested equivalent in Greek
פגה (hard) פגה	פגה	–
בוחל (when head becomes white) בוחל	בוחל	ἀκμαῖα
צמל (fully developed) צמל	בגר	ὑπέρακμος

Now ἀκμαῖος would not be sufficient to describe stage three or to give the correct connotation of צמל, which literally means "contraction or wrinkling," neither would it adequately express the name given to a girl who had reached that stage of development, namely בגר, whose root also means "to be wrinkled, to be rough or harsh." St. Paul, therefore, used the intensified form of ἀκμαῖος with the addition of the prefix ὑπερ- indicated by the Hebrew original.[92]

Whence, however, did this term arise and was it ambiguous (suggesting old age) when used out of context? Jastrow[93] demonstrates that the wrinkling does not refer to old age but to the wrinkling of the nipples. This idea is reflected in the following paragraph in Nidd. (5:8): "What are the tokens in her that she is past her girlhood?" R. Jose the Galilean says, "When the wrinkle appears beneath the breast . . . ." Thus צמל applies to the condition of the breast and at that stage of development the girl is known as בגר (literally, the one who is wrinkled) and as "the one who has come forth complete (יצתה מלאה)" (Nidd. 47a).

Hence it is understandable that Paul used the prefix ὑπερ- bearing the connotation "complete and/or wrinkled." Indeed, grammatically it would be possible to read

---

[88] *Art. cit.* "Levirate marriage . . . ."

[89] Arndt and Gingrich under *huperakmos.*

[90] Liddell and Scott under ὑπερακμάξω.

[91] Danby, trans., Mishna, Oxford, 1933, Nidd. 5:7.

[92] בהד would apply to a woman from puberty until she became an "old woman" (defined in Nidd. 1:5) and therefore the term can be used in the childbearing period but does not necessarily indicate whether she is past the prime of her youth or not. I have been unable to find the term ὑπέρακμος in a Greek-Jewish writer.

[93] Jastrow under עמל.

ὑπέρακμος in the clause ἐὰν ᾖ ὑπέρακμος as an anarthrous
adjectival noun and to translate "even if she is a בגר,"
that is even if she has reached the age when levirate
marriage is incumbent on her (Nidd. 5:9).[94] For a *bogereth*
was a girl of twelve and one-half plus one day or over: at
this age she was no longer a minor.

The critical age was between twelve and twelve and one-
half years. Finkelstein notes[95] a controversy which may
well have made itself felt in Corinth among the different
parties.

> We do not know what the Sadducean civil law was or
> how the pre-Maccabean Temple Courts functioned.
> However, there are hints in the *Book of Jubilees* and
> the *Testaments of the Twelve Patriarchs...* that one
> issue between the Hasideans and the Proto-Saddacees
> concerned interpretation of the word *na'arah* (maiden)
> in the Bible. According to the Hasideans, in this in-
> stance followed by the *Book of Jubilees* and the *Testa-
> ment of the Twelve Patriarchs*, the term referred only
> to a pubescent girl, i.e. one above the age of twelve but
> not yet twelve and a half (B. Nidd. 65 a cf. Mishna,
> *ibid.* v. 8). The Pharisees held such a girl to be a grown

[94] I meant to add a note on the Syriac text of Ep. 2., chapter 2 of the
Pseudo-Clementine Epistles on Virginity where there seems to be a
similar difficulty and it is not known whether there should be a reference to an "old woman," a "rich woman" or "a woman about to be
married." Brock has given me many valuable suggestions on the two
epistles as a whole but as neither of us have access to the best manuscripts it was felt preferable to put forward this note so that others
may work on it if they find it of use. ("A Note on the Rabbinic
Background of St. Paul's use of ὑπέρακμος (1 Cor. 7:36)" submitted
to the *Journal of Jewish Studies* forthcoming, where further details
will be found. Since coming to this conclusion I note that Isaksson
has come independently to the same, *op. cit.*, p. 136, n. 3.

[95] L. Finkelstein, *The Pharisees*, Philadelphia, 1962, p. 78 f.

woman, only partly under the authority of her father. After she became twelve and a half her father's rights over her ceased completely. Thus fines paid for rape (Deut. 22:29) or seduction (Ex. 22:16) or slander (Deut. 21:19) of his daughter belonged to a father only until she was twelve and a half years old. Only before that age could he choose her husband (*ibid.* 22: 13). If the father sold her into concubinage (an institution probably already archaic and considered only for theoretical exegesis of the biblical passages) before she was twelve, she could leave her "husband" on reaching that age, whether he agreed or not (Ex. 21: 7 and Mekilta, Mishpatim, c. 3 p. 257). If she remained with him she would not be considered a concubine or maid servant, but his wife (Ex. 21:10 and Mekilta, Mishpatim, c. 3 p. 258).

ὑπέρακμος may be another word important for the interpretation of the passage.

(3.) The phrases

(a.) οὕτως ὀφέιλει γίνεσθαι

(b.) μὴ ἔχων ἀνάγκην

(c.) ἐξουσίαν δὲ ἔχει περὶ τοῦ ἰδίου θελήματος [96]

All these phrases indicate some external pressure impending on the man, and Chadwick [97] suggests that this might be pressure from an ascetic group. This explanation would account for pressure on a father or a guardian or a fiancée, but it does not account for the man putting pressure on the girl or the free character of the counsel toward a celibate life. On the other hand, levirate marriage

---

[96] Yeb. 12. shows that the levirate was the concern of the community. See again Prof. Daube's article (cit.) just above the citation quoted above p. 91.

[97] Chadwick, *op. cit.*, p. 267.

was regarded as a duty and that duty would be enforced on an individual by the immediate family and, failing their success, the whole community, especially the *beth din*.[98] Indeed the *halizah* had to be performed in public and the man refusing the widow received public degradation. Further, certain conditions increased the obligation on the part of the man, for example, if his brother had been merely betrothed to the woman; if the marriage had not been actually consumated; if the woman were childless or without a son. The obligation would probably be most strict where the man had no more brothers to take the woman.[99] But even if there were brothers, it is possible that *halizah* had to be performed with all the brothers (Epstein p. 114) or the performance of *halizah* frees all brothers from the obligation and all sisters from incest (*ibid.* p. 130). Contact with a man outside the family would be adultery for the woman awaiting *halizah* (*ibid.* p. 106 and p. 122).

St. Paul, in this passage, appears to stress the fact that the ordinary social obligations must be fulfilled and that, only if no scandal is caused, may the man perform the *halizah* instead of taking the woman.

(4.) If there really is a case of levirate marriage here, then the pronoun αὐτοῦ (*v.* 36 and *v.* 38) is perfectly understandable because the woman is actually the man's possession by right of inheritance. The woman was in the state of *zikah*, that is she was chained to her dead husband and "given by heaven" to the *levir*, but he had not come into possession of her. *Zikah* was rather like the state of

[98] *Beth din* (Lit. house of law or judgment): a gathering of three or more learned men acting as a Jewish court of law. (Glossary, TB: Soncino, trans.).
[99] See *JE* under "levirate" and Epstein, pp. 77–144.

betrothal, but betrothal gave legal ownership whereas *zikah* comprised right of ownership (Epstein pp. 104 ff.)

(5.) Perhaps the most puzzling grammatical point in this passage, namely the use of $\gamma\alpha\mu\epsilon\acute{\iota}\tau\omega\sigma\alpha\nu$ in *v.* 36 (let them get married) and $\gamma\alpha\mu\acute{\iota}\zeta\omega\nu$ in *v.* 38 (give her in marriage) is solved by the exegesis of levirate marriage for this section. It is only in levirate marriage[100] that the man has both the choice of taking a woman in marriage or giving her away either to another brother or to another man. Later actual ceremonies for "marriage" with the levirate woman were added, but the essence of the procedure was *ma'amar*, a promise or pronouncement, not *erosin* (betrothal) or *kiddushin* (marriage). *Ma'amar* had a legal effect like the betrothal of a minor orphan girl, (Epstein pp. 117–119). Hence it is understandable how the Pauline marriage (1 Cor. 7:36–40) exercised exegetes as to whether it concerned a "daughter" or a "fiancée": levirate seems to bear the characteristics of both.

(6.) We note that the phrase $\tau\eta\rho\epsilon\tilde{\iota}\nu$ $\tau\grave{\eta}\nu$ $\pi\alpha\rho\theta\acute{\epsilon}\nu o\nu$ may be used in the sense of "support financially."[101] It would point to the solemn responsibility of the brother-in-law to provide for the levirate lady even if he does not marry her. The levir must support the woman even before marriage (Epstein p. 119). There is no new *ketubah* but the old one remains in force. Here St. Paul appears to recognize the justice of the *kethubah*.[102]

---

[100] Or, as Rev. J. J. O'Rourke reminds me, in slave marriage a man has also the opportunity to give or receive the same woman in marriage; see J. J. O'Rourke, "Hypotheses Regarding 1 Corinthians 7: 36–38," *CBQ* XX, no. 3 (July, 1958) pp. 292–298.

[101] See Arndt-Gingrich under $\tau\eta\rho\epsilon\tilde{\iota}\nu$. Also Liddell and Scott $\tau\eta\rho\eta\tau\rho\alpha$, $\tau\acute{\alpha}$ expenses of guarding an oliveyard.

[102] *Kethubah*, a wife's marriage settlement which she was entitled to on the death of her husband or on divorce.

Finally *vv.* 39–40 form a fit conclusion to the whole chapter. They run smoothly on from *vv.* 36–37 if these concern not virginity, but widowhood. There would be no point in these verses if the preceding section dealt with absolute celibacy, and in addition the reference to the death of a husband supports the hypothesis of levirate marriage. The woman had the right to *halizah* instead of marriage on "any pretext whatsoever," but she might be declared a "rebellious wife" and lose her *kethubah* (Epstein p. 122). The *levir* and widow could privately arrange for no marriage and no *halizah* (*ibid.* p. 136); however, for the dissolving of *zikah*, *halizah* must be performed. Physical compulsion could be brought on the levir to free the woman (*ibid.* p. 137).

In St. Paul's usual manner he considers both parties in the marriage. He has considered the obligations of the man (*vv.* 36–38) and now (*vv.* 39–40) turns to those of the woman. As with the man, he leaves the decision about remarriage as an open choice to the woman. St. Paul's phrase ἐλευθέρα ἐστὶν ᾧ θέλει γαμηθῆναι is similar to Josephus' statement ἡ ᾗ ὥπερ ἄν βουληθῇ τινι τῶν δεομένων γαμείσθω (Ant. 4:256). One notes, however, that she is bound to her husband "as long as he lives": this is in agreement with Christ's teaching on divorce in the synoptic gospels; it is not consonant with the Jewish ideas of divorce.

If this passage really does concern levirate marriage, then this is an interesting incident of new converts' adapting themselves to their new faith and trying to decide which practices they should retain and which omit. The practice of monogamous levirate marriage is permitted by canon law in Africa today. The Jewish context of the passage may well have been forgotten when Jewish laws became less important. Crehan notes that a similar case is found concerning the questions submitted to the Council of Jerusalem in Acts 15:20. The decision is given over four points of Jewish Law (taking πορνεία to refer to Jewish marriage impediments) and sent, not to the Church at large, but to areas (containing non-purebred Jews) where such questions of Jewish law might arise. In the later manuscripts and in patristic references,[103] πνικτοῦ is omitted, *porneia* is taken in the moral sense and the decisions are read as general laws binding the whole Church.[104] Likewise as the Church spread among the Gentile peoples the question of levirate did not arise and gradually the passage would be interpreted in a different way. The time elapsing between the composition of this epistle and its inclusion in the canon is quite sufficient to allow the specific case in Corinth to fall into oblivion.[105]

III   OTHER NEW TESTAMENT TEXTS CONCERNING "CELIBACY"

It is necessary to devote some space to a discussion of the other texts in the New Testament which concern celibacy.

[103] Irenaeus, Ephraem, Ambrose, Ambrosiaster, Augustine *et cetera.*
[104] It might be observed that the fact that St. Paul did not mention the Apostolic decree to the Corinthians might mean that community was predominantly Jewish and, as such, the directives of the Decree were not applicable to them.
[105] The theories and practices concerning the levirate and *halizah* and which was preferable varied during the different epochs and in the different schools of thought (cf. Epstein, p. 123). Epstein observes that *halizah* became quite acceptable and that the "tragedy of a man's name being lost because of childlessness became less alarming than in former days either from an *eschatological* or patriarchal point of view." The eschatological motive may have influenced St. Paul's discussion of the point.

I have already mentioned[106] Luke 14:26f and suggested a Rabbinic parallel (cf. Matt. 10:27–38). But St. Matthew does not include "wife" among those whom a man must not love more than God. It is interesting that St. Matthew omits the reference to "wife" (unlike Luke) and that he uses the masculine "*ō*" whereas St. Luke uses "*tis*," which is neither masculine nor feminine). This is consonant with St. Matthew's allusion to male celibacy in Matt. 19:10–12.[107]

St. Matthew's reference in 24:19 "And alas for those who are with child . . ." is not really a reference to celibacy but falls into the category of circumstances which will delay flight, like winter or the sabbath, *v.* 20. Matt. 24:38—"For as in those days before the flood they were eating and drinking, marrying and giving in marriage, until the day when Noah entered the ark"—has a more ascetic savor. Nevertheless, it does not appear to envisage celibacy as a perpetual state but to be an eschatological counsel. A parallel is found in Taan. 12b. Here if prayers for rain are not heard, more penance is performed among which is abstinence from coition. The passage continues: "If these passed and there was [still] no answer to their prayers then business is restricted as also is building, planting, betrothal and marriage; and men greet one another as people labouring until divine displeasure . . ."; all this is part of the practice of "affliction of soul" rather than adopting celibacy for its intrinsic value.

In considering *Rev.* 14:4 *supra* p. 16, I suggested that these men are the "once-married." It would be possible to understand the passage in a metaphorical sense as does

[106] *Vide supra*, pp. 51 f.
[107] Cf. pp. 101 f. *infra*.

Farrer,[108] but it seems probable that the metaphor is connected with "teachers" and that the background of this passage may be the Midrash Rabbah on the Canticle of Canticles. (This is discussed in more detail *infra* pp. 102 ff. It is sufficient to note here that *v.* 5, "And in their mouth was found no lie; they are without blemish," supports this hypothesis.

The most important Gospel reference for this theme is Matt. 19:11, 12 which has no parallel in the other Gospels. Lagrange[109] distinguishes between the three types of eunuch and quotes Rabbinic parallels to the first two. It is the third which is of particular interest to Christians and which seems to be the innovation. It denotes as Lagrange[110] states" ...*la continence absolue et perpétuelle. Le mot 'eunuques' indique en effet une situation qui ne peut plus être changée, un propos perpétuel....*" Lagrange notes the aorist tense (εὐνούχισαν) and comments that Jesus indicates that some had already realized that state, for example John the Baptist or St. John the Disciple. The word, however, would apply to Christ himself (cf. Tertullian, *infra* p. 209).

It was this word εὐνοῦχος (not παρθένος) that denotes complete abstinence from marriage and that was used by the early Fathers[111] when they wished to refer to celibacy. One notes, however, that it is masculine and could never be applied to women as *parthenos* could apply to both

108 Austin Farrer, *The Revelation of St. John the Divine*, Oxford, 1964, pp. 159–161 and *A Rebirth of Images*, Glasgow, 1949, p. 48 f.
109 M. J. Lagrange, *Evangile selon Saint Matthieu*, Paris, 1948, pp. 371 f.
110 *Ibid.*, p. 371.
111 *Vide, PGL* under εὐνοῦχος and εὐνουχία where full references are given to the meaning of "eunuch" in the sense of one who embraces absolute celibacy.

genders. It cannot be doubted that Christ spoke about celibacy as a meritorious and voluntary state, but one cannot produce any dominical statement which counsels celibacy for women. This was to arise as a constituent part of emancipation and education of women. In Talmudic times the following quotation possibly expresses the mind of many: "... a foolish pietist, a cunning rogue, *a female pharisee* and the plague of Pharisees bring destruction on the world" (Sotah 20a). Religious women may have appeared as a peculiarity.

In summarizing the texts which appear to refer to the practical aspect of the celibate life, one concludes that in the Corinthian correspondence St. Paul appears to be treating practical issues concerning marriage. Within these discussions, one finds a clear tendency to advocate continence and/or abstinence from second marriage, because of the eschatological tension of the times. There does not appear to be any reference to *virginitas intacta* either for men or women. The same advocacy of eschatological continence appears in Luke 14:26f; Matt. 10:37–38 and Matt. 24:19. Matt. 19:10–12 seems both to fall into a slightly different category and to show preference for male celibacy or continence as a more permanent state. Rev. 14:4 is ambiguous but may refer to purity of teaching; furthermore the term "parthenos" may have been applied to those who were without blemish in the purity of their doctrine. But the text defies any unequivocal interpretation. If, however, it does refer to purity of teaching, it bears some similarity to the Philonic concepts concerning "virginity" and the pursuit of genuine wisdom (*vide supra* pp. 21 f.).

It is this aspect, the symbolic sense of *parthenos*, that may provide a new interpretation of the Parable of the Foolish

Virgins (Matt. 25, 1–13).[112] This parable is eminent for its peculiarities.[113] It presents a picture of a very strange wedding. Firstly, it appears that the central figure, the bride, is absent;[114] secondly, the bridegroom arrives at a most unusual hour, namely, midnight, and finds waiting for him not his male escorts, the bridegroom's friends, but a solitary group of maidens who seem to be well aware of the probable unpunctuality of the bridegroom, for they have equipped themselves with lamps and settled down to sleep. Thirdly, there is no sign of celebrations, guests, parents of bride or groom, master of ceremonies—indeed, the only words which suggest that the parable concerns a wedding are τοῦ νυμφίου and γάμους. When the bridegroom does appear, those who had the forethought to bring oil for their lamps refuse to share it with their companions who are sent out to a store which is expected to give day and night service. Finally, the selfish maidens mysteriously disappear behind a closed door with the bridegroom. The other maidens are rudely refused entry. Yet there is one more remarkable feature in this parable, namely it is the only place in the Gospels where Jesus utters any criticism either direct or in metaphorical lan-

[112] This exegesis was read at a staff seminar in the Department of Religious Studies, Makerere University College, University of East Africa on July 7, 1965. The writer wishes to express appreciation for valuable help from Professor David Daube.

[113] A previous attempt to explain the parable is found in 'Zum Verstandnis' von Matt. 25:1–13, F. A. Strobel, *Novum Testamentum* vol. 11, fasc. 3/4, pp. 199–227, in which the author finds the setting of the parable to be that of Passover night. One would, however, question whether Passover night was regarded as a nuptial night. However, the Canticle may have been recited about the time of the Passover. See *JE*, vol. 8, pp. 429–431.

[114] The bride is not mentioned according to the best manuscript authority.

guage against women. This is emphasized by the fact the characters in the other "watching" parables are all male. One is obliged to ask what necessitated female *personae dramatis* and what kind of wedding did Jesus mean to depict?

There is one situation in which the Jews were obliged to play a feminine role and one theme in which they allowed the use of erotic symbolism normally prohibited for profane use.[115] This situation and theme was the nuptial relationship between Yahweh and his bride Israel. This erotic imagery finds its most fervent and uninhibited expression[116] in the Canticle of Canticles, traditionally regarded as the great love song between Yahweh and his people Israel: the love romance around which this song is woven is the story of the Exodus—the wooing, courting and final union between the two. It is a theme consonant with the *Heilsgeschichte* according to St. Matthew, who from the beginning of his Gospel depicts Jesus as the second Moses and redemption as the fulfillment of the Exodus.[117] Therefore, it would not be surprising if the second to the last parable[118] in his Gospel dealt with this theme. However, the appreciation of Matthew's treatment and the justification for my thesis hinge on an explication

[115] It was prohibited to sing the Canticle of Canticles as a drinking song.

[116] Cf. for example, Y. Yadin, *The War Scroll of the Sons of Darkness against the Sons of Light*, Oxford, 1962, in which he suggests that Cant. 2:4 should read "his leg over me in love" rather than "banner over me in love."

[117] Cf. for example, the work of W. E. Davies, *The Setting of the Sermon on the Mount*, Cambridge, Eng., 1964.

[118] One notes that these parables in chapters 21–25 are separated from the block of parables in chapter 13. It would seem, therefore, that they have a particular *Sitz im Leben* as Jesus draws to the close of his ministry.

of the progressive movement of the Exodus motif of the Canticle as it appears in Canticle Rabbah.

(a.) Israel as "bride" is a frequent epithet: "R. Berekiah and R. Helbo in the name of R. Samuel b. Nahman said: In ten places in Scripture Israel is called *bride*, six here [in the Song of Songs], and four in the prophets..." (Cant. R. IV. 10 p. 212f.);

(b.) The courtship begins in the land of Egypt as illustrated by: Commenting "*I adjure you, O Daughters of Jerusalem... what will ye tell Him?*' 'That I am love-sick.' As a sick person yearns for healing, so the generation in Egypt yearned for deliverance." (Cant. R.V. 8 para. 1 p. 238).

(c.) In Cant. R. IV. 8 para. 1, p. 205, Yahweh calls his prospective bride from Egypt:

Come with Me from Lebanon, My Bride, with Me from Lebanon.... We have learnt elsewhere: "A virgin is allowed twelve months from the time the bridegroom claims her to prepare herself for the wedding". I, however, did not observe this rule, but while you were still busy with bricks and mortar I hastened to redeem you![120] This interpretation is possible because there is a play on the word "Lebanon" read as *lebenim* (bricks).

(d.) The coming forth from Egypt is read into Cant. vi. 8., for in (Cant. R. VI 9 para. 4, p. 267) it stated: "The Rabbis applied the verse to the Israelites who went forth from Egypt. There *are threescore queens*: these are the sixty

[119] Text, Midrash Rabbah, trans. *op. cit.* Cf. also Cant. R. IV: 12 para. 2, p. 221 f. Here the bride Israel is said to present thirteen presents to Yahweh, but he presented her with twenty-six, "as it is the custom of the bridegroom, to double the wedding-gift of the bride."

[120] Cf. Exod. R. 23:5, p. 282 f. and also the play on Lebanon and stones in Git. 56b where Lebanon is used as name for Temple.

myriads who went forth from twenty years old and up-
wards. *And fourscore concubines*: these are the eighty
myriads who went forth twenty years old and under. *And
maidens without number*: there is no end and no number
to the proselytes."

(e.) In Cant. R. IV 9, p. 212, Israel is described as ravish-
ing Yahweh's heart by the Red Sea: "Thou *hast ravished
my heart* . . . . 'Ye had one heart by the Red Sea and ye
gave Me two hearts'. . . when ye stood before Me at
Mount Sinai and said, 'All that the Lord hath said will we
do and obey'" (Ex. 24:7).

(f.) Cant. I. 2: *"O that you would kiss me with the kisses of
your mouth"* is the subject of various interpretations by
Rabbis of different generations. It is, however, in general
interpreted of the consent which Israel gave to obey
Yahweh's commandments, hence he kissed her on the
mouth, (Cant. R. I, 2 para. 1, pp. 20–30).

(g.) Israel is depicted as sleeping while Moses, the best
man, delayed with God on the mountain.[121] Commenting
on Cant. *v.* 3, R. Johanan said in the name of Resh
Lakish: ". . . *I have put off my coat, how shall I put it on!*
But why in fact is this said? Because sleep at Pentecost
time [when the Law was given on Mount Sinai] is sweet
and the night is short. R. Judan said: They were not
bitten by fleas either." Cant. R. p. 234 n. 6 comments
"Yet Israel awoke to receive the Law."[122]

(h.) Yahweh comes down like a bridegroom and meets his
bride Israel and the consummation of their union is
affected by the setting up of the Tent of Meeting in which
Yahweh communes directly with his people and in which
his Shekinah rested.[123] Hence the giving of the Law on

[121] Cf. S-B, vol. I., p. 970 quoting *PRE*, 41.
[122] Cant. R. 1:12, para. 2, pp. 79 f.

Mount Sinai was known as the "Day of Espousals":

In the day of his espousals: this was the day of Sinai, when Israel were like bridegrooms. *And in the day of the gladness of his heart*: this refers to [when they received] the Torah, as it says, . . . another explanation: *On the day of his espousals*: this refers to [the consecration of] the Tent of Meeting. . . [123] (Cant. R. III. 11, par. 2 pp. 174f.).

(i.) Yet the Rabbis do not overlook that the children of Israel sinned on the very day of their espousals: "R. Simeon b. Halafta said: Shame on the bride who misconducts herself in her very bridal chamber! (That is, made the Golden Calf at Sinai itself). . . . they lost the good counsel which was given at Sinai. . ." (Cant. R. VIII, 5, 1 p. 305).

Thus the Song of Songs according to the many sections of the Midrash [124] is predicated of Israel as a whole. Yet it was the Jewish scholars who were attracted above all to the Canticle, in fact so much so that they prohibited men to study it until they had reached a certain stage in their academic course: "undergraduates" were not permitted to be introduced into the mysteries of the Song or the Chariot. The popularity of the Canticle by the time of R. Akiba is shown by his own exclamation:

[123] The connection between the Covenant on Sinai and the nuptial imagery probably depends on *chatham*.

[124] Most of the quotations above are not attached to the names of Rabbis; hence one might assume (although there is no certainty) that they are early material collected by R. Meir. In all quotations I have named the Rabbi where possible as an indication of dating. These Rabbis are, of course, after the New Testament but some of the sentiments they express may antedate their tradent or author. If, however, a Rabbinic saying casts light on the New Testament, this might suggest that the idea, although not necessarily the form in which it is expressed, may have been known in New Testament times.

...no man in Israel ever disputed about the Song of Songs [that he should say] that it does not render the hands unclean, for all the ages are not worth the day on which the Song of Songs was given to Israel; for all the Writings are holy, but the Song of Songs is the Holy of Holies. . . .[125]

With unparalleled audacity, the scholars appear to have appropriated almost every phrase of the Canticle either to the details of the Torah or to descriptions of themselves.[126] "The daughters of Jerusalem" served to denote the Sanhedrin. "*O ye daughters of Jerusalem.* The Rabbis say: Read not *benoth* (daughters) but *bonoth*-ye that build Jerusalem; by this is meant the great Sanhedrin of Israel who sit and instruct them in every difficulty and point of law" (Cant. R. I, 5 para. 3 p. 53 and so on). The ornaments of the beloved in the Canticle refer to the leaders of Judaism:

"Thy neck with beads" refers to " . . . the seventy members of the Sanhedrin who were strung after them (Moses and Aaron) together like pearls on a string" (Cant. R. I. 10 para. 2 p. 73).

"Thy cheeks are comely with circlets (torim): when the words of Torah are recited on their due occasions

[125] Mishna, Yadim 3.5, trans. by Danby, *op. cit.*

[126] The present article should be compared with Raphael Loewe's article, "Apologetic Motifs in the Targum to the Song of Songs," in *Biblical Motifs: Studies and Texts*, vol. III, ed. by A. Altmann, Cambridge, Mass. (1966) pp. 159–196. Loewe summarizes the Targum of the Canticle the *redaction* of which he dates in the seventh century. The whole article is germane to the present study. Particularly relevant to this theme are: section B I–V which deal with the Sinaitic Revelation to the significance and the oral Torah and section C I–II which deals with the "office-holders and sundry classes" in Israel.

(torim).[127] The laws of Passover on Passover, the laws of
Pentecost on Pentecost, the laws of Tabernacles on Tabernacles [the word *tor* being used as in] *Now when the turn
(tor) of every maiden was come* (Est. 2:12). *Thy neck in
pearls*: R. Levi said in the name of R. Hama b. R. Hanina:
This refers to the various sections of the Torah, which are
linked with one another, or lead on to one another..."
(Cant. R. I. 10 para. 3 p. 75).

"*Thy cheeks are comely with circlets*: these are the Rabbis.
Thy neck with pearls (harizum): These are the disciples
who strain (*hozrim*) their necks to hear the words of
Torah... when they link the words of the Pentateuch
with those of the prophets..." (Cant. R. I. 10 para 2
p. 74).

"*Thine eyes are as doves*: *Thine eyes*: these refer to the
Sanhedrin who are the eyes of the congregation, as it is
written. *If it be hid from the eyes of the congregation* (Num.
15:24). There are two hundred and forty-eight limbs in
the human body, and they move only by the direction of
the eyes. So Israel can do nothing without their Sanhedrin"
(Cant. R. I. 15 para. 2 p. 86 cf. IV. 1 para. 2).[128]

The scholars were not content to be but jewels around the
neck of the bride of Israel; rather they compared themselves to the bride:

> R. Huna and R. Halafta of Caesarea said in the name of
> R. Simeon b. Lakish: Just as a bride is adorned with
> twenty four ornaments (see Is. 3:18–24) and if one is
> missing she cannot pass muster, so a Rabbinical scholar
> should be conversant with the twenty four books of the

[127] Raphael Loewe pointed out to me the pun on חודה and הוד.
[128] Cf. Matt. 6:22, 23. This may be a reference to the Sanhedrin.
Raphael Loewe drew my attention to the play on עין (eye) = number
seventy ע = Sanhedrin.

Scripture, and if he is not conversant with one of them he cannot pass muster. R. Huna said in the name of R. Simeon b. Lakish: Just as a bride must be modest, so a Rabbinical scholar should be modest. R. Halafta said in the name of Resh Lakish: Just as the bride sits on the couch and says: "See for yourselves that I am pure, and here is my proof that testifies for me", so a Rabbinical student should be liable to no reproach . . . (Cant. R. IV 11, para. 1 p. 214).

R. Johanan said: If one discourses on the Torah in public and his words do not give as much pleasure to his hearers as a bride gives pleasure to the beholders when sitting in her bridal chamber, it were better that he had not delivered them. Resh Lakish said: If one discourses on the Torah and his words do not give as much pleasure to his hearers as a *bride to her husband when she enters the bridal chamber, it were better that he had not delivered them.* (Cant. R. IV 11, para. 1 p. 215; italics are mine).

For the scholars, the Tent of Meeting became "the chamber of my teaching" (deriving *horathi* from *hora'ah*, teaching, Cant. R. II. 3 para. 5 and note 4 *ibid.*, p. 101); and they appropriated to their own merits the inmost portion of the Tent: "*The inside thereof being inlaid with love*: R. Judan said: This refers to the merit of the Torah and the merit of the righteous who study and practice it . . . . *The inside thereof being inlaid with love from the daughters of Jerusalem*" (*ibid* p. 167). The commentator adds in note 1 (*ibid.*) "The addition from the daughters, etc., hardly seems relevant, and it is not quoted at this stage in the preceding section. Perhaps, however, the Midrash desires to draw attention to the scholars in Jerusalem."

Further Cant. 6:8 which formerly referred to all the people of Israel who left Egypt (*vide supra* p. 105 f.) is transferred to the scholars themselves:

> R. Isaac applied the verse to the sections of the Torah. *There are threescore queens*: these are sixty tractates of *halachoth. And fourscore concubines*: these are the eighty sections in Leviticus. And *maidens without number*: There is no end of additional *halachoth. She is one*: the students argue with one another, but all base themselves on one principle... R. Judan b. Il'ai applied the verse to the Tree of Life and the Garden of Eden. *There are threescore queens*: These are the sixty companies of the righteous who sit in the Garden of Eden under the Tree of Life and study the Torah.... *And fourscore concubines*: these are the eighty companies of the fairly good who sit and study the Torah outside the Tree of Life. *And maidens without number*: there is no end of the disciples (Cant. R. VI 9 para. 2–3 pp. 265f.).

The rabbis introduced themselves into the bridal chamber by interpreting the verse, "*Let my beloved come into his garden*" (Cant. 4. 16) and "*I come to my garden...*" (Cant. v. 1) as *ginnuni* (bridal chamber) not *ganni* (garden). "R. Menahem, ... in the name of R. Simeon b. Jusna [states]: "It does not say here, 'I am come into *the* garden,' but *I am come into my garden (ganni)*: as if to say, to my bridal chamber (*ginnuni*): to the place which was my real home originally; for it was not the original home of the Shechinah in the lower realm ... (i.e. on earth)" (Cant. R. IV. 1, para. 1 p. 228 cf. *ibid.* I, 4 para. 2 p. 43). Four Rabbis are supposed to have entered the chamber (Cant. R. I, 4 para. 1 p. 46 f.).

Since it is apparently against this background that the

Parable of the Foolish Virgins is told,[129] Jesus may have thought that the scholars monopolized the nuptial imagery of the covenant on Sinai and tended to exclude the less learned from an intimate relationship to God. The parable's *Sitz in Leben* appears to fit this interpretation. Jesus tells the parable against the hypocrisy of the Jewish teachers.

The *Sitz in Leben* seems to arise from the dispute over Jesus' authority in Matt. 21:23. In the controversy, Jesus illustrates his points with parables which contain symbols obviously known to the chief priests and scribes, for they realize that the parables are told directly against them (*v.* 45). Moreover the symbols are carefully chosen.

The *vineyard* (Matt. 21:28, 33 ff.) may apply to Israel generally, but more particularly it was applied to the Sanhedrin ("... *A vineyard* this is the Sanhedrin, as we have learnt elsewhere" [Ed. 2:4]). "R. Ishmael testified to three things before the Sages in the vineyard in Jabneh, and they accepted his statements. Now were they sitting in a vineyard? The fact is that the Sanhedrin is so called because it was arranged in rows like a vineyard" (Cant. R. VIII. 11, para 2 p. 315).

The marriage feast (Matt. 22:1–15) may be a symbol of the completion of the study of Torah; compare, for example, R. Eleazar who supposed that Solomon made a feast to celebrate the completed study of the Torah (Cant. R. I. 1, 9 and note 2, p. 13). Further in the Midrash (Cant. R. VIII, 2) still commenting on the "vineyard," the narrators compare God to a king who gave his daughter (Torah) in marriage. The mingling of the themes of vineyard (Cant.

---

[129] Cant. R. I. 3:3 p. 39 f. gives various interpretations of *'alamoth* (maidens), e.g., "with youthful energy"; "penitents"; "proselytes"; the "generation of destruction," etc.

8, 11, 12) and marriage would not be unfamiliar to the scholars. It is, for example, found at the end of Taanith 4.8 where "day of espousals" is interpreted as the giving of the Law.

The wedding garment may be a scholar's cloak to which Strack and Billerbeck draw attention (vol. 1 p. 882). One may also compare the fascinating study *The Divine Garment and Shi' ur Qomah* by Raphael Loewe who comments that the wrapping of the Deity in the garment of light or radiance seems to be "explicitly connected with God's own biblical scholarship, it is to be noted that the targumist's formulation seems to hint that the wrapping on of the garment is an invariable (and indeed indispensable?) preliminary to the study of the Bible—almost a 'scholar's gown' . . . ." [130]

This section in Matthew culminates in the two great precepts of charity which is Jesus' epitomy of Torah and in the forced admission of the Pharisees that Christ must be Lord. This theme is further expanded in Matt. 23 which contains the woes directed not against the teaching of the leaders of Israel, but against their lack of good deeds which fail to accompany their teaching. The climax of these is reached in the lament over Jerusalem which is possibly a direct address to those who were known both as the "daughters of Jerusalem," that is, the Sanhedrin, with the play on "daughters" and "builders" (*vide supra* p. 108). The irony of the passage lies in the fact that they are destroyers rather than builders.

Matt. 24 treats of false teaching, false Christs and the cosmic upheavals preceding the coming of the Son of Man. There is a fairly close parallel to this section in the

[130] R. Loewe, *HTR*, vol. 58, no. 1 (January, 1965) p. 157.

114   *A Trilogy on Wisdom and Celibacy*

same Midrash Cant. R. II. 13, 4, pp. 126–127. It speaks of the Torah being forgotten in Israel.[131] However, the *locus classicus* in the Little Apocalypse is Sotah 9:15.

Hence one sees that the whole section from Matt. 21:23 to 24 preceding the watching parables centers around teaching—good teaching, bad teaching, deceptive teaching but above all teaching unaccompanied by good deeds. This sets the stage for the watching parables of which the most poignant is the parable of the virgins.

These parables, the watchful householder and the faithful and wise servant, strike the initial note according to which the scholars appropriated to themselves the whole of the Song of Songs. They quoted the test "*Seest thou a man diligent in his business? He shall stand before kings, he shall not stand before mean men*; (Prov. 22:29): this applies to the righteous who labour in the work of the Holy One, blessed be He. Therefore, '*he shall stand before kings,*' which means that they stand firm through adherence to the Torah, as it says. . . ." A lengthy discourse (Cant. R. I 1 1–6 pp. 1–5) on Prov. 22:29 forms the prelude to the Midrash on the text of the Canticle; similarly St. Matthew's two parables of the men "diligent in their

---

[131] One might suggest, too, that Matt. 24:32–35 may be inspired by the following sections of Cant. R:

a) Cant. R. II, 13, para. 1 "'*The fig tree putteth forth her green figs*:' this refers to the sinners of Israel who died in the three days of darkness. . . ;"

b) "'. . . *winter is past*. . .'; this refers to the forty years which Israel spent in the wilderness";

c) "'*the rain is over and gone*:' this refers to the thirty-eight years during which Israel were as if under a ban (therefore could not speak to their teacher cf. *Ta'an* 30b) in the wilderness, as God did not speak with Moses until that generation had passed away. . .";

d) Lev. R. 19:2, p. 238, on the indestructability of the words of the Torah.

business" serve as an introduction to the more startling parable of the Foolish Virgins.

In this parable Our Lord appears to depict not an ordinary marriage but men who apply themselves to the study of Torah and hope to be led into the bridal chamber, the chamber of instruction.

The symbols are apt. The number of the virgins is ten—ten is the required number to make up a quorum for the synagogue; ten for the courts of ten in Temple law (Sanh. 1. 3); but, most important of all, ten for the circles of study, for example, in the Qumran community (*C.D.* 10. 4).

The time is night. Day and night study was highly recommended. In the Qumran community one finds the members taking turns to study one-third of the night.[132] Frequent references to night study are extant; for example, R. Johana said: "The full crop of the Torah is garnered only at night, for so it says, '*She riseth also while it is yet night*'" (Prov. 31. 15) and it is also written, "'*Arise, cry out in the night*' (Lam. 2:19).[133] Both these verses were understood to refer to the study of Torah at night," (Cant. R. V. 11, para, 1 pp. 239f.).

The passage from Lamentations R. is particularly interesting. Here David is said to sleep until midnight and then rise to study Torah (Lam. R. 11. 18–19, para. 22). Thus midnight is deemed the special hour of revelation at which time the scholars should be at their scrolls. Thus the "*cry at midnight*" in the parable has a wealth of biblical exegesis behind it.

The virgins hold lamps. Krauss[134] comments that it is

[132] *C.D.* 10:4. Cf. also Lev. R., 19:1–2, pp. 236 f.

[133] Cf. Cant. R. V:11, para. 1 f., pp. 239 f.

[134] Krauss, S., *Talmudische Archaologie*, vol. 2, reprint, 1966, p. 38.

only from Matt. 25 that one learns of the custom of holding lamps at a wedding.[135] The detail seems deliberately introduced as a necessary feature of this spiritual marriage theme. The lamp is symbolic of the Torah. *"Thy word is a lamp to my feet"* (Ps. 119. 105); and according to Ex. R. 36. 3, p. 439 "The Man who does not occupy himself with Torah stumbles and all because he has no lamp in his hand' . . . God said: 'Let My lamp be in thy hand and thy lamp in my hand'" (i.e., "Do Thou keep my Torah and I will keep thy soul" [Ex. R XXXVI 3, para. 3]).

Now the virgin-scholars are not reprimanded for sleeping during the night, for they follow the example of David who rose at the cry of midnight. Neither are they reprimanded because they do not hold lamps (the Torah). Indeed, the crux of the parable lies in the fact that they even go so far as trimming their lamps, and it is this action which may be the essential part of the parable, for there is probably a play on "trimming" (t-b literally "improving") and "[speaking] well". In Cant. R. II. 14 (para. 4 p. 131) commenting on *"For Sweet is thy voice"* the following passage occurs:

> This refers to what they said after the Commandments were given, as it says, *And the Lord heard the voice of your words . . . and said . . . they have well said all that they have spoken* (Deut. 5.25). What is meant by *"they have well (hetibu) said all that they have spoken"*?
> Hiyya b. Adda and Bar Kappara gave different ex-

---

[135] Cf. J. Jeremias, "Lampades Mt. 25:1, p. 3 f., 7 f., *"Zeit. N.T. Wiss*, 56 (3–4 1965) pp. 196–201 who finds a parallel in present day Arab weddings where "torches" (not lamps) are used. However, one might reflect that in Israel today shopkeepers appear to sleep on the premises of their shops and in the light of this custom it might have been possible for goods to be purchased during the night in New Testament times.

planations [of the word "well"]. One compared it to the trimming (*hataboth*) of the lamps . . . . (The same comment is made in Cant. R. IV. 4 para. 1 p. 183.)

Up to this point in the parable the scholars have fulfilled their duties. One last thing they lacked, that is oil. The lamp is the symbol of Torah, but the oil is symbolic of good deeds, for example, in Num. R. XIII 15, p. 535 commenting on the phrase "mingled with oil," the Midrash reads, "the study of Torah must be mingled with good deeds.[136]

The oil represents the good deeds for the deficiency of which Jesus reprimands the scribes and Pharisees even though they have trimmed their lamps, that is have spoken and taught well. But why did the five wise virgin-scholars with good deeds to their credit refuse to give to those who had none? The apparent reason is that one's good deeds cannot benefit another person, not even one's sons or daughters for "no amount of good deeds *are sufficient* for oneself." [137]

Thus the wise scholars with their good deeds hasten to the nuptial chamber, the Tent of Meeting, when they are roused from sleep at midnight even as Moses roused Israel from "gazelle-sleep" on Mount Sinai when God came as bridegroom to meet and claim his bride Israel.[138]

Those who followed up their well-spoken words with the "making of the Golden Calf" are shut out from the nuptial chamber. The Lord says: "I know thee not." This seems to bear a threefold meaning:

[136] Cf. also Bacher W, *Ag. Pal. Amor.*, vol. 1, p. 223 and vol. 2, p. 466 where students are called "sons of oil." See also *JE* under "oil."
[137] Lev. R. 4:1–2, p. 50.
[138] S-B, vol. 1., pp. 969–70.

a) I know thee not (in the nuptial sense);

b) I do not recognize thee;

c) I know thee not, i.e., Jesus proclaims in Rabbinical language the refusal of a Rabbi to admit a disciple.[139]

Thus Matt. 26 fits admirably into the theme of the parable because it shows the sheep and the goats divided according to their performance of good deeds.

Thus at the end of Jesus' fifth discourse, St. Matthew records a parable which reflects a theme common to all three evangelists, namely Jesus as bridegroom.[140] In Matthew the parable stands as the climax of the Exodus motif. Jesus comes like God on Mount Sinai on the "day of espousals," He comes to draw Israel to Himself in the New Covenant and to the virgin-scholars says, as God said on Sinai, ". . .when you take the Torah, you are taking Me, as it were" (Ex. R. 33. 6–7). According to Lev. R. 11. 9, those who receive him will dance as maidens pointing their finger and saying: "This, this is our God and we will rejoice in Him."

Christ, like Solomon, referred to in the Canticle, is able to "take in large numbers" (i.e., or "wives") and "yet sin not" (Cant. R. I, 1, 1 p. 17). For when "Solomon did cleave unto them in love" (Cant. R. I, 1, 10 p. 16), it meant (according to R. Jose b. Halafta) to "make them beloved (to God, to bring them near to God, to convert them and to bring them under the wings of the Shekinah."

The rather unusual exegesis of this parable outlined above will raise various questions in the minds of readers. Firstly, they will question the dating of the Rabbinic material controlling the exegesis, and secondly, they will not wish

---

[139] One notes that St. Luke says "I do not know *whence* thou comest" (Luke 13:25).

[140] Matt. 9:14–15; Mark. 2:18–22; Luke 5:33–39.

to admit such allegorical interpretation of parables in face of the classical books on the subject.[141] These are certainly just criticisms. Most of the material which has been used in the exegesis is undated (unnamed) or comes from a period later than the New Testament; some of it is post-Tannaitic. In addition to this, even though some of it may antedate its tradent or author, this does not prove that it ascends in substantially its present form to New Testament times.[142] However, given the retentive and precise memory of the Rabbinic schools and the methodology of their learning,[143] one cannot exclude the possibility that ideas such as those discussed above may have been in circulation in apostolic days. If, for example, tannaitic thought throws light on the New Testament, then this is one argument toward finding in it earlier thought. It is unlikely that Judaism borrowed from Christianity.

After stating that there survive some examples of exegetical treatment of the Canticle by named Tannaitic figures including R. Akiba "in which the reading of the Song as a dialogue between God the lover and Israel the beloved maiden is taken for granted," Loewe[144] also notes that

---

[141] C. H. Dodd, *The Parables of the Kingdom*, rev. ed., 1961, and J. Jeremias, *The Parables of Jesus* (1963), trans. by S. H. Hooke from the German, *Die Gleichnisse Jesu*, 6th ed., 1962.

[142] Krister Stendahl, *The School of St. Matthew and Its Use of the Old Testament*, Uppsala, Sweden, 1954, pp. 11–12. Cf. P. Carrington, *The Primitive Christian Catechism*, Cambridge, 1940 p. 69, who also refers to the Matthaean school and compares the teachers to the *tannaim* of contemporary Judaism.

[143] Gerhardsson, *op. cit.*, with which thesis the writer is in general agreement.

[144] Raphael Loewe, *op. cit.*, p. 161. Mr. Loewe has kindly allowed me to see his manuscript before publication. I should add here that he is not entirely in agreement with my exegesis and I am indebted to him for his helpful criticism over several points.

there is a trace of the "same exegetical approach" in 2 Esdras (IV) v. 24–26 (100 B.C.). He points out that Akiba's defense of the canonicity of the Song presupposes the allegorical interpretation.[145] Moreover Loewe[146] comments that Jewish circumspectness as recorded by Origen regarding the Canticle when combined with R. Akiba's recorded dictum[147] concerning it may suggest (but certainly does not prove) that this sort of exegesis of the Canticle was current in Pharisaic-Rabbinic circles in apostolic times.

The earliest Christian commentary seems to be one by Hippolytus[148] and it is reported that his commentary was so popular that it was translated into Syriac.[149] It is possible that the Canticle was confined to a small circle of Christian exegetes, as it was reserved for the more advanced Jewish students; perhaps this is the reason it is not quoted in the New Testament, although, on the whole, it seems that one cannot entirely rule out the possibility of the exegetical use of the Canticle by early Christians.

The second objection concerning the allegorical use of the Canticle is perhaps the more serious obstacle.[150] While it is important to be cautious about the allegorical interpretation of parables, Loewe again has much to contribute. He makes a clear distinction between the Rabbinic use of allegory and the patristic use. In Rabbinical exegesis the literal sense is not opposed to the allegorical:

[145] *Ibid.*, p. 161.
[146] By correspondence.
[147] *Vide supra*, p. 108.
[148] Hippolytus, *MG*, 10 cols: 627–630.
[149] *Ibid.*
[150] Père X. Leon Dufour has also discussed this question in "La parabole des vigerons homicides," *Sci. Eccl.*, 17 (3/65) pp. 365–396. He finds allegorical details in this parable.

. . . we ought not to expect rabbinic literalism to admit a distinction between the literal and allegorical senses as supposedly being mutually exclusive, precisely because it exploits the resources of the letter in order to re-inforce its own variety of allegorical interpretation by adding thereto colourful verisimilitudes and these are sometimes discovered by a remorseless insistence upon one literal (or possible) meaning of a single word, in a sense paradoxical to the context as naturally under-stood. In discussing rabbinic exegesis, therefore, we ought perhaps to distinguish the idiosyncratic meaning of the term "literal" here by putting it into quotation marks, for the letter is not, as in Christian exegesis, the potentially jealous stepmother of allegory, but rather her willing handmaid or research assistant.[151]

Indeed the importance of the "word" has been exposed by M. Gertner whose passage is worth quoting *in extenso*:

Yet a midrash is not only based on a biblical text, to which the author normally refers, but also relies on certain techniques in handling this text and on various methods of interpreting it. Of the various techniques applied in midrash, mention will be made here only of those which are of interest in the discussion below. These are the following six techniques: "*al tiqrey*," that is, a changed or double reading of a word; "*tarety mashma*," that is a different or twofold meaning given to a word; enriching, that is, illuminating one passage of Scripture by another; *muqdamme'uhar*, that is, re-arranging the chronological, or contextual, order of the chapters in a book or the parts in a passage; changing

[151] *Op. cit.*, p. 159–162. Cf. also his article, "The Jewish Midrashim and Patristic and Scholastic Exegesis of the Bible," *Studia Patristica*, 63, vol. 1 (1957) pp. 492–514, but especially pp. 494, 503–508.

the grammatical or logical subject-object structure of a sentence; and, finally midrashim based on the homiletical interpretation of names.[152]

It is the "covert midrash" behind the parable which this exegesis has tried to trace.

It has been suggested that the Midrash is from the Canticle and the most likely chapter seems to be chapter 5: "I come to my garden, my sister my bride [*v.* 1]...I slept, but my heart was awake. Hark my beloved is knocking... [*v.* 2] I rose to open to my beloved... [*v.* 5], 33 or I 2–4 especially "...The king has brought me into his chambers [*v.* 4]." There may also be double meanings attached to "rose up," i.e., be spiritually elevated (*v.* 7)[153] and "lit their lamps," i.e., "spoke well" *v.* 7.[154]

If one can find this methodology in St. Matthew's parable (or parables), this is not to say that the other evangelists used the same method or even understood Jesus' use of it. All three evangelists refer to Christ as the bridegroom,[155] but it is St. Matthew who appears to bring this theme to a climax. To him may belong a peculiarly Rabbinical method of "parabolic" exegesis. Stendahl's thesis "The School of St. Matthew" is compelling. Although he quotes E. von Dobschutz[156] that Matthew may have been a Rabbi trained in the school of Johanan ben Zakkai, his own thesis, namely that a school created Matthew, presupposes a greater possibility of traditional Jewish influence from higher education in the *beth hamidrash*. If this were so,

---

[152] M. Gertner, the Midrashim in the New Testament, *Journal of Semitic Studies*, vol. 7, no. 2 (Autumn 1962) pp. 267–292. The passage is quoted from p. 270.
[153] Lev. R. 32:2, p. 409. Eccles R. 10:20, p. 281.
[154] *Vide supra*, p. 000.
[155] Matt. 9:15, Mark. 2:19 and Luke 5:34.
[156] Stendahl, *op. cit.*, p. 30.

then St. Matthew might have had access to teaching concerning the Canticle. In commenting on the use of Midrash,[157] Stendahl observes that

> The degree to which a quotation is exactly cited cannot be determined in a general statement consistent to the whole of the New Testament. We have already established that texts, if apocalyptic in nature, seldom contain quotations in the strict sense while at the same time, it is just these texts which are abounding in allusions which, with supreme freedom and skill, have been woven into the context. Revelation is itself a striking example of this. Without a single true quotation, nevertheless interwoven with O.T. material to a greater extent than any other writing in the New Testament. In the apocalypse of the gospels, as in their sayings of apocalyptic nature, we have found the same phenomenon. Consequently, there is no attempt to quote exactly in this form, and the citing is certainly freely given from memory. The prophet-spirit creates, it does not quote in order to teach or argue.

This section has attempted to discover the allusion which with supreme freedom and skill have been woven into the parable alone recorded by St. Matthew.

Now one must ask whether Jesus used the parable with the intention I suggested. It does not seem to the present writer to be beyond the bounds of possibility that Jesus did tell this parable to the Jewish leaders in approximately the form in which St. Matthew records it. Matthew, realizing its true import, incorporated it into his gospel according to the purposeful structure of that Gospel. The early church did not completely understand its message

---

[157] *Ibid.*, p. 158–159; cf. also pp. 183 ff.

or indeed the full meaning of the preceding parables and thus the "Foolish Virgins" became a watching parable instructing the people to be prepared for the coming of Christ, hence the addition of *v.* 13, (although, it is observed that in the other parables the servants do not sleep). Later the parable was appropriated by those who advocated male celibacy, for example, Aphraat who used it when speaking to the "sons of the covenant."[158] Still later it was used as a parable especially fitting for women virgins. By this time it had probably lost all connection with the Canticle.

The brief "allegorical" use of the Canticle which I suggest this parable formed and which was directed against Jewish teachers found a fuller allegorization first in Hippolytus and then in Origen. If Loewe's thesis is correct,[159] the next movement on the side of the Jews was the Targum as a polemic against the Christian use of the Canticle. Loewe notes the prominence of the Torah, especially the Oral Torah, in the Targum; although the scholars themselves are not the central attraction, yet scholarship itself is certainly stressed and praised. For example:

(1) ". . . God's praise of Israel is prefaced by an appeal for her return to Him, to Jerusalem, to the house of study and to a receptivity towards true prophetic teaching and a rejection of the false prophets" (p. 171 on 7:11);

(2) ". . . When eventually the Messiah is commissioned to take up his kingdom and reveals himself to Israel, he is welcomed by an invitation to join Israel in proceeding

---

[158] Aphraat, *"Demonstratio Sexta," De Monachis, M.P. Syriaca,* vol. 1., part I, cols. 239–240. See especially note 1.

[159] *Op. cit.,* (Apologetic Motifs in the Targum to the Canticle of Canticles).

to Jerusalem to attend a Talmudic discourse the unnamed guest lecturer being presumably the Deity himself..." (p. 172 [7:12–18. 14]);

(3) The Targum "reads an eulogy on the scholars of the Sanhedrin who possess the near-esoteric knowledge of astronomy for calculating (*heshbon*) matters of inter-calculations..." p. 176 on "*Your eyes are pools in Heshbon...*");

(4) The "kisses on the mouth" (1.2) have to do with the two tablets of the law, the six orders of the Mishnah and the Talmud. Finally commenting on the important verse 1. 4 "*The king brought me to his chambers*" the Targum reads "Draw us after Thee... and draw us near to the base of Mount Sinai, and give us Thy Torah from Thy treasure house (*min ganzakh*) of heaven..." p. 177.

Loewe comments:

> I suspect that it is rather a deliberate counter assertion of the enduring validity of Torah, and of the adequacy of the Sinaitic revelation, against the claims here made by patristic exegetical tradition for a new and superior revelation through Christ: and that the Targumist subtly insinuates his apologia by himself adopting (or reclaiming) Paul's metaphorical reference to all treasures of wisdom and knowledge hidden in Christ. Conceivably, too, an additional motive for the Targumist's identification was provided by the well-known words of Jesus himself (Matt. 5. 19) regarding laying up for yourselves treasures in Heaven.... (p. 180).

Thus it would seem that even in the seventh-century redaction of the Targum, there still remained a certain polemical note against the Christian idea of wisdom and a certain defense of Rabbinic scholarship and the importance of the Oral Torah. Therefore it might have been possible that this formed the original "*Sitz in Leben*" of the parable.[160] The purpose of this rather detailed exposition of the "Parable of the Foolish Scholars" is twofold. Firstly, the writer senses a certain connection between incipient Jewish mysticism as it is found in the midrash on the Canticle and the "symbolic" use of the term "virgin" in Rev. 14:4 and Matt. 25:1–13. To these texts, one might also add St. Paul's use of "virgin" in 2 Cor. 11:2: ἡρμοσάμην γὰρ ὑμᾶς ἑνὶ ἀνδρί, παρθένον ἁγνὴν παραστῆσαι τῷ Χριστῷ.

The marriage motif in religions became the chief vehicle in conveying profound union between the earthly community (synagogue and church) and the deity, but in contrast to "Gnosticism" one finds no disparagment of the *copula carnalis*. (This will be further discussed in the "Epiloque," *infra* pp. 216 f.)

Secondly, one sees the "symbolic" sense of virginity preceding its practice. Indeed, as will be seen in the following chapters, the theological import of virginity is appreciated to some extent, but the practice is the practice of continence rather than virginity. The importance of the "typological" interpretation of the "Parable of the Foolish Virgins" will be further expanded in the next section on the Greek writings, namely the Shepherd of Hermas.

A Note on Celibacy in the Greek and Roman Worlds

In Greece one finds that marriage was regarded as a duty

---

[160] Since the completion of this section has appeared the Rev. C. H. Cave's article, "The Parables and the Scriptures," *TS*, 11 (July, 1965) pp. 374–387. In this study the Rev. Cave exposes the scriptural readings behind some Marcan parables. This gives the parables a certain typological interpretation: it might be better to speak of "typology" in parables rather than of allegory in parables.

to the gods[161] and in the eyes of some philosophers it was a way of securing immortality. Marriage was a duty in Sparta; Lycurgus passed laws concerning this:

> The civil rights of unmarried men were curtailed; thus they were not allowed to take part in the festival of naked boys (gymnopaedia); in the winter they were ordered to go round to the market, while they sang a song of ridicule attacking themselves, declaring that they deserved what had happened to them, as they had disobeyed the laws of their country; and they were also deprived of the respect and attention which was usually shown by young people to their elders.[162]

Plato, also, makes marriage a legal demand and he would like punishment to be inflicted on those who live a single life.[163] According to Ariston not only bachelors but men who married late were punished.[164]

Roman law also legislated against bachelors and penalized childless men.[165] Statements against celibacy are found in Cicero *De leg.* 2; Valerius Maximus, 2, 9, 1; Livy, *epit.* 59, Gellius 1. 6. Augustus had to stress his laws against celibacy (Suetonius *Aug.* 34). But although one reads of the objections of men to these marriage laws, this does not mean that they wished to live single lives. No marriage for the Roman probably meant concubinage and the reasons for not desiring marriage were normally selfish, not God-inspired.[166]

[161] Hans Licht, *Sexual Life in Ancient Greece*, London, 1956, p. 34 refers to Plato, *Laws*, 6. 773.

[162] *Licht, op. cit.*, p. 35.

[163] *Laws*, 4. 721; 6. 774.

[164] See Licht *op. cit.*, p. 34. He refers to Stobaeus, *Sermones*, 67. 16.

[165] See Otto Kiefer, *Sexual Life in Ancient Rome*, London, 1963, p. 34.

[166] Further information about Roman "celibacy" is given by Kiefer (*ibid.*), pp. 30–39.

Perhaps the only people who advocated a respectable celibate life were the philosophers. Epictetus spoke persuasively of celibacy but was refuted by Musonius and neither of them quoted any individual examples of celibate men or women.[167] Rome provided the example of the Vestal Virgins, but these women did not embrace the life voluntarily and were permitted to marry when their term of service was completed. Their life was not one of ascetism if one judges by their privileges at circuses *et cetera*.

This note is added to allow for the possibility of pagan influence toward celibate lives in Corinth and among the early Christians generally. However, there does not seem to be sufficient evidence to prove that this could be the case.

[167] E. V. Arnold, *Roman Stoicism*, London, 1958, p. 368. Arnold quotes both Epictetus, "In the present state of things, which is like that of an army placed in battle order, is it not fit that the Cynic should without any distraction be employed only in the ministration of God? To say nothing of other things, a father must have a heating apparatus for bathing the baby; wool for his wife when she is delivered..." (Epict., *Disc*. 3.22, 69–75) and Musonius, "Marriage was no hindrance to Pythagoras, Socrates or Crates; and who were better philosophers than they?... He who would destroy marriage, destroys the family and the commonwealth..." (*Stob*. 4.22, 20). See the *Oxford Classical Dictionary*, Oxford 1957, under *Vesta* and also A. Pauly, *Real-Encyclopedia der classischen Alternumwissenschaft*, ed. G. Wissowa, Stuttgart, 1893 ff.

CHAPTER 5

Celibacy in the Writings of the Subapostolic Fathers and Apologists

I SUBAPOSTOLIC FATHERS

Any statistical survey of material from patristic sources[1] must of its very nature be superficial because of the paucity of extant works. Nevertheless one is immediately struck by the dearth of references to παρθένος and its cognates[2] and the apparently apposite text, 1 Cor. 7:25, 36–38 in the earliest Christian writers. The accompanying table[3] shows the approximate rise in the popularity of virginity from the first to the fourth century. The scanty references in the first and the second century are more marked when they are contrasted with the many complete works devoted to the subject in the later centuries.

A   The Epistle of Barnabas and the Epistle of Diognetus

There is no allusion whatsoever to those living in celibacy or virginity; neither the word παρθένος or

[1] See the accompanying chart, pp. 230 ff.

129

εὐνοῦχος³ occurs; furthermore, 1 Cor. 7 and Matt. 19:11, 12 is not quoted.

B   The Shepherd of Hermas⁴

The setting of the *Shepherd of Hermas* appears to be so Jewish that one would not expect to find "consecrated virgins" (men or women) within the context. Nevertheless the numerous references to παρθένοι (feminine) and the section in Sim. IX. 10:6 to 11:8 concerning Hermas' night with the virgins present a difficulty. However, it would appear that even here the Jewish background prevails, and it is possible that the chief source of the author's imagery is a writing akin to the Midrash on the Canticle of Canticles.⁵ Although the Greek of individual words in the *Shepherd* varies frequently from the LXX version of the Canticle, there are numerous common themes.⁶ In both occur the familiar themes of shepherd,⁷ flock,⁸

---

² *Εὐνοῦχος* is used for male celibates in Clement of Alexandria. Origen appears to prefer the masculine παρθένος.

³ E. J. Goodspeed, *Index Patristicum sive clavis patrum apostolicorum operum*, Leipzig, 1907, does not record the use of εὐνοῦχος in the Apostolic Fathers. I regret that I have been unable to consult his second volume containing the fathers after the apostolic and sub-apostolic age. There are, however, several references to εὐνοῦχος in *PGL*.

⁴ Text—*The Shepherd of Hermas*, ed. by Miss M. Whittaker, Berlin, 1957.

⁵ Soncino translation, *op. cit.* Cf. also the Midrashic background to the *Shepherd* discussed in the author's "Thou art 'Abraham' and upon this rock..." (Matt. 16:16 ff.), *Heythrop Journal* (July, 1965) pp. 298 f.

⁶ It should also be remembered that the original of Hermas might have been in Ethiopic or Coptic although these seem to be versions rather than originals.

⁷ Cant. 1:8; Sim. VI. 2.

stones,[9] towers,[10] love,[11] wisdom,[12] kissing,[13] embracing,[14] singing,[15] dancing,[16] mountains,[17] hills[18] and sister-brides.[19] Neither the *Shepherd* nor the Canticle may be taken literally and it seems most reasonable to align one-self with those scholars who see the *Shepherd* as a sus-tained allegory:[20] the portion about the virgins should not be excepted from this, despite the arguments of Daniélou and Achelis.[21] It would seem that here, once again, one meets the themes of virginity (in its symbolic sense) and wisdom which was noted in Philo (pp. 21 ff. *supra*), in the Essenes and the Therapeutae (pp. 34 ff. *supra*) and in the "Parable of the Foolish 'Scholars'" (pp. 102 ff. *supra*). The *Shepherd* illustrates a combination of both Hellenistic and

---

[8] Cant. 1:7; Sim. VI. 1.

[9] Cant. 5:14; Sim. IX. 8.

[10] Cant. 7:4; Sim. IX. 10.

[11] Cant. 2:10; Sim. IX. 11.

[12] Cant. 1:2 (*vide infra*, pp. 133 ff. for the interpretation); Sim. IX. 11.

[13] Cant. 1:2; Sim. IX. 11.

[14] Cant. 2:6; Sim. IX. 11.

[15] Cf. Cant. 1 and 4; Sim. IX. 11.

[16] Cf. Cant. 2:8; Sim. IX. 11.

[17] Cant. 2:8; Sim. IX. 14.

[18] I have made some attempt to explain the "strange mixture" of metaphors from architecture and obstetrics in the paper mentioned above (note 5). I believe the same explanation may be applied to the *Shepherd* and, perhaps to the Cant. of Cant. My explanation orig-inates from the play on the Hebrew words "build" and "beget," "sucklers" and "builders."

[19] Cant. 5:1; Sim. XI. 11.

[20] For a recent summary of some of the interpretations of the Cant. of Cant., see L. Cantwell, "The Allegory of the Canticle of Can-ticles," *Scripture*, vol. 16 (July, 1964).

[21] Achelis, *Virgines Subintroductae, Ein Beitrag zu 1 Cor. 7*, Leipzig, 1902 (chapter III *supra*, p. 89 f.). J. Danielou, *The Theology of Jewish Christianity*, vol. 1 *A History of Early Christian Doctrine*, London, 1964, pp. 351 ff.

Jewish thought—the two working in perfect harmony.
The virgins are probably figurative agents of the precepts
of God, teachers of wisdom and revelation. They are
adaptations of the theme of Wisdom as a woman,[22] as a
virgin in Philo [23] and of the prophets compared to women
in the Midrashim: [24]

> *If Thou know not, O Thou fairest among women* means,
> Thou fairest among prophets, thou most eminent of
> prophets. R. Jose b. Jeremiah said: Why are the proph-
> ets compared to women? To show that just as woman is
> not ashamed to demand from her husband the require-
> ments of her household, so the prophets were not
> ashamed to demand the requirements of Israel from
> their Father in heaven.

The following are some of the similarities which may be
found between the *Shepherd* and Midrash Rabbah, Song
of Songs.

(1.) The first of these is the kissing theme. (Sim. IX. 11:4).
" . . . began to kiss and embrace me . . . and to play with
me" (cf. Cant. 1.2). In the Midrash "kisses" [25] are interpreted as the precepts of the Lord, or the Holy Spirit, and
are used to convey the idea of the reception of Torah
directly from God, not through an intermediary: [26] " . . .
'Our master, Moses, would that God might be revealed to
us a second time! Would that He *would kiss us with the
kisses of His lips*! Would that He would fix the knowledge
of the Torah in our hearts as it was!' He replied to them:

[22] Prov. 9; Wisdom 7, *et cetera*.
[23] Philo, Cher. 49–50.
[24] Cant. of Cant. R. 1:7, 2–3, p. 64. One notes that the same passage
(p. 63) speaks of shepherds as leaders of Israel.
[25] Cant. of Cant. R. 1:2, 1–2, p. 21 f. This theme becomes popular
in later writings, e.g., Ambrose.
[26] *Ibid.* 1:2, 4, p. 26; see notes 2 and 3 *ibid.*

'This cannot be now, but it will be in the days to come . . .'"
(Cant. R.I. 2, para. 4).

(2.) The "love" imagery in this section of the *Shepherd*
can be paralleled in Cant. R. 1, 3 (pp. 40–41). Commenting
on "Therefore do the maidens (*'alamoth*) love thee" (Cant.
1:3), the Midrash reads, "With youthful energy (*almuth*
and vigour . . . . What is the meaning of [*'almuth*]? In two
worlds ([*'alamoth*]) He will guide us—in this world and
the next. Another explanation of *al-muth* is, with energy
(*alimuth*) and vigour. Another explanation of *'al-muth* is,
like those maidens of whom it says, In the midst of
damsels ('alamoth) playing upon timbrels." (*ibid.* 68. 26).
This thought may also be the basis for the *Shepherd*, XX,
11, 5: "I too, had, as it were, become young again and
began to play with them myself, for some were dancing,
others were gavotting, others were singing, and I walked
in silence with them round the tower and was merry with
them." [27] One may compare this theme of merriment and
youth, which is prominent both in Cant. of Cant. and in
the *Shepherd*, with that in the Midrash [28] "We will be glad
and rejoice in Thee" where one finds the "ten expressions
of joy" in connection with Israel.

(3.) The maidens who help in the building of the Tower
may represent the "daughters of Jerusalem." [29] The citation reads: "*O Ye daughters of Jerusalem*. The Rabbis say:
Read not *benoth* (*daughters*) but *bonoth*—ye build Jerusalem: by this is meant the great Sanhedrin of Israel who sit
and instruct them in every difficulty and point of law . . . .
What is meant by daughters? Towns . . . Israel are compared to a female . . ." The maidens, therefore, represent

[27] I used the Loeb translation, Kirsopp Lake, 1913.
[28] Cant. of Cant. R. 1:4, 1.
[29] Cant. of Cant. R. 1:5, 3 (Cant. of Cant. 5. 1).

teachers—the figure of speech being taken over from a Jewish play on the words "daughters" and "builders." The fact that they are teachers is evident from the words of Hermas in reply to the *Shepherd*,[30] "...I supped, Sir, ...on the words of the Lord the whole night."[31]

(4.) The theme "sister-bride" occurs frequently in the Cant. of Cant. In the Midrash,[32] Israel is found as both "bride" and "sister"; in addition the Rabbis or teachers are compared to brides.[33] However, the text which is closest to the *Shepherd* is Cant. of Cant. 8:1 "O, that you were *like a brother* to me...If I met you outside, I would *kiss* you, and none would *despise* me."[34] With this may be compared the *Shepherd* XI. 11. 3: "'You shall sleep with us...as a *brother and not as a husband*, for you are our brother and for the future we are going to live with you, for we love you greatly'. *But I was ashamed* to stay with them ... Then the shepherd came and said to the maidens: 'Have you done him any despite....'"

Hermas's night with the maidens is akin to the interpretation of Cant. of Cant. 1:4 "The King hath brought me into his chambers." "We learnt elsewhere: Four entered the Garden ..."[35] (that is studied the mysteries of the Creation and the Divine Chariot).[36]

There is also a similarity to Cant. 5:1, "I am come into my garden." "It does not say here, 'I am come into the garden,' but *I am come into my garden* (ganni): as if to say, to my bridal-chamber (*ginnuni*): to the place which was

---

[30] "Shepherd" is often used in the sense of teachers.
[31] Sim. IX. 11. 8.
[32] Cant. 4:12; 5:1.
[33] Cant. of Cant. R. 4:10, 1 and *vide supra*, pp. 109 ff.
[34] The italics are mine.
[35] Cant. of Cant. R. 1:4, 1.
[36] *Ibid.*, note 5.

my real home originally; for was not the original home of
the *Shechinah* in the lower realm? . . . . "[37]
A similar idea is found in Philo where commenting on
Abimelech is seeing Issac sport with his wife (Gen. 28:8)
he says " . . . a divine pursuit, the wise man making merry
with her who waits patiently for all that is beautiful"
(Plant. 169f.).

(5.) Further "sleep" (Sim. IX. 11. 3) may be given an
allegorical sense, for example, from the same Midrash, "I
sleep, but my heart waketh . . . I sleep in respect of righteous
deeds, but my heart is awake [in desire] to do them."[38]

(6.) If this section of the *Shepherd* were an example of the
practice of *subintroductae*, one should expect Hermas to be
attached to one particular maiden, not many maidens.[39]
But the number of maidens surrounding him may be
interpreted in a similar way to the "fourscore concubines" (Song 6:7)—"*And fourscore concubines*: these are
the eighty companies of the fairly good who sit and study
the Torah outside of the Tree of Life. And the *maidens
without number*: there is no end to the disciples."[40] This
whole section, therefore, could be an allegory expressing
the mystical bestowal of spiritual wisdom; this would be
in keeping with the main theme of the whole treatise,
namely the spiritual education of Hermas.

In Sim. IX. 1:2 there occurs the phrase ὡς ὑπο παρθένου.
The whole passage reads "For since you were too weak in
the flesh, it was not shown to you by an angel. But when
you were strengthened by the spirit, and made strong in

[37] *Ibid.*, 5:1, 1. *Vide infra*, pp. 223 f.
[38] *Ibid.*, 5:2, 1.
[39] Polygamous *subintroductae* relationships would hardly be possible.
[40] Cant. of Cant. R. 6:9, 1–3.

your strength, so that you could see an angel, then the building of the tower was shown to you by the Church. You saw all things well and holily as if from a virgin. But now you see them from an angel, yet through the same Spirit." Here again "virgin" may be used in the sense of teacher but one who ranks lower than the angels. Kirsopp Lake[41] observes, "The point is that the form of the Vision was accommodated to Hermas' powers. It was at first sent in the form of a human being (the emphasis is on the humanity, not the virginity) and afterwards when he was stronger spiritually in the form of an angel." One cannot tell whether $\pi\alpha\rho\theta\acute{\epsilon}\nu o\varsigma$ is masculine or feminine, but if it is feminine then it may refer to the maidens in Sim. IX. 10–11. $\Pi\alpha\rho\theta\acute{\epsilon}\nu o\varsigma$ may also convey the meaning of "one who is free from emotion and passion," for Philo says that Sarah became a "youth" after "the custom of women had ceased."[42] That is, she was no longer swayed by passion. Rachel is called "ever-virgin."[43] The meaning is possibly that such women remain emotionally stable and, like a pubescent, unaffected by lust. If this interpretation is correct, one must conclude, then, that the *Shepherd of Hermas* does not contribute any information about the history of consecrated virgins or the theology of virginity. It is a Hellenistic Jewish-Christian allegory which uses the symbolism of virginity.

C   The Didache

Whatever date one suggests for this work, its antiquity may be supported by the absence of the mention of

---

[41] *Op. cit.*, p. 217, note 1.
[42] Philo, *Post.* 134.; *Cher.* 40–50.
[43] *Ibid.*

παρθένος [44] or εὐνοῦχος and any reference to 1 Cor. 7 or Matt. 19:11, 12. This makes one hesitate to accept Daniélou's statement.[45]

The prophet has no possessions and lives on alms, and in addition he seems to preserve virginity.[46] This seems to be the meaning of a passage in the *Didache* not so far considered: "And every prophet approved and found true, if he doeth ought as a cosmic mystery of the Church, and yet teacheth not others to do all that he himself doeth, shall not be judged by you" (XI, 11).

In addition Daniélou says that "the expression 'cosmic mystery of the Church' seems to stand in opposition to a 'heavenly mystery of the Church'. This latter mystery is the celestial marriage of Christ to the Church, which also finds its expression in this world." Daniélou then supports his argument by reference to "spiritual unions which existed in Jewish Christianity between prophet-apostles and a sister" and further substantiates it by quotations from Hermas, Sim. IX, 10:6–11:8; 1 Cor. 7:36 ff;. and the practice of the Gnostics (*Adv. haer.* I. 21:3). I have dealth with both 1 Cor. 7:36 ff. and Hermas Sim. IX, 10:6 and 11:8 and have suggested that neither passage is connected with the subject of *subintroductae*. As far as the Gnostic influence is concerned, one might say:

(1.) it is still a moot point whether it can be identified with "Jewish-Christianity";

(2.) one cannot align prophet and Gnostic too closely; the Gnostic had esoteric knowledge, the prophet normally wished to instruct the ordinary members of the Church;

(3.) the early Fathers were at pains to oppose this practice

[44] But Eve is also called *parthenos* in 12:8.
[45] Danielou, *op. cit.*, pp. 351.
[46] The italics are mine.

of *subintroductae* and also the aberrations of the Gnostics about marriage;

(4.) the allusion to marriage and virginity or continence is not found in this passage of the *Didache* (c. XI);[47]

Consequently, the interpretation of Père Audet,[48] who sees in the cosmic mystery of the Church a type of prophetic *ôth*, appears to be more possible. The *Didache*, therefore, like the *Shepherd*, does not contribute to the history or theology of virginity.

D   I Clement

If a group of virgins lived in Corinth at the time of St. Paul, it would be natural to expect St. Clement to mention them in his epistle; but, although the subject of families and marriage is touched upon (for example chapters 1, 3, 6) and various dissensions are mentioned, there is not a word about virgins. This is even more surprising since there is a reference to continence (38) "Let him that is pure (ἀγνός) in the flesh not grow proud of it, and boast knowing that it was another who bestowed on him the gift of continence (ἐγκράτειαν)." A similar phrase "Having kept the flesh pure" (τὴν σάρκα ἁγνὴν τηρήσαντες) occurs in the second epistle 8:4–6 and here it is connected with baptism, "He means, then, this: Keep the flesh pure (ἁγνὴν), and the seal of baptism (ἄσπιλον), undefiled, that we may obtain eternal life." But, again, there is no mention of virginity.

---

[47] Cf., however, *infra*, p. 223 for a discussion of the "cosmic mystery" in Jewish mysticism. The Jewish character of the *Didache* might suggest that influence came from this direction. On the other hand, the Jewish influence would not give any encouragement to celibacy.

[48] J. P. Audet, *Le Didache*, Paris, 1958, pp. 447–453.

""Aγνος" means pure or holy but not necessarily virgin.[49]

E Epistles of Ignatius and of Polycarp

Exactly the same situation is found in the Epistles of Ignatius and Polycarp. The only references to virgin here are:

Smyrn. 1:1 (the virgin Mary); Smyrn. 13:1 (*vide supra* pp. 16 f.); Polycarp, *Ad Phil.* 5:3 (where the feminine παρθένος is opposed to νεώτεροι, young men). There is, however, a reference to continence which is similar to the one quoted above in 1 Clement, "If anyone can continue in a state of purity (ἀγνεία), to the honour of the flesh of the Lord (εἰς τιμὴν τῆς σαρκὸς τοῦ κυρίου), let him so remain without boasting" (*Ad Poly.* 5:2).

However, the most important evidence in these epistles is to be found in the "House Codes" for which tables are given below (pp. 140 ff.). One should see that "virgins" only occur in the "House Codes" which can be dated later than the subapostolic age. For the New Testament "House Codes" one cannot do better than consult Selwyn's[50] Tables especially Tables 7 (p. 416), 10 (p. 423), 11 (p. 427), 12 (p. 430), 13 (p. 432). In these, eunuchs and virgins have no place and widows do not appear there but rather in a separate passage, namely 1 Tim. 5.

The situation is not changed in 1 Clem, for in c. 21 the following "house code" is found:[51]

" . . . let us esteem those who have the rule over us; let us

---

[49] I. Clement is perhaps too Jewish to conceive of celibacy. Cf. the author's "To the Corinthians or to the Hebrews?" *CBQ* (October, 1966).

[50] E. G. Selwyn, *The First Epistle of St. Peter*, London, 1958.

[51] I take just a representative group of codes.

honour the aged (or the presbyters) among us; let us train up the young men in the fear of God; let us direct our wives to that which is good. Let them exhibit the lovely habit of purity [in all their conduct]; . . . let your children be partakers of true Christian training. . .";

or in the *Epistle of Polycarp*:[52]

". . . your wives [to walk] in the faith given to them . . . to train up their children. . . . Teach the widows to be discreet. . . (τας χήρας σωφρονούσας περὶ τὴν τοῦ κυρίου πίστιν) knowing that they are the altar of God (θυσιασ-τήριον θεοῦ), and that all offerings are tested (καὶ ὅτι πάντα μωμοσκοπεῖται)";

and

". . . the deacons be blameless . . . let the young men also be blameless . . . and 'the young girls'";[53]

and

". . . let the presbyters be compassionate and merciful."[54]

Thus, it is only widows who have a special mention.

The genuine epistles of St. Ignatius show little difference from the New Testament and from the works quoted above, but both the longer recension and the spurious epistles exhibit considerable change in church order and in the emphasis on asceticisim:[55]

Genuine epistles	*Longer recension (C. 4)*[56]	*Spurious epistles*
Ad Phil. c. 4. ". . . as there is one bishop, along with the presbyters and deacons, my fellowservants: do this and you will do after God's bidding . . . ."	". . . and one bishop, with the presbytery and deacons . . . wives be subject to your husbands . . . and *ye virgins*, to Christ in purity (αἱ παρθένοι τῷ χριστῷ ἐν ἀφθαρσία) not counting marriage an abomination, but desir-	*Ad Phil.* c. 15 col. 940 " salute the company o virgins and the order o widows of whom may have joy."

Genuine epistles	Longer recension (C. 4)[56]	Spurious epistles

Longer recension (C. 4)[56]

ing that which is better, not for the reproach of wedlock, but for *the meditating of the law* (ἀλλ ἔνεκα τῆς τοῦ νόμου μελέτης). "Children ... servants ... husbands ... *Virgins, have Christ alone before your eyes* and His Father in your prayers, being enlightened by the Spirit ...." "May I have pleasure in your purity (ἁγνεία) as that of Elias, or as of Joshua,[57] ... Melchizedek, Eliseus, Jeremias[58] John the Baptist, the beloved disciple ... Timothy ... Titus ... Evodius ... Clement, who departed this life in perfect chastity. (τῶν ἐν ἁγνεία ἐξελθόντων τὸν βίον). Not, however, that I blame the other blessed [saints] because they entered the married state ... Abraham ... the *prophets* ... Peter and *Paul* and the *rest of apostles that were married men*[59] .... Let governors be obedient to Caesar; soldiers ... deacons ... presbyters .... Let not the widows be wanderers but ... like Judith ... like Anna ...."

Ad Smyrn. c. 12

"... families of my brethren, with their wives and children and the *virgins who are called widows* (τὰς παρθένους τὰς λεγομένας χήρας)."

"I salute the families of my brethren with their wives and children, and those that are ever-virgins, and the widows[60] (καὶ ἀειπαρθένους καὶ τὰς χήρας)".

Ad Tarsians 9, col. 896

c. 9. "Husbands ... wives ... children. Honour those (who continue) in virginity (τὰς ἐν παρθενία τιμᾶτε) as *priestesses* of Christ (ὡς ἱερείας χριστοῦ.) and the widows that persevere in the gravity of behaviour

142　A Trilogy on Wisdom and Celibacy

Genuine epistles	Longer recension (C. 4)[56]	Spurious epistles

(τὰς ἐν σεμνότητι χήρας) as the altar of God (ὡ θυσιαστήριον) . . . ser vants . . . masters . . . ." *Ad Antioch. col. 905 c. 8* ". . . presbyters . . . dea cons . . . peoples . . . Le the virgins (Αι παρθένοι known to whom the have consecrated them selves (γινωσκέτωσαν τίνι καθιέρωσαν ἑαυτάς). c. 9. ". . . husbands . . . wives. . . parents . . . children . . ." c. 10. ". . . masters . . . ser vants . . ." c. 11. ". . . let widows not live a life of pleasure . . . ." *Ad Antioch. col. 908* c. 12. "I salute the holy pres bytery . . . sacred dea cons . . . sub-deacons . . readers . . . singers . . . doorkeepers . . . exor cists . . . deaconesses in Christ (τὰς ἐν χριστῳ διακόνους . . . χριστολή πτους παρθένους, ὧν ὀνα ἱμην ἐν κυρίῳ Ἰησοῦ)." *Ad Hero. c. 5.* ". . . Watch over the virgins (παρθένους φυλατ τε) as the precious trea sures of Christ . . . (ὦ χριστοῦ κειμήλια)."

For footnotes see page 143

These tables show that during the subapostolic age the virgins did not constitute a distinct class as they did in *circa* 380 A.D. when these epistles in the longer recension and the spurious epistles were written. If a class of "virgins" is not found in the subapostolic age, then it is highly improbable that they could be found at the time when St. Paul wrote 1 Corinthians. It is interesting to observe that the virgins in the long recension and the spurious epistles are feminine and also that they begin to take precedence over the widows.

The Pseudo-Clementine literature is not within the scope of this thesis, but it is perhaps worth remarking that the *Homilies and Recognitiones* have a great deal about chastity but nothing about virginity whereas the two Epistles concerning Virginity[61] stress eunuchs and virgins (feminine) and chapter 6 in Epistle 1 is very similar to the longer recension of Ignatius *Ad Phil.* c. 4. They serve to form a contrast with the earlier literature that I have been discussing.

[52] *Ad. Phil.*, 4:3.

[53] *Ibid.*, chap. 5.

[54] *Ibid.*, chap. 6.

[55] Text Migne, *PG*.

[56] See Altaner, *op. cit.*, p. 58 f.

[57] Cf. Tertullian (*supra*, p. 196).

[58] I think that this is the first reference to Jeremiah as a celibate. I do not think that any of the Jewish texts mention him as such; Tertullian omits him.

[59] Cf. pp. 70 f *supra* (Chapter III), where there is a discussion of St. Paul as a married man.

[60] See my discussion on this point pp. 21 ff, Chapter II. It is interesting that the phrase "ever-virgin" should appear.

[61] Dr. S. Brook informs me that where the masculine of "virgin" is used in the Syriac, the Coptic has "eunuch."

II   THE APOLOGISTS

The Apologists give a few hints that some Christians did embrace a life of continence; however the following quotations are the only sources which provide material to work from:

A.   Justin Martyr, *Apol.* c. 15

> For not only he who in act commits adultery is rejected by Him, but also he who desires to commit adultery; since not only our works, but also our thoughts, are open before God. And many, both men and women, who have been Christ's disciples from childhood, remain pure (ἀφθόροι) at the age of sixty or seventy years; and I boast that I could produce such from every race of men.

The statement does not stress eunuchs or virgins and, indeed, the last clause suggests that Christian morality is not necessarily higher than other "races."

B.   Athenagoras, Supp. c. 33

After speaking of chaste wedlock, Athenagoras states:
> Nay, you would find many among us, both men and women, growing old unmarried (καταγηράσκοντας ἀγαμούς) [or as widows] in hope of living in closer communion with God. But if the remaining in virginity (ἐν παρθενία) and the state of an eunuch (ἐν εὐνουχία) brings nearer to God, while the indulgence of carnal thought and desire leads away from him, in those cases in which we shun the thoughts, much more do we reject the deeds. For we bestow our attention, not on the study

of words, but on the exhibition and teaching of actions
—that a person should either remain as he was born
(οἶος τις ἐτέχθη) or be content with one marriage (ἐφ'
ἑνὶ γάμῳ); for a second marriage is only a specious
adultery (ὁ γὰρ δεύτερος εὐπρεπής ἐστι μοιχεία).
This is the first passage which clearly indicated Christians
living in virginity according to the teaching of Christ in
Matt. 19:11, 12 (not 1 Cor . .),[62] but the practical emphasis seems to be on widowhood (cf. ἀγαμούς, supra).

C.

Irenaeus, even though he speaks highly of the virginity
of Mary (for example, in Bk. V. c. 19), does not seem
to advocate the life of celibacy.

D.

Hippolytus of Rome, in spite of the fact that he speaks
about the Essenes' and the Montanists' views of marriage does not mention orthodox Christian eunuchs or
virgins. He has no reference to 1 Cor. 7 or Matt. 19:11, 12.
The result, therefore, seems to be that there is only one
clear reference in these early works to Christians living in
celibacy (Athenagoras, supra); but there are, however,
several references to continence and to those who live in
purity of the flesh, e.g., I. Clem. c. 38; Ig. Ad. Poly. c. 5;
Just. Martyr Apol. 29. These people in Clement and Ignatius are warned not to boast or to be proud: this warning
may suggest that only a few embraced this way of life and
that, as it was fairly rare, there was a tendency for these
people to try to be singular in their behavior.

[62] Theophilus of Antioch has no information on this point.

CHAPTER 6

Celibacy in the Writings of Clement
of Alexandria and Origen

I CLEMENT OF ALEXANDRIA[1]

It is Clement of Alexandria who first devoted a complete section of a work to continence, namely in *Stromata* Bk. 3. The section shows that the Church was too concerned with fighting heresies which disparaged marriage to advocate too strongly the state of virginity for her own members. Bk. 3 of *Strom.* is devoted to a polemic—on the one side against those who treated marriage as sinful, and, on the other, against those who indulged in licentiousness.[2] Clement is obliged to find the golden mean between both:

[1] Text MG, vols. 8 and 9. Translation in *Alexandrian Christianity* (Library of Christian Classics), vol. II trans. by J. E. L. Oulton and H. Chadwick, London, 1954, pp. 15–165.

[2] See Chadwick, *op. cit.*, pp. 15–33. In the text see chapters 1, 2, 3, 4 and 12. Chadwick notes the relationship between election and predestination and chastity. The Valentinians believed that the "elect" could marry but those less gifted with spiritual graces should abstain from marriage, pp. 30–32. Predestination is another "heresy" which had to be suppressed before celibacy could be established as a practice for many.

146

he recognizes the celibate life but tends to advise marriage.[3] He speaks of *ἐγκράτεια*[4] and *ἀγνεία* in their widest sense of abstinence from desire[5] including coitus; moreover, he recognizes that the duties of marriage are just as much things belonging to the Lord as the duties of a continent life,[6] " . . . Both celibacy and marriage have their own different forms of service and ministry to the Lord . . ." (3:79).

It is significant that 1 Cor. 7. *vv*. 25, 36–38 are not used by the heretics in support of their misogamy. Their "proof texts" are Matt. 19:12; 22:30; Rom. 6:14; 1 Cor. 7, 5, 39 and 40 and the *Gospel of the Hebrews*. Clement, on the other hand, employs 1 Cor. 7:2, 5, 27 in defense of marriage[7] and uses these in combination with 1 Tim. 4:1–3. Further he finds it necessary to allegorize Matt. 24:5, 37 ff.; Luke 8:8 and Isa. 56. In c. 6. speaking of "Woe to those who are with child" he says, " . . . a saying, I admit, to be understood allegorically."

Clement finds a spiritual meaning for the word "eunuch" and the word "virgin": "a eunuch, then, does not mean a man who has been castrated, nor even an unmarried man, but a man who is unproductive of truth . . .";[8] " . . . the Lord's Scriptures, which bring forth the truth and yet

[3] See H. Chadwick, "All things to all men" (1 Cor. 9:22) NTS, no. 4, 1 (May, 1956) pp. 261–275, especially pp. 263–270 and the references cited there.
[4] Col. 1164 B and trans. (*op. cit.*) c. 7.
[5] *Ibid.*
[6] C. 12:79. See also c. 5: "If it is lawful to live any sort of life one likes, obviously one may live in continence; or if any kind of life has no dangers for the elect, obviously one of virtue and self-control is far less dangerous. . . ."
[7] Clement's arguments suggest that he sees "concession" in 1 Cor. 7:6 as a concession to "abstain," not "to marry."
[8] C. 15:99.

remain virgins, hiding within them the mysteries of the truth . . . ."[9]

Clement's source for these ideas is probably Philo, for example, when he says that the Eunuch of Pharaoh is the mind incapable of begetting wisdom[10] and when he refers to Sarah as wisdom whose virginity "is not of the ever-virgin type but she typifies those who pass from woman-hood to virginity (*Post.* 134)." Clement shows acquaintance with 1 Cor. 7. 36, for he refers to it at the beginning of c. 12[11] and stresses St. Paul's two conditions for abstinence: firstly, there must be a limit to the duration lest the partners should fall into sin; secondly, abstinence should be practised only by mutual consent, "lest anyone should dissolve his marriage":

> If by agreement marriage relations are suspended for a time to give opportunity for prayer, this teaches continence. He adds the words "by agreement" lest anyone should dissolve his marriage, and the words "for a time" lest a married man, brought to continence by force, should then fall into sin; for if he spares his own wife he may fall into desire for another woman.[12]

After this discussion of 1 Cor. 7:5 and continence within marriage, Clement turns immediately to a discussion of 1 Cor. 7:36 without alluding to any change of subject:

> On this principle he said that the man who thinks he is not behaving properly if *he brings up his daughter to be unmarried, does right to give her in marriage.* Whether a

---

[9] C. 16:94; cf. Bk. 7., c. 12:72: "They are virgins who abstain from evil."

[10] Cf. Philo, *Leg. All.*, 3:236–241.

[11] Col. 1179–1180.

[12] The Greek text reads:

Ὧ λόγῳ καὶ τὸν ἀσχημονεῖν ἑαυτὸν ἐπὶ τῇ παρθενοτροφίᾳ ὑπολαμβά-νοντα καλῶς εἰς γάμον ἐκδώσειν τὴν θυγατέρα ἔλεγεν.

man becomes a celibate (εὐνουχίσαντος) or whether he joins himself in marriage with a woman for the sake of having children, his purpose ought to be to remain unyielding to what is inferior. If he can live a life of intense devotion he will gain to himself great merit with God, since his continence is both pure and reasonable. But if he goes beyond the rule he has chosen to gain greater glory, there is a danger that he may lose hope.[13]

The text requires some comments.

Firstly, Clement seems to be quoting from memory or paraphrasing: the words underlined indicate variations from the New Testament text. The inexactitude of the rendering requires that one does not place too much reliance on Clement's understanding of the text.

Secondly, it is remarkable that Clement introduces the word θυγάτηρ in apposition to παρθένος: there appears to be no manuscript authority for this. This addition of θυγάτηρ increases the difficulty of the text, for immediately after referring to a virgin daughter, Clement speaks of the man keeping himself from marriage: ἑαυτὸν εὐνουχίσαντος; but if it is a father who gives in marriage, there is no question of his remaining chaste himself unless an incestuous union is contemplated; this is impossible.

Thirdly, the above inconsistency may stem from Clement's recognition of the difficulty of reconciling the two verbs γαμείτωσαν (v. 36) and γαμίζων (v. 38). Levirate marriage would not be a practice with which the Greek Clement would be familiar, and consequently he added the word "daughter" in his attempt to elucidate the text.

---

[13] The Greek text reads:

Ἡ πρόθεσίς τε ἑκάστου τοῦ τε ἑαυτὸν εὐνουχίσαντος τοῦ τε αὖ γάμῳ διὰ παιδοποιίαν συζεύξαντος, ἀνένδοτος πρὸς τὸ ἧττον διαμένειν ὀφείλει. Εἰ μὲν γὰρ ἐπιτεῖναι οἷός τε ἔσται τὸν βίον, μείζονα ἀξίαν ἐν

Fourthly, Clement's phrase ἐπὶ τῇ παρθενοτροφία[14] probably translates τηρεῖν τὴν ἑαυτοῦ παρθένον in 1 Cor. 7:37. The Latin translation reads "*quod virginem alat.*" Both the Greek and Latin suggest that τηρεῖν is used in the sense of maintenance or support (financially and economically) of the virgin. *Τηρεῖν* is used for maintainance or board in kind or money.

Even if Clement of Alexandria is vague about St. Paul's meaning in 1 Cor. 7:36–38, he is quite clear about the general tenor of the apostle's teaching on marriage and continence. He summarizes this in c. 12. (col. 1188) (para. 86):

> In general all the epistles of the apostle teach self-control and continence and contain numerous instructions about marriage, begetting children and domestic life. But they nowhere rule out self-controlled marriage. Rather they preserve the harmony of the law and the gospel and approve both the man who with thanks to God enters upon marriage with sobriety and the man who in accordance with the Lord's will lives a celibate (εὐνουχιᾳ) life, even as each individual is called, making his choice without blemish and in perfection. (12:86 M6, col. 1188).

In Clement's own view St. Paul[15] and the daughters of Phillip[16] are married and the apostles took their wives

---

θεῷ αὐτὸς ἑαυτῷ περιποιήσεται, καθαρῶς ἅμα καὶ λελογισμένως ἐγκρατευσάμενος εἰ δὲ ὑπερβὰς ὅν εἵλετο κανόνα εἰς μείζονα δόξαν, ἔπειτα ἀποπέσε πρὸς τὴν ἐλπίδα.

[14] Liddell and Scott comment that this word is peculiar to Clement of Alexandria.

[15] C. 6., col. 1156. See also the notes in the Migne text.

[16] Clement does not state that he is referring to Philip the Evangelist, but it seems likely that he has Acts 21:9 in mind.

around with them like sisters.[17] The passage reads as follows:

> Or do they also scorn the apostles?. . . Peter and Philip had children and Philip gave his daughters in marriage. . . . Paul addressed his consort (Phil. 4:3). The only reason why he did not take her about with him was that it would have been an inconvenience for his ministry. Accordingly he says in a letter: "Have we not a right to take about with us a wife that is a sister like the other apostles?" But the latter, in accordance with their particular ministry, devoted themselves to preaching without any distraction, and took their wives with them not as women with whom they had marriage relations, but as sisters, that they might be their *fellow-ministers* (συνδιακόνους) dealing with housewives. It was through them that the Lord's teaching penetrated also the women's quarters without any scandal being aroused. We also know the directions about women deaconesses which are given by the noble Paul in his second letter to Timothy (1. Tim. 5. 9f.).[18]

One should observe here that Clement's attitude toward women is one of high regard and there is no trace of Philonic misogyny. It would be interesting to know whether any Rabbis took their wives with them when, like R. Akiba, they became peripatetic.[19] At least, in this passage Clement sees the apostles and disciples conducting themselves in a manner similar to the Jewish teachers who adopted "scholastic continence."

Clement's own view about marriage is expressed thus:

[17] C. 6., col. 1157.
[18] C. 6.
[19] Akiba himself does not seem to have done so if one judges from the length of time he left his wife, *vide supra*, p. 49.

"Our view is that we welcome as blessed the state of abstinence from marriage (εὐνουχίαν) in those to whom this has been granted by God. We admire monogamy and the high standing of single marriage, holding that we ought to share suffering with another and 'bear one another's burdens', lest anyone who thinks he stands securely should himself fall. It is of *second marriage* that the apostle says, 'If you burn, marry.'" (col. 1104) Clement remarks in c. 12 that remarriage is not wrong but that it is more perfect not to remarry; and again in c. 12, after quoting 1 Cor. 7:34, he immediately speaks of second marriage:

> the unmarried woman cares for the things of the Lord, that she may be. . . so also the married woman cares in the Lord for the things of her husband and the things of the Lord, the one as a wife, the other as a virgin.[20]
> But to put to shame and to discourage those inclined to contract a *second marriage*, the apostle appropriately uses strong language and says at once: "Every sin is external to the body, but he who commits fornication sins against his own body".

These references to second marriage suggest that Clement did not think that St. Paul emphasized celibacy.

Clement's view of "celibacy" is bound up with his idea of the true Gnostic (c. 6:100). This type of man lives with his wife as with a sister, that is the best Christians are married but do not use marital rights.[21] Clement probably means that they abstain after the birth of several children. This seems likely when one reads that Clement ridicules those who abstain from coition on the pretext that they have

---

[20] Clement appears to use the word "virgin" in reference to an unmarried woman.
[21] Cf. Bk. 7.

already attained the resurrected state; he tells them that, according to their reasoning, they should not eat or drink either. He also says that there are some people "now who rank the widow higher than the virgin in the matter of continence, on the ground that she scorns pleasure of which she has had experience."[22] The same is said of the man, "And true manhood is shown not in the choice of a celibate life (ἐν τῷ μονήρη); on the contrary the prize in the contest of men is won by him who has trained himself by the discharge of the duties of husband and father and by the supervision of a household... he who has no family is in most respects untried...."[23]

Clement, therefore, while approving the continent life tends toward *moderation* in *celibacy* rather than moderation in marriage. In this he is consonant with the teaching of St. Paul and his line of thought runs parallel to such Rabbis as Akiba and Ben Azzai. Yet it cannot be doubted that the "scholastic" or "philosophic" continence which he advocated for his true Gnostic must have come through the medium of middle Platonism wedded to Judaism in Philo but without misogamy.

II   ORIGEN[24]

Origen did not write a complete work on celibacy or virginity and there is no evidence in his writings that celibates either formed a numerous group in the Church or were subject to either special discipline or were recip-

[22] C. 16:102.

[23] Bk. 7., c. 12., col. 497.

[24] In this section I have dealt only briefly with Origen because Henri Crouzel has recently dealt with this subject at length in his book, *Virginité et mariage selon Origen*, Paris, 1962. Text for Origen's Fragments on 1 Corinthians: Claude Jenkins, "Origen on 1 Corin-

ients of special privileges.[25] Nevertheless Origen supports
the statement of Athenagoras[26] concerning those who
embraced "purity" for he speaks of some Christians who
"from the time they accept the word become more reasonable and reverent, so that some of them through a desire
for a higher chastity and for a purer worship of God do
not even indulge in the sexual pleasures that are allowed
by law."[27] Further Origen mentions some who "practise
perfect virginity" (ἀσκοῦσι τὴν παντελῆ παρθενίαν)[28] and
he interprets the "solid food" (στερεαν τροφήν) of 1 Cor.
3:1–3 as the "more perfect moral precepts" (ἐν ἠθικοῖς
τελειοτέρα διδασκαλία). In addition he specifies these as
chastity (ἀγνείας), virginity (παρθενίας) or self-control
(σωφροσύνης).[29]

In Origen's mind absolute celibacy is superior to continence (that is abstention from second marriage or abstention within marriage). This view is seen, for example, in
Ad Rom. lib. 9. col. 1205 where he states that virginity has
"first rank" among the living sacrifices offered to God:
but Origen insists that it is not the only offering which a
Christian can make. Again in *In Num. Hom.* 11. col. 647, he
calls the virgins of the Church the first fruit. This view of
virginity may be contrasted with Tertullian's view, for he
believed that "widowhood" is more meritorious than

thians," *JTS* 9 (1908) pp. 231–247 and pp. 353–372. This will be
abbreviated Jenkins, *JTS*.

[25] Cf. Crouzel, *op. cit.*, p. 195.

[26] Athen., *Suppl.*, c. 33.

[27] Translation from Origen, *Contra Celsum*, and introduction and
notes by Henry Chadwick, Cambridge, 1953.

[28] *Contra Celsum*, 7:48. One notes the qualification of "virginity,"
cf. pp. 10f. *supra*.

[29] Jenkins, *JTS*, p. 241.

virginity because it involves sacrificing something of which one has already had experience.[30]

Origen insists that the state of celibacy must be entered upon through one's free choice.[31] This, again, is in contrast to Tertullian who sees abstinence from digamy as a matter of obligation whereas Origen makes the special point that St. Paul did permit digamy.[32] Yet Origen also stresses that celibacy and virginity are preferable to the married state; he argues that the body is not only for coition, that Adam did not know Eve until they left paradise, "For the preferable thing is to keep chaste ($\dot{\alpha}\gamma\nu\varepsilon\dot{\nu}\varepsilon\iota\nu$) and pure and to have leisure for prayer."[33] When he discusses Anna, the prophetess from Luke 2, he says: "If one has not the grace of virginity then take the opportunity of widowhood or resolve to do so even if your husband has not died yet."[34] Origen confirms the evidence for the marital status of St. Paul, for he says[35] that there is a tradition that St. Paul was called with a wife to whom he refers in Phil. 4:3; but Origen appears to think that with her permission he abstained in order to devote himself more to Christ,[36] "*qui quoniam ab ipsa ex consensu liber effectus est, servum se nominat Christi.*"

[30] Clement's view is the same as Tertullian's *vide supra*, p. 153. This is not to deny that Tertullian in theory ranks virginity higher than continence, e.g., cf. *Exhort. Cast.* 1. 4.

[31] Jenkins, *JTS*, p. 370:

Virginity is to accomplish more than one is in duty bound to do. Cf. *Ad Rom.* lib. X, col. 1275. There is a trace of misogamy in *In Num. Hom.* VI, col. 610 and also in *In Lev. Hom.* III, col. 425 (lines 10–13).

[32] Jenkins, *JTS*, p. 370 on 1 Cor. 6:12. One notes, however, that Origen says that St. Paul did not *absolutely* forbid digamy.

[33] *Ibid.*

[34] *In Lucam Hom.* XVII, pp. 108–109 (GCS).

[35] Cf. pp. 70–71, *supra.*

[36] Jenkins, *JTS*, p. 504, lines 31–39.

Origen is very insistent that virginity of body should be accompanied by a virtuous life without which it is useless, for example, in *Comm. Ad. Rom. lib.* 1. col. 840 "... *Est et vocata virgo, sed non electa virgo, quae scilicet non fuerit sancta corpore et spiritu* ..." and *Ad Rom. Lib.* 9. col. 1205 where he teaches that the offering of the body is useless if it is accompanied with pride, envy *et cetera*. The whole import of virginity should be not to be conformed to this world but to renew oneself[37] by the practice of wisdom, meditation on the word of God "*et legis eius intelligentiam spiritualem,*" especially by reading Scripture daily.

Origen's teaching here seems to be the key to the whole theology of virginity and the clue to its origin. While the writer cannot feel that Origen was influenced by the same type of Judaism as Tertullian,[38] one knows that he consulted Jews and took the greatest interest in the culture and religion from which Christianity was nurtured. To examine how far Origen regarded Jesus as the New and Living Torah[39] would be outside the scope of this thesis, but it is noticeable that he advocated virginity and continence for the same reasons as R. Akiba and colleagues who abstained from their wives. Similarly as the Rabbis adapted the practices of their religion to a society in which animal sacrifice at Jerusalem was impossible after the Destruction of the Temple,[40] so Origen finds in

[37] *Ad Rom.* lib. 9, col. 1204 (645).

[38] For Origen's connections with Jewish teachers, see G. Bardy, "Les traditions juives dans l'oeuvre d'Origène," *RB* 1925, pp. 149 ff. and J. Daniélou, *Origène*, Paris, 1948, pp. 175–198. Although points of contact between Origen and Rabbinic teachers can be demonstrated, when compared with the influence of Alexandrian Judaism the Rabbinic influence is slight. Bardy does not feel convinced that Origen's knowledge of Hebrew was exceptionally good.

[39] *Vide infra*, pp. 218 ff.

[40] This was particularly the work of Johannan ben Zaccai; see

the details of the sacrificial system a lasting spiritual value because he sees them as the type of the spiritual offering of the individual's body and soul to God as a living sacrifice. The details are elaborated in *Ad Rom.*[41] and in *Lev. Hom.*[42] where after speaking of Jesus as the fulfillment of the sacrifices of the Old Law, he encourages Christians to offer chaste bodies and souls to God.[43] This is not found in a developed form in earlier patristic writings. Origen's ideas appear to be derived from Philo as one would expect.[44] Understandably, in view of his castration, Origen does not stress Matt. 19:11, 12 but in his *Commentary on Matthew*[45] passes over it quickly by explaining that "celibacy" (τὴν παντελῆ καθάρευσιν) is expedient and is a gift from God. Origen emphasizes that when Jesus said "to whom it is given" (Matt. 19:11), He did not suggest that it was impossible for people to master their passions but that by

---

J. Neusner, *A life of Rabban Johanan ben Zakkai*, (ca. 1–80, C.E.) Leiden, The Netherlands, 1962.

[41] *Ad Rom.*, lib. 9., col. 1205.

[42] In *Lev. hom.*, cols. 410 and 411.

[43] See also *In Num. Hom.* 11., col. 647 and *Hom in Exod.* 13 col. 394 where Origen says that the "incorruptible wood" (Exod. 35:24) is *"incorruptionis et virginitatis gratia, apud rarum quemque invenireo potest, sicut et Dominicus dicit; Non omnes capiunt verbum istud, sed quibus datum est."* The text is interesting both because it indicates the paucity of persons embracing absolute celibacy and also because Hippolytus of Rome refers to the same Old Testament text but applies it to the Virgin Mary. He speaks of the "incorruptible wood," i.e., the "flesh of the virgin" out of which the Ark was made. Crehan kindly provided me with this interesting reference. It is the earliest patristic reference to the Assumption of Mary and in a fragment of Hippolytus preserved by Theodoret on Ps. 22:7 (GCS I [Hippolytus] I. 2. 147).

[44] E.g., cf. Philo, *Spec. Leg.* 1., para. 166 (vol. 7 [Loeb]) and Origen *Ad Rom.* 9., col. 1205, both on Lev. 22:21 ff.

[45] *Comm. in Matt.*, Bk. 14., c. 25 (ANF, vol. 9., pp. 511–512).

prayer one might well acquire this gift from God. Therefore God will give the good gift, perfect purity in celibacy
and chastity, to those who ask Him with the whole soul,
and with faith, and in prayers without ceasing."

A   Origen's exegesis of 1 Cor. 7[46]

Origen does not use 1 Cor. 7 frequently to encourage a life
of virginity, but fortunately there is one extant commentary
on this chapter.[47]

(1.) Origen's exegesis of 1 Cor. 7 notes firstly the circumstances in which that section of the epistle was written.[48]
There had been a dissension (ἀκαταστασία) among the
Corinthians,[49] for men and women were trying to practice
too much continence in marriage.[50] The clause (καλὸν
ἀνθρώπῳ γυναικός μὴ ἅπτεσθαι) was written by the Corinthians[51] to St. Paul[52] and he replies[53] to them by
warning them that there must be mutual consent about
abstinence or one or other of the marriage partners will be
led into sin.[54] Sin is committed in two ways, by omitting
to obey precepts or by excessive zeal in observing them:[55]
in the light of this neither marriage or *parthenia* must be

[46] Text: Jenkins, *JTS*, pp. 500–514.

[47] It is, of course, possible that the fragment does not belong to
Origen. Père Crouzel, *op. cit.*, accepts it as genuine.

[48] *JTS, ibid.*, pp. 500–501.

[49] *Ibid.*, line 11.

[50] *Ibid.*, line 12.

[51] *Ibid.*, lines 13, 22–23.

[52] Cf. pp. 66 f and also contrast St. Athanasius' view, Frag. in *Ep. I,
Ad Cor.* (33) *PG* 27, col. 1403–1404. Athanasius thought the Corinthians were sinning in the opposite direction, that is, licentiousness.

[53] *JTS, ibid.*, pp. 500–501, line 14.

[54] *Ibid.,* lines 8–10 and p. 501, lines 29–30.

[55] *Ibid.,* para. 121, p. 500.

disparaged.[56] The whole import of St. Paul's exhortation is to modify excessive abstinence and to stress equality and justice in the marriage bond.[57]

(2.) The meaning of "concession" ($\sigma\nu\gamma\gamma\nu\dot{\omega}\mu\eta$).[58] In the Fragment under survey,[59] Origen does not discuss fully 1 Cor. 7:6 ($\tau o\tilde{\nu}\tau o$ $\delta\grave{\varepsilon}$ $\lambda\acute{\varepsilon}\gamma\omega$ $\kappa\alpha\tau\grave{\alpha}$ $\sigma\nu\gamma\gamma\nu\acute{\omega}\mu\eta\nu$...), but Père Crouzel,[60] noting other texts of Origen, mentions the diversity of opinion among exegetes as to whether the concession refers to marriage or continence and he states that Origen himself thinks that it refers to marriage.[61] However, Père Crouzel's statement,[62] "*L'état normal du chrétien serait la virginité*," would seem to need a little modification. The subject of the passage in which 1 Cor. 7:6 occurs has little to do with virginity, but it is a question of abstinence within marriage[63] and Origen appears to think that the concession refers to second marriage,[64] not to first marriage. One may compare, too, Crouzel's statement[65] "... *il ne lui est donc pas difficile de transformer en precepte ce qui dans la pensée de l'Apôtre était une autorisation, ou tout au plus un conseil*"; however, this, too, would seem to refer to Origen's abhorrence of digamy (successive polygamy) rather than marriage.[66] Thus one

---

[56] *Vide supra*, pp. 14–19 where I have discussed the meaning of *parthenos*. There is a possibility that here also $\pi\alpha\rho\theta\varepsilon\nu\acute{\iota}\alpha$ might mean abstaining from successive polygamy.

[57] *JTS, ibid.*, p. 501, lines 34–49; cf. p. 158, *supra*.

[58] 1 Cor. 7:6.

[59] *JTS, ibid.*, p. 502, lines 34–37.

[60] Crouzel, *op. cit.*, p. 54.

[61] *Ibid.*, p. 58 f.

[62] *Ibid.*

[63] *Ibid.*, 59; see *Comm. in Matt.*, Bk. XIV, c. 23.

[64] Cf. Crouzel, *op. cit.*, p. 80.

[65] *Ibid.*, p. 54.

[66] *Ibid.*, p. 92 and p. 146. Cf. C. H. Joyce, S. J., *Christian Marriage*,

concludes that Origen's thought is consonant with Justin, Athenagoras and Tertullian, who look upon second marriage as "decent adultery." [67]

(3.) Further it should be observed that the word παρθενία and its cognates only occur five times in the Fragment. The argument in all these cases is hypothetical, that is Origen does not seem to be thinking of a group of virgins at Corinth. Two references are cited in connection with *v.* 25,[68] but even here the discussion is quite general and no allusion is made to *vv.* 36–38. In general Origen appears to attribute the masculine gender to virgin, probably even when alluding to *v.* 25,

"Ἐὰν δὲ παρθένος μείνω, οὐ κελευσθεὶς οὐδε διαταχθείς, οὐκέτι λέγω ἐπὶ τῷ τῆς παρθενίας κατορθώματι δοῦλοι ἀχρεῖοί ἐσμεν, ὃ ὀφείλομεν ποιῆσαι πεποιήκαμεν.[69]

This must apply to Origen himself or to St. Paul, whom Origen considers to be a married man or widower: or the argument might be purely hypothetical.

(4.) Therefore in this Fragment, Origen's attention is chiefly directed toward men (not women) who wish to embrace continence (or virginity). The words referring to continence here are ἀγνεία, ἐγκράτεια, καθαρεύειν and their cognates. I should hesitate to translate ἀγαμος by "*celibataires*" as Crouzel does[70] although Crouzel himself ob-

London, 1933, p. 581. Joyce quotes Origen's assertion that digamists are not crowned but this perhaps refers to not wearing a crown at the liturgical wedding service rather than crowns in heaven. Cf. also *JTS, art. cit.*, p. 505, lines 57–71.

[67] This point is discussed *supra*, p. 145 and *infra*, pp. 208 ff.

[68] *JTS, art. cit.*, p. 509, lines 12–13.

[69] *Ibid.,* p. 509, para. 146.

[70] Crouzel, *op. cit.*, p. 85. See also *JTS, art. cit.*, p. 506, but see also *PGL* for later references which appear to refer absolute celibacy.

serves that ἄγαμος appears to refer to widower rather than virgin with reference to St. Paul.[71]

Further in Origen's allegorization of the meaning of circumcision and slavery,[72] which he sees as symbolic of those freed from marriage,[73] it is those who have been separated from their wives (τὸν ἀποβεβληκότα τὴν γυναῖκα),[74] not those who have never married, about whom Origen speaks. Origen's allegorization, even if extravagant, makes the whole of 1 Cor. 7 absolutely coherent and consistent. This exegesis is also consistent in that he speaks mainly about continence and not virginity.

In view of the lack of some original texts of Origen and also his tendency to allegorize, I am not able to decide whether Origen always uses παρθενία in the sense of *virginitas intacta* or whether he uses it in the sense of *continentia* as well. Certainly in his commentary on 1 Cor. 3:1–3a,[75] he uses the phrase ἁγνείας τελείας and then refers to παρθενίας or σωφροσύνης (self-control) as if he used celibacy in the first rank and self-control in the second. Further in *Contra Celsum*[76] the phrase ἀσκοῦσι τὴν παντελῆ παρθενίας suggests that virginity could, in a sense, be imperfect.[77] However, in Origen's commentary on Luke[78] the verb παρθενεύειν is contrasted with χηρεύειν.

---

[71] Crouzel, *op. cit.*, pp. 116, 133 and *JTS, art. cit.*, p. 504, lines, 31–49.
[72] *Ibid.*, pp. 506–508, (on 1 Cor. 7:18–20).
[73] *Ibid.*, pp. 506–507.
[74] *Ibid.*, p. 506, line 7.
[75] Jenkins, *JTS*, pp. 241–242.
[76] *Contra Celsum*, 7:48.
[77] See p. 11 ff. *supra* where the texts from the Babylonian Talmud show the use of "perfect virginity" and "partial virginity." I mention this as a parallel but do not suggest that Origen was directly influenced by it.
[78] Orig., *In. Luc. Hom.* XVII, pp. 108–109 (GCS).

This suggests that Origen does use *parthenos* in the sense of *virgo intacta* (*intactus*) although he finds it necessary to qualify it on some occasions.

In this connection it is interesting to observe that Origen is perplexed over the reading καὶ ἡ παρθένος ἡ ἄγαμος in 1 Cor. 7:34. Crouzel[79] expresses Origen's belief that true Christian virginity must be embraced solely for the service of God, not merely because one has not found a spouse. He continues:

> Un fragment des Stromates Origéniens, conservé dans la marge d'un manuscript de l'Épître aux Romains[80] l'exprime en essayant de trouver un sens valuable à une leçon impossible de 1 Cor. 7:34. Ainsi dans le quatrième livre des Stromates (Origène) rapportant cette leçon, l'explique en ces termes. L'addition de ἡ ἄγαμος à παρθένος paraît superflue. Cependant les exemplaires les plus exacts écrivent: καὶ ἡ γυνὴ ἡ ἄγαμος καὶ ἡ παρθένος ἡ ἄγαμος. Voici ce qu'il faut dire: on ne peut appeler femme non mariée celle qui veut se marier, même si dans le present elle semble non mariée; ni vierge non mariée celle qui se marier et est soumise à des sollicitations de ce genre. C'est pourquoi il n'est pas inutile d'écrire: La femme non mariée et la vierge non mariée se préoccupent de ce qui concerne le Seigneur'. 'Quoi qu'il en soit de ce texte invraisemblable, trouvé dans 'les examplaires les plus exacts', l'explication est conforme aux intentions de l'Apôtre. Se consacrant au Seigneur, la vierge ou la veuve assume volontairement sa virginité ou son état de veuve: elle a rejeté toute idée de mariage et a offert à Dieu se chasteté comme un don irrevocable.

[79] *Op. cit.*, p. 104.
[80] *Texte und Untersuchungen.*, XVII, 4, 1899, no. 78, p. 64.

Origen is right that this reading is by far the best attested, even given by 𝔓[46]. The adjective ἄγαμος qualifying παρθένος may well have been omitted because it appeared a contradiction in terms although to the Jew the combination was certainly legitimate as has been seen.[81] Origen probably was not acquainted with the terminology of the Palestinian Jews[82] and therefore was obliged to find some plausible explanation for this reading. This correct but difficult reading is perfectly consistent with the levirate interpretation of 1 Cor. 7:36–40.

B   The Virgins in Revelation

These seem to interest Origen more than any virgins possibly alluded to in 1 Cor. 7. He refers to the text in *In Num. Hom. 11.*[83] and gives a fuller exposition in *In Ev. Joannis Tomus I.* Here the virgins not defiled with women do not come from the physical seed of Israel: they are the ones who do not fall from the truth.[84]

C   Organization of Virgins

Crouzel observes[85] that Origen has little to say about the concrete life of celibacy. "*L'Alexandrin ne dit rien de la vie concrète des ascètes de chaque sexe*" and also "*Origène ne s'interesse guère aux institutions ecclésiastique*" (*ibid*). It would seem that the cause of this was the fact that very few embraced a life of complete celibacy and these would

[81] See pp. 13 f., *supra.*
[82] See note 38, *supra.*
[83] Col. 647.
[84] Cf. Philo, *Post.* 130–136 and *Cher.*, 49 and Appendix, p. 483 on Jer. 3:4. Also cf. pp. 100 f, *supra.*
[85] Crouzel, *op. cit.*, p. 195.

be mainly men, as indicated by the gender of παρθένος. I shall discuss the difficulty of women embracing celibacy in the concluding chapter of this thesis. Origen treats the subject of "virginity" on the whole quite academically, as in his commentary on the Cant. of Cant., but it is noticeable that in this treatise he has not one reference to 1 Cor. 7. Origen probably stressed abstinence from remarriage rather than virginity although he recognized this as the higher life and his theory of virginity, for example, its connection with wisdom and the sacrificial system of the Old Testament perhaps did much to influence the later writers.

Yet with Origen there is notable development concerning the idea of virginity; the word παρθένος seems to be used in a more precise sense; virginity is extolled above widowhood and there seem to be definite signs that more Christians were embracing this form of life. But St. Paul is regarded as married and the fragments on 1 Corinthians do not indicate clearly that there was a group of women virgins at Corinth.

CHAPTER 7

Celibacy in the Writings of the Latin Fathers: Phrygian Montanism and the Jewish Background of Tertullian's Thought

I   THE JEWISH BACKGROUND OF PHRYGIAN CHASTITY

The origins of the "montanist" heresy are far from clear.[1] This much is known, that it began in Phrygia (or Mysia) and the date of its commencement must have been before 172 when Montanus had his visions and before the prophetess Maximilla is said to have died.[2] It is also conjectured that "Montanism," a name which does not occur before the fourth century, may have been a title attached to the heresy later[3] and that the earlier names "the New Prophecy" and the "Phrygian or Kataphrygian heresy" are more exact connotations for the movement. Of the two names the first is perhaps to be preferred, for

[1] See, for example, A. Faggiotto, *L'eresia dei Frigi*, Rome, 1924, p. 4 f. P. De Labriolle, *La Crise Montaniste* and *Les Sources de l'histoire du Montanisme*, Paris, 1913 (pp. 1–12 of the first work). W. Schepelern, *Der Montanism und die Phrygienne Kulte*, Tubingen, 1929, pp. 1–7.
[2] Labriolle, *La Crise*, p. 12.
[3] Schepelern, *op. cit.*, p. 3 f.

"the New Prophecy" does not seem to have been a heresy in its beginnings: doctrinal aberrations came only in the later centuries.[4] In view of these facts it is legitimate to ask whether "the New Prophecy" was a Judeo-Christian group which broke off from the Church and still later became heretical, that is that the movement in essence existed before the time of Montanus and his ladies but that it was only in his day that it became a separate movement.[5]

It is striking that both Phrygian Montanism and its later branch "Tertullianism" existed and flourished in areas which were thickly populated with Jews. In a most informative article "The Jews in Phrygia,"[6] W. M. Ramsay has shown how vast the population of the Jews was in Phrygia; for example he quotes Reinach's[7] calculation that in the town of Apameia alone where the tax was only two drachma per Jew a total of 75,000 drachma was collected. In addition Ramsay cites the towns, especially those inhabited by Jews, and indicates the amount of evidence for their presence by numerous inscriptions and Jewish names:[8] in Akomonia the inscriptions are more numerous than all the inscriptions in Phrygia combined; furthermore a special law was passed for the protection of Jewish graves.[9]

The Jews of Apameia were brought to Phrygia by Antiochus the Great in 200 B.C. from Babylonia.[10] These

[4] *Ibid.*, p. 25 f.; Faggiotto, *op. cit.*, p. 8.

[5] I do not think that anyone has suggested before that Montanism was a Jewish-Christian heresy, but I have intimated this ("St. Paul the Philogamist" *NTS* [April, 1965] pp. 326–348).

[6] W. M. Ramsay, *Cities and Bishoprics of Phrygia*, Oxford, 1897 i part ii, pp. 667 ff. ("The Jews in Phrygia").

[7] *Ibid.*, p. 667 (Th. Reinach, Mnn. Juives, 72n).

[8] Ramsay, *op. cit.*, p. 673.

[9] *Ibid.*, p. 668.

[10] Josephus, *Ant.* 21., para. 148.

Jews seem to have been somewhat unorthodox, for they engaged in superstition and magical arts and syncretized to some extent with the imperial cult.[11] Thus the Phrygian Jews were considered by their more orthodox brethren as a separatist group divided from their land and people: indeed, so far were they divided that they even forgot their own language.[12] Yet the Phrygian Jews did not participate in Alexandrian philosophy and education like their confrères in Egypt. Instead they seem to have been attracted to Christianity.[13] The towns around this region, for example, Iconium,[14] Pisidian Antioch and Colossae, seem to have mixed populations; however, the Jewish element is not of the "Alexandrian" type. Even when they adopted Christianity, they do not seem to have been willing to relinquish all their Jewish practices and one knows from the New Testament[15] that St. Paul had trouble with his converts at Colossae who still adhered to dietary laws, festivals, new moons and sabbaths and were interested in angels and visions. Indeed, as Ramsay points out,[16] the converts to Christianity flocked to the synagogue in the time of St. Paul: there is no reason to believe that this stopped after his time. From the fact that the Jews and Christians, according to inscriptions which Ramsay cites, shared cemeteries, one may infer that there was constant intercourse between Jews and Christians and that they shared beliefs and practices in other ways.[17]

[11] Ramsay, *op. cit.*, p. 672.

[12] *Ibid.*, p. 674.

[13] *Ibid.*

[14] *Ibid.*, p. 667, note 3. Acts 13, 14, 16 and 2 Tim. 3:11. Iconium was originally Phrygian: its name being Kawania (*NBD*).

[15] Col. 2:16–19.

[16] Ramsay, *op. cit.*, p. 675.

[17] For a detailed description of the Jewish faith and mission, see

With this background one may ask what similarities can be found between the "New Prophecy" and Judaism of the sectarian type.[18] The New Prophecy may be linked with three branches of sectarian Judaism: Qumran, the Therapeutae and the Karaites.[19]

A

There are some interesting similarities between Qumran and the New Prophecy.

(1.) According to Sozomen and Pseudo-Chrystostom,[20] the Montanists used the solar calendar. Schepelern[21]

D. Georgi, *op. cit.*, Die Gegner des Paulos im 2. Korintherbrief, Neukirchen-Vluyn, 1964, pp. 83–137. He mentions especially the importance of the Synagogue as the medium of the mission, pp. 87 ff.

[18] In suggesting a Jewish influence, I argue against Schepelern, *op. cit.*, pp. 90–128, who finds a purely pagan influence, for example, influence from the Phrygian Spring Festival, p. 105; the taurobolium, p. 113 f; the weeping of Attis, p. 127. Labriolle, *op. cit.*, p. 90, thinks these theories are exaggerated, despite the fact that Schepelern is in agreement with many scholars.

[19] The Karaites are thought to belong to the eighth century A.D.; see *ODCC, ERE, JE, SJE*; but Naphtali Wieder, *The Judean Scrolls and Karaism* (London, 1962) has convincingly shown similarities with the Judean Scrolls. See the review in *Rev. de Q.* no. 14, fasc. 2, 4 (May, 1963) pp. 297–310.

[20] Soz., *H.E.* 7. 12, 18. Ps. Chrysostom, Ep. 7. (*M.G.* LIX. 747).

[21] Schepelern, *op. cit.*, p. 49 f.: "There exists another heresy—Montanism—who still continued to celebrate Easter with the Jews who simultaneously broke with the Church to its own harm. They hold the fourteenth of the first month (i.e., the seventh month according to the Asiatic Kalender) but not the fourteenth day of the moon. 'Ich weiss nicht, woher sie diese Regel bekommen haben. Denn was Gottes eingebornen Sohn betrifft, so war es am Osterfest der Juden, am 14 Tag des Mondes im 1 Monat, an diesen 14 Tag, am Osterfest der Juden war es, dass Christus litt. Woher kommt es denn, dass diese abscheuliche Haeresie den 14 Tag nach dem sonnenmonat und nicht nach dem lunaren Monat hervorgehoben hat? Ist

remarks on the singularity of this which seems in one way to be like and in another to be unlike the Jews.

It is known that the writer of *Jubilees*, possibly the members of Qumran,[22] the Samaritans[23] and some of the early Christians used the solar calendar. For evidence of the early Christian use of the solar calendar, one turns naturally to the work of Mlle. A. Jaubert[24] whose conclusions are summarized here:

> les deux points de vue, synoptique et johannique sont donc a priori différents. Les deux traditions ne parlent pas de la même Pâque. Ces considerations pourraient expliquer en partie le silence des synoptiques à propos des fêtes juives officielles. Elles jettent beaucoup de lumière sur les querelles pascales posterieures. Une tradition liturgique dans la ligne de la catechese palestinenne conservée dans les synoptiques n'avait aucune raison de célebrer la Pâque selon le jour officiel mobile —mais selon le jour de la semaine. Telle la liturgie romaine, appuyée sur une catechese du type de Marc. En defendant—avec trop de rigueur—le dimanche pascal, le pape Victor suivait bien, comme il l'affirment, une tradition apostolique (*H.E.*, V. 23. 1:24. 9–10).
>
> Mais les Asiates suivaient non moins bien une tradition johannique! L'évangile de Jean ne mentionnait que la Pâque du 14 Nisan, fête officielle des Juifs. Il était assez

---

es nicht augenscheinlich, dass der Betrug eines Demons daran schuld ist?'." Schepelern writes before the work of Mlle. A. Jaubert, *La Date de La Cêne*, Paris, 1957. He writes, of course, before the discovery of the *DSS*.

[22] As reported in *BA* 194 (1956) p. 93 and *R.B.* 63 (1956) p. 65.

[23] For a comprehensive study of biblical calendars see J. Van Goudoever, *Biblical Calendars*, 2nd. ed., Leiden, The Netherlands, 1961.

[24] See note 21 above.

normal que le seul anniversaire de la Pâque fut pour
eux ce 14 Nisan, jour du crucifiement. Ils "gardaient le
14e jour de Pâques, *selon l'évangile*," à la suite de Jean
et de Polycarp (*H.E.* V. 24. 3–6).[25]

Therefore according to these findings there were differences among the early Christians. The Phrygian Montanists seem to have followed a Johannine tradition, which
used the solar calendar of Judaism and kept the Passover
on Nisan 14.

The fact of following the Johannine tradition for the
calendar is important when one considers that Phrygian
Montanism bore other characteristics resembling Johanine
primitive Christian "theology." Their prophecy, as Faggiotto[26] and others show, breathes the same atmosphere
as the Revelation of St. John and the Phrygian eschatology seems but an exaggeration of that which one finds in
Revelation.[27]

(2.) Schepelern[28] has ascribed the prominent position of
women in the Phrygian movement to the influence of the
pagan priestesses. It is, however, far more likely that this
peculiar and enlightened mark in the Phrygian Montanism
was due to the relationship between the Jews (and/or the
Jewish Christians) in Phrygia and the imperial cult, which
did not disdain educated women.[29] The most potent influence may have come from Julia Severa[30] who was high
priestess of the imperial cult even though she was a Jewess;

[25] Jaubert, *op. cit.*, p. 111.
[26] See, for example, Faggiotto, *op. cit.*, p. 17 f.; Schepelern, *op. cit.*,
chapter 10.
[27] *Vide infra*, pp. 181 f.
[28] *Op. cit.*, p. 7 ff. and pp. 113 ff. (Schepelern).
[29] See Georgi, *op. cit.*, p. 101 ff. for influential women and the Jewish
faith.
[30] Ramsay, *op. cit.*, p. 675.

moreover such women as Cornuta[31] and Poppaea would also inspire rivals and followers among their women devotees. One's thoughts turn naturally, too, to the Therapeutae and Qumran where women also were allowed a part in the religious community, although there is no suggestion that they were priestesses. Neither at Qumran or among the Therapeutae does one find women excluded from "education" or community exercises.

B

One complaint against the Montanists is that they introduce peculiar fasts:[32] this also may be explained by reference to the Jewish fasts. In *De Jejun.* 2, Tertullian meets this objection by reference to the Day of Atonement in the Old Testament (a fast not kept by Christians). This may be the further particular fast day referred to by Tertullian[33] but which he leaves unnamed. Indeed, Schepelern has suggested that the seven white-robed virgins bearing torches and wailing in the Montanist service may have its origins in the weeping of Attis.[34] However, one observes that the Day of Atonement was not always a complete day

[31] Ramsay (*ibid.*) refers to inscriptions nos. 530 and 551. Cf. also Labriolle, *op. cit.*, p. 23–29 who refers to the prominence of women in Asia Minor but who does not refer to Jewish women. Labriolle says that the municipal regime favored their (Asian women's) accession to public honors, although they were under civil disabilities. He mentions that numerous inscriptions show us that they were in charge of certain liturgies, *"Il eut même des femmes prytanes, des femmes hipparques dignities qui, il est vrai, étaient à cette epoque à peu pres purement nominales."*

[32] Hipp., *Phil.*, 10. 25; *cf.* 8. 18; Theodor., *Haer. fab.*, 3. 1. Origen, *De Princ.*, 2. 7, 3; cf. *In Ep. ad Tit.*; Epiph., *Pan.*, 48. 8.

[33] Tert., *De Jejun.*, 14; *De Orat.*, 18; Schepelern, *op. cit.*, p. 54.

[34] *Ibid.*, p. 127.

of mourning but some Jewish groups kept it with wailing and dancing of virgins.[35] Thus St. Chrysostom (who disliked the Jews) complains that some of the Christians partook of these celebrations[36] and may possibly be referring to the "Montanists."

Further one notes that the Montanists were accused of prolonging their fasts to the end of the day[37] rather than finishing at the ninth hour. This appears to be akin to the Jewish habit of fasting until sunset.[38] These practices were particularly followed on the station days. Wieder[39] has indicated both the Jewish influence on the Christian practice of station days and the observing of these near cemeteries. The Karaites[40] visited the cemeteries on *Yom Kippur* and, according to Wieder, this was taken over by the Christians on their station days. Orthodox Christians would possibly shorten the fast so that they could celebrate the Eucharist, but the Montanists probably adhered to the Jewish custom more strictly. Two minor points may be inserted here. Hippolytus tells us that the Montanists ate dishes of radishes. The radish features in the Passover *haggadah* and also in the subject of discussion in the Mishna. Further Cyril (*Cat.* 16) accuses the Montanists of

[35] Wieder, *op. cit.*, p. 163 ff. and p. 186. (*Ta'an.* 4, 8; *Ta'an.* 31a).

[36] Wieder, *op. cit.*, p. 171. It is interesting that Chrysostom should make this observation and that a reference to the Montanist use of the solar calendar should also be found in a work attributed by some to the same author, *Ep.* 7. (Ps. Chrysostom).

[37] Schepelern, *op. cit.*, p. 54. Tertullian, *De Jejun.*, 15; cf. c. 10. The fasts lasted to the last quarter of the day, not until the ninth hour.

[38] Cf. the Therapeutae, Philo, *De Vit. Cont.*, c. 1 and c. 4.

[39] Wieder, *op. cit.*, p. 191.

[40] *Ibid.*, p. 191 f. Wieder remarks that Chrysostom found that it was a very old custom in his day and that he could not find a Christian origin. It might have originated in the service on the Great Sabbath preceding Easter. Yemenite Jews apparently visited the cemeteries to pray for rain, p. 192.

murdering children at the Eucharist, this—an accusation made against the Jews—was tossed onto the Christians in the first century and, I suggest, was retained as Jewish-Christians against the Montanists.

The origin of the Montanist *xerophagia*,[41] especially the avoidance of juices, moist food and wine, may be found in Jewish practices. Such vows of abstinence are found both in the tractate *Nedarim* and in the tractate *Nazir*. The subject of the vows is akin to the principles of the Rechabites[42] and in some ways to the Nazirite asceticism, but one would hesitate to see too close a link with Nazirite practices, since there is no allusion to the growing of hair or avoidance of defilement by the dead. This kind of *xerophagia* does not seem to occur in other heretical Christian sects which avoided the use of wine. Furthermore, the Montanist prohibition does not seem to have extended to the use of wine at the Eucharist[43] which would have been the case if they regarded wine as intrinsically wrong. Another Montanist practice which may be traced to Judaistic origins is the practice of abstaining from bathing[44] as complementary to their eating dry food. Abstinence from bathing is recorded in MK 93[45] where it is reproved; moreover it is found in Judeo-Christianity,

[41] Schepelern, *op. cit.*, p. 54. Tertullian, *De Jejun.* 1 and 13. *De Mon.*, 15.

[42] See M. Black, *The Scrolls and Christian Origins*, Edinburgh, 1961, pp. 15, 43, 58, 107 who speaks of the Rechabites with reference to the Jewish sectarians.

[43] Cf. Cyprian, Ep. 63.

[44] Schepelern, *op. cit.*, p. 54; Tertullian, *De Jejun.* 14. and *De Orat.* 18.

[45] The reference is to "one under a ban." *M.K.* (*Mo'ed Katan*) 15b, p. 93, a mourner is forbidden to wash oneself, "... as it is written. And anoint not thyself with oil, and bathing is implied in anointing." The mourner does not cohabit but one "under a ban" does.

at least Hegesippus[46] says that James of Jerusalem did not drink wine, cut the hair or use oil or the bath (*H.E.* 2. 23, 5). One may also compare the Essenes who did not use oil (connected with bathing), for they counted it as a defilement.

Another "unorthodox" characteristic of the Montanists, the members of Qumran and the Karaites was their attitude to the prophets of their respective communities and to the oral tradition, which comprised the interpretation of Torah by competent and authorized scholars and which is now in written form in Mishna, Gemara and other extra-biblical writings of the othodox Jewish authorities. Both Qumran and the Karaites rejected[47] this oral tradition, but, unlike the Sadducees, they replaced it with another unwritten tradition which arose from their own prophets and from their own method of *pesher exegesis.*[48] They regarded the precepts arising from their new tradition as obligatory in character but the authority on which this tradition rested was the prophetic authority depending on divine inspiration given to persons of their community who received revelation but did not necessarily understand the full implications of their own teaching.[49] The Karaites complained that prophecy had ceased in Rabbinic Judaism, but they maintained that perfect continuity in prophecy had been kept from the Babylonian community as this was now represented by the Karaites.[50] One also notes that it was this Babylonian form of Judaism with which

[46] Jean Daniélou, *Théologie du Judeo-Christianisme*, Tournai, 1958, p. 426 f.
[47] Wieder, *op. cit.*, p. 79.
[48] *Ibid.*, p. 259.
[49] Cf. 1 Cor. 14 where there may be a similar situation.
[50] Wieder, *op. cit.*, p. 263.

the Montanists were closely related at least genetically.[51]
The Karaites maintained that they alone knew and practiced the "hidden things" (*nistaroth*).[52] By *nistaroth* they
did not mean esoteric doctrines but practical issues which
could be expounded correctly only by the Karaite
scholars.[53]

Thus both Qumran and the Karaites separated themselves
and formed an elect community in which they regarded
their prophets[54] as genuine and the Rabbinic prophecy of
Orthodox Judaism as false and in which they practiced
disciplines which were not regarded as obligatory by other
Jews.

The situation is not dissimilar to that of Montanism and
its relationship to the orthodox Christian Church. Both at
one time were inseparable, the Montanist element being
merely the type of prophetic Christianity represented, for
example in 1 Corinthians, in the Apocalypse of St. John
and in the *Shepherd of Hermas*. However a section of this
broke away, not because the Church disagreed with
prophecy as such[55] but because some of the prophets
refused to submit to the judgment of the Church on their
prophecy and because these prophets rejected the orthodox oral tradition and replaced it by one of their own
making. Hence one finds that Montanus and his followers
were not condemned with ease by the bishops who disagreed with them but that many of the faithful supported
them in opposition to the bishops; consequently, one has
the impression that long disputes ensued before any

[51] *Vide supra*, p. 166.
[52] Wieder, *op. cit.*, p. 50.
[53] *Ibid.*, p. 57.
[54] Cf. also Georgi, *op. cit.*, p. 119–124.
[55] *Ibid.*, cf. 1 Cor. 11 and 14.

apology was committed to writing: indeed, the bishops seemed to hesitate lest they should deny a true element in Christianity.[56]

The type of prophecy thus evolved in sectarian Judaism and Montanism is not unlike that which is described by Celsus.[57] It is a prophecy analogous to Old Testament prophecy before the classical period of Amos and his successors. Preclassical prophecy[58] was ecstatic in character accompanied by frenzy, unintelligible words, visions and trances. The prophets were originally in bands and are thought by some scholars to have had cultic functions. The individual prophets, such as Elijah, Elisha and Micaiah, who stand midway between the early bands of ecstatic prophets with their non-Israelitish characteristics and the classical prophets with their individual call, their awareness of history, their discernment of events before they came to pass, their ethical and social concern and, in most cases, their eschatological emphasis, are the kind of category into which one could place the individual prophets of the Essenes, the Therapeutae, the members of Qumran, the Karaites and the Montanists.

Celsus speaks of the existence of this type of prophet in Origen's day which is contemporary with the Montanist period. The prophets are inspired by the *Ruach* of God

[56] Cf. the scruples of the anonymous writer Euseb., *H.E.* 16., 1–5.

[57] *Contra Celsum* 7. He says that there are several kinds of prophecy and that many with ease assume the conduct of inspired persons. "These are accustomed to say each for himself 'I am God, I am the Son of God or I am the Divine Spirit'. They say that the world is about to perish, they predict fire falling on cities *et cetera*, to these prophecies are added strange, fanatical and unintelligible words. . . ." Cf. Georgi, *op. cit.*, p. 120.

[58] See A. R. Johnson, *Cultic Prophet in Ancient Israel*, Cardiff., 1944. A. Haldar, *Association of Cult Prophets among the Ancient Semites*, 1945. C. Kuhn, *The Prophets of Israel*, Edinburgh, 1960.

which is a driving force[59] and is variously named Father, Son or Spirit both by Celsus[60] and by the Montanists.[61] The latter's identification of the Father, Son and Spirit is analogous to the identification of the Spirit of Yahweh with his Word (cf. the Logos) and His Power (cf. the Spirit of *dunamis*).[62] This seems to be another Judaistic feature of Montanism.

In the Old Testament the *Ruach* is not separate from Yahweh even when it is evil.[63] Against this background can be seen the difficulty of the orthodox church in deciding whether an evil or a good spirit inspired the Montanist prophets. The criterion of good or false prophecy in the Old Testament seems to rest upon the fulfillment of the prophecy; if what was foretold came true then the prophet was true. This is the criterion applied to the New Prophecy:[64] Maximilla is thought to be false for the very reason that the wars and catastrophes which she foretells have not come to pass within thirteen years. One may also compare the anxiety of the Essene Menehem (Manaemus)[65] that his prophecy should be precisely fulfilled as regards the place and death of Antigonus.

The prophets and the Montanists in general emphasized the role of the Spirit and it was one of the offices of the

[59] Cf. the "active" (not passive) use of the word "Paraclete" in 1 John 2:1. My attention was drawn to this by Joseph Crehan, S.J.
[60] Cf. *Contra Celsum* (note 52 *supra*). Also Schepelern, *op. cit.*, p. 154 who says that Celsus confused Jesus and the Paraclete but even St. John gives the name Paraclete to both Jesus and the spirit.
[61] The Montanists eventually lapsed into Trinitarian heresies but even before that it does not seem clear who was speaking through the prophets and prophetesses.
[62] Eusebius, *H.E.* V. 16, 17.
[63] Cf. for example, the evil spirit which came upon Saul.
[64] Cf. Euseb. *H.E.* V. 16, 18 f., where the bishops try to refute the spirit in Maximilla.
[65] Joseph., *Ant.*, 15. 373 ff.

paraclete to show the things to come as Betz[66] remarks: "*Es ist kein zufall, dass der 'Paraklet' Montan das nahe Endgericht verkundigt und eine starke eschatologische Bewegung aus gelost hat.*"

The elements of ecstatic prophecy are also found among the Therapeutae. They have visions[67] and are carried away "by a heaven-sent passion of love, remain rapt, and possessed like bacchanals...[68] and corybants until they see the object of their yearning." They have a consecrated room[69] in which they take nothing, "either drink or food or any other of the things necessary for the needs of the body, but laws and *oracles* delivered through the mouth of prophets, and psalms and anything (or 'the other books') else which fosters and perfects knowledge and piety... even in their dreams the picture is nothing else but the loveliness of divine excellence and powers.... Indeed many when asleep and dreaming give utterances to the glorious varities of their holy philosophy." This is not dissimilar to the Montanist oracles and visions.[70]

One cannot help feeling that the genuine and desired prophecy about which St. Paul speaks is different from this type of prophecy. I should concur with Leaney's[71] suggestion that it was perhaps this ecstatic prophecy which St. Paul was concerned with when he forbade women to speak in church.[72] Clearly in 1 Cor. 11:5, he envisages women prophesying.[73]

[66] O. Betz, *Der Paraklet*, Leiden, The Netherlands, 1963, p. 192.
[67] Philo., *De Vit. Cont.*, c. 2, 11, 12.
[68] Note again the mention of "madness."
[69] Philo., *De Vit. Cont.*, c. 3, 25.
[70] Cf. the vision of the "sister" who sees the soul, *De Anima*, c. 9.
[71] Suggested by correspondence.
[72] 1 Cor. 14:34. But see the convincing exegesis of Isakkson, *Marriage and Ministry in the New Temple*, Lund, 1965, pp. 153–186.
[73] Cf. also the daughters of Philip, Acts 21:9.

While one cannot postulate a direct influence of either Qumran or Karaism or the Therapeutae on the Phrygian heresy, one may suggest that the rather heterodoxical Jewish background of Asia Minor, especially of Phrygia, provided material and practices which the Montanists could adopt and which at first went unsuspected by the Church. It was thus that continence became of utmost importance in the eyes of the new prophets and prophetesses, partly because of the eschatological character of their beliefs but partly because, as shall be noted below,[74] continence was imputed to the prophets of the Old Testament by the extrabiblical Jewish writings and indeed became an indispensable requisite for their proper functions.

The Phrygian prophetesses are accused of leaving their husbands. Their action seems to be stimulated by the expectation of an imminent *parousia* and to bear some resemblance to the conduct of Jeremiah. Their motives are at one with St. Paul's. It would be interesting to know whether they continued in continence when their hope of the *parousia* became less fervent:[75] when one turns to Montanist continence in Carthage, the motive is entirely different. Thus Phrygian Montanism presents an adaptation of an Essene and prophetic continence. It seems to have functional and temporary character and consequently adds very little to a "theology of virginity."

II   THE JEWISH BACKGROUND OF TERTULLIAN'S THOUGHT

Now that the writer has offered a few indications of a possible link between the Asiatic "New Prophecy" and

[74] *Vide infra*, pp. 198 ff.
[75] It must have been disappointed when Maximilla's prophecies were not realized.

various forms of Judaism and has suggested that the
continence of these Christian prophets came from such a
milieu, one turns to the "New Prophecy" as it is represented by Tertullian.[76] Perhaps a more succinct and pregnant sentence concerning Tertullian's Montanist Christianity could not be found than that with which Hanson
ends his article, "*Notes on Tertullian's Interpretation of
Scripture*":[77]

> The tendency to turn Christianity into a baptized Juda-
> ism, observable in many aspects of the life and the
> thought of the third-century church, finds its earliest
> exponent in Tertullian.

Indeed, the environment Tertullian lived in could not
but bring him into constant contact with various expressions of the Jewish faith but a Jewish faith which had
little in common with the Alexandrian Diaspora.

Simon[79] demonstrates that Carthage was the center of
African Judaism and that the presence of the Jews in this
important city stimulated the writing of polemical works
against them by the Christian fathers, especially Tertullian,
Cyprian and Lactantius: he mentions also the danger
presented to the faithful by these Jews avid for converts.[80]
It was a Judaism originating in the remote past, for according to Jewish and Arab traditions the ancestor of

[76] It is tantalizing that Tertullian's seven books *De ecstasi*, a defense
of the ecstatic speech of the Montanist prophets, are lost. (B. Altaner,
Patrology, Edinburgh, 1960, p. 178).

[77] R. P. C. Hanson, "Notes on Tertullian's Interpretation of Scripture," *JTS*, n.s., 12 (1961) pp. 273–279.

[78] See Marcel Simon, *Recherches d'Histoire Judeo-Chretienne*, Paris,
1962, pp. 30–87 (especially). See also, Victor A. Tcherikover, "The
Decline of the Jewish Diaspora in Egypt in the Roman Period," *JSS*,
14 (1963) pp. 1–33. This may account for the lack of influence.

[79] Simon, *op. cit.*, pp. 31–33.

[80] *Ibid.*, p. 33.

these Jews was either Ham or Esau,[81] Abraham or Noë. Their ancestry made them tenacious in their beliefs and practices on the one hand, but on the other they welcomed syncretism and indulged in magic and prophecy.[82] Their relations with Christianity were very close[83] and Simon[84] conjectures that either Christianity was first preached from the synagogues or that Jewish Christianity was tolerated by the Jews. The Jews appear to have given the privilege of burial to the Christians at a time when Christians were not allowed cemeteries.[85] Indeed, Jewish-Christian sects seem to have appeared of which two notable examples for this thesis are the Abelonians and the Caelicoles.[86] It seems possible that Tertullianism, like the Asiatic "New Prophecy," emanated from Jewish-Christian circles.

Nevertheless this conjecture would be obliged to meet the objection that Tertullian wrote against the Jews and that his type of "Montanism" differs from the "New Prophecy" especially in its lighter emphasis on prophecy, the omission of the mention of Pepuza and the concomitant lack of interest in an imminent *parousia*. If one may express it so, Tertullian's eschatology is "realized" rather than "futurist" and is characterized by a legalism which is disconsonant with a belief in the imminent coming of Christ. It is possible that Tertullian was not always interested in

[81] *Ibid.*, pp. 35, 38 f., 39–40 f.

[82] *Ibid.*, p. 34.

[83] *Ibid.*, p. 33.

[84] *Ibid.*

[85] *Ibid.* See also W. H. C. Frend, "The Seniores Laici and the Origins of the Church in North Africa," *JTS*, n.s., 12 (1963) pp. 280–284 who points out the effect of Jewish-Christianity and Judaism on the organization and discipline of the Church in North Africa.

[86] Simon, *op. cit.*, pp. 54–57. Thus one finds a difference between St. Paul's eschatological approach to "celibacy" and remarriage and Tertullian's condemnation of remarriage for all time.

Judaism and that it was during that period that he wrote *Adversus Judaeos*.[87] A study of his Catholic works shows little evidence of Jewish influence and even quotations from the Scripture are comparatively infrequent.[88] Interest in Scripture and in Judaism seems to appear first in Tertullian's writings against Marcion and it becomes deeper and deeper as he enters more into his Montanist phase. It is possible in his defense against Marcion and against the heretic's objections to the Old Testament God and the Law that Tertullian found himself inadequately equipped for his task and, as a true scholar, repaired to Jewish teachers to make certain enquiries. These would not be difficult to find in Carthage. It is known that Judaism in the time of Tertullian had undergone the momentous change occasioned by the Fall of Jerusalem[89] and by the establishment of Jamnia together with the resurgence of literary activity which was preceded by the travelling of Rabbis to the great centers of civilization to collect Mishnaic material. The most remarkable scholar of the period following 70 A.D. was Rabbi Akiba[90] whose compilation of Mishnaic

[87] Chapters 9–14 of *Adversus Judaeus* are thought to be spurious. In chapters 1–8 is a mild apology of Christianity against Judaism and is compared, for example, with works like the *Epistle of Barnabas*. Tertullian states in *Adv. Jud.* that one need not keep the Mosaic law. His attitude is different in *De Jejun*. It might be possible that *Adv. Jud.* was written in two parts, one when Tertullian was more favorable to Judaism.

[88] I had thought of producing some statistics on this point, but on reflection I decided that they would prove little as quotations from Scripture depend so much on the subject matter under discussion.

[89] It is worth remarking here the observation of Simon (*op. cit.* pp. 10–15) that the Fall of Jerusalem reinforced the hopes of the Jews concerning a new Jerusalem that would replace the old one which was destined to pass away. The belief described by Simon is not unlike the expectation of the Asiatic New Prophecy.

[90] L. Finkelstein dates Akiba c. 40–137 A.D. (see his essay, "Akiba,"

material and interest in the broad fields of sociology, juristic philosophy and religion must have attracted such men of the type represented by Tertullian, the lawyer and philosopher. Tertullian must have been born some forty or more years after the death of Rabbi Akiba [91] who is known to have visited Carthage; moreover Rabbis Isaac, Hanan and Abba are called "of Carthage." [92] Akiba himself is famed for gathering disciples [93] and it is possible that his influence was still felt in Carthage in the period of Tertullian's *floruit*. Several points of similarity are found between Tertullian's later teaching and Akiba's principles, for example, Akiba supported the emancipation of women but, at the same time, he insisted on very strict marriage laws especially with regard to "incest" (*zonah*): [94] he adopted "scholastic continence" [95] and he and the other rabbis exhibited zeal for martyrdom approximating Tertullian's Montanist view that one must not flee from the city of martyrdom. [96]

The evidence suggests that Tertullian may well have availed himself of the scholarship of the Jewish teachers in Carthage during the time in which he was seeking to rebut Marcion's heresy, and if one takes a representative group of Tertullian's Montanist works, one can show Tertullian's acquaintance with Jewish thought. This provides an in-

---

no. 5, pp. 121–152 in *Great Jewish Personalities*, ed. by Simon Noveck, London [1962].) Tertullian died after 220 A.D.

[91] Simon, *op. cit.*, p. 48.

[92] *Ibid.* See the references there given.

[93] Yeb. 62b, p. 417 "... R. Akiba had twelve thousand pairs of disciples...."

[94] See Finkelstein, *art. cit.*, p. 141. A more detailed study is found in the same author's, *Akiba, Scholar, Saint and Martyr*, New York, 1936.

[95] *Vide supra*, p. 50.

[96] In his earlier works Tertullian does not insist on surrender.

teresting background to Tertullian's views on marriage and continence and especially to his exegesis of 1 Cor. 7.

Jewish influence in *Adv. Marcion*: the desecration of the Sabbath

(1.)   *Adv. Marc. II. 18 and 19*

Tertullian discusses the Jewish laws, for example, *lex talionis*, the dietary laws, sacrifices and so on and in defending them says that these were ordained so that the people would be bound to God and would be ever mindful of God's presence by their performance of detailed requirements laid upon them. Similarly the Rabbis do not advance individual reasons for biblical precepts[97] but merely see them as an expression of God's will: this is particularly evident in the tradition of Johanan ben Zaccai and his disciples, Akiba and Hanan, who came to Carthage.[98] The affinity between Tertullian's arguments and the Rabbis' on these points may be accidental, but one detail in chapter 19[99] indicates that Tertullian may have been acquainted with details of controversial points. Discussing Josh. 6:15 where Joshua appears to desecrate the Sabbath by walking around Jericho, Tertullian defends his action thus: it was "*opus . . . sacrosanctum . . . et ipso tunc dei praecepto utique divinum*" (c. 21. 2). A similar reason is given in Num. R.:[100] "If a man should say to you: 'How is it that Joshua desecrated the Sabbath?'—he did it at the bidding of the Holy One. . . ."[101]

---

[97] E.g., Yeb. 23a, p. 138, n. 3.
[98] See Num. R. 19:6–8, p. 757.
[99] *Adv. Marc.* II, c. 19 ff.
[100] Num R. 19:1, p. 565.
[101] In the same context Tertullian mentions the prohibition of the

(2.) *Adv. Marc. II. 20 — The Spoiling of the Egyptians.*[102]

This has long been a puzzle to many scholars, but the chapter entitled "Jewellery"[104] in Daube's recent book[103] fully explains this as the "substance" due to slaves on their release from their masters. Now this is precisely the way in which Tertullian explains the morality of the Hebrews, namely that the Egyptians owed them compensation (*compensatio*) for the hard labor which the Hebrews had performed. I do not think that this can be pure "guess work" on the part of Tertullian who was a lawyer and must have been acquainted with Semitic law pervading Africa. Moreover, his explanation is followed by other fathers.

(3.) *De Anima—The Concept of Soul*[105]

Similarly in *De Anima* there is also evidence that Tertullian's thought is consonant with the Jewish idea of the "soul." This treatise is directed against a Hellenistic view of the soul; however, while explaining Christian (or Montanist) views, Tertullian says that they agree to some extent with Stoic view (*paene nobiscum*),[106] but he does not say that the Stoic views are the source of his philosophy

---

gathering of sticks (Num. 15. 32): this is reminiscent of Gen. R. 11:2. (note 2, p. 90).

[102] Ex. 12:36.

[103] D. Daube, *The Exodus Pattern in the Bible*, All Souls Studies, Oxford, 1963.

[104] *Ibid.*, pp. 55–61.

[105] In suggesting Jewish influence on this work, the writer does not wish to deny other influences; cf. J. H. Waszink, *De Anima* with trans. and commentary, Amsterdam, 1933.

[106] *De An.*, 5:2.

or identical with it. Indeed, on certain points he disputes
with the Stoic, for example he argues against those who
say that the soul comes into the body as the fetus is born
and breathes the cold air [107]; he further states that this
is a Stoic viewpoint which he is opposing. [108] His answer is
consonant with the Rabbinic opinion expressed in Gen.
R.: [109] "When was the soul implanted in the body?"
Answer, "when it left the womb". Objection, "Leave meat
without soul for three days, will it not putrefy?" (that is, the
fetus would not live *in utero* without the soul). In the same
chapter Tertullian identifies "blood" and "soul": "the
blood will not be without the principle of the soul." This
is a completely Hebraic thought. [110] Further Tertullian
identifies "breath" and "spirit" with soul. Again this is
Hebrew, not Stoic, thought, [111] for in Hebrew *neshamah* is
often identical with *ruach*. Again Tertullian argues that
the soul does not sleep [112] whereas to the Stoic sleep is a
relaxation or weakening of the spirit. [113] In Deut. R. [114]
one finds a view similar to Tertullian's. I do not doubt
that there are other examples of the influence of Jewish
thought in *De Anima*, but the above examples indicate the
confirmation of Tertullian's statement in the beginning of
this treatise: [115] "*Deliquit, opinor, divina doctrina ex Judaea
potius quam ex Graecia oriens.*"

[107] *De An.*, 25.
[108] For an account of the Stoic philosophy of the soul, see E. Vernon
Arnold, *Roman Stoicism*, London, 1958, pp. 238–272.
[109] Gen. R. 34:10–11, p. 275.
[110] See, for example, Lev. 17:11, 14.
[111] Cf. Arnold, *op. cit.*, p. 243 f. Tertullian does not mention fire
as a constituent "part" of the soul.
[112] *De An.*, 45.
[113] Arnold, *op. cit.*, p. 261.
[114] Deut. R. 2:37.
[115] *De An.*, 3:3.

(4.)   *De Resurrectione*

Here one finds three major arguments used by the Rabbis for the resurrection of the body: [116]

(a.) if God created the world from nothing, how much easier is it for him to resurrect the flesh (c. 11.); [117]

(b.) the analogy of day from night and season from season (c. 12.); [118]

(c.) the analogy of the Phoenix which may come either from Jewish or pagan sources but more probably from sources which wish to illustrate the resurrection of the body rather than the immortality of the soul, that is Jewish philosophy. [119]

(5.)   *De Idolatria*

It is unnecessary for me to treat this in detail as Elmslie has already made a close examination between the Mishnah on Idolatry and this treatise on the same subject by Tertullian. [120]

(6.)   *De Corona*

I cite one important example. In Sot. 49a, [121] one reads:

[116] One may, for example, contrast Tertullian's work with the *De Resurrectione* of Athenagoras who only gives one of these arguments.

[117] Ber. 15b, p. 91 "as the womb takes in and gives forth, so the grave takes in and will give forth again."

[118] Cf. Shabb. 88b and Ber. 60b where the prayers on walking are particularly instructive.

[119] Cf. Gen. R. 14:4–5, p. 151.

[120] W. A. L. Elmslie, *The Mishna on Idolatria, Aboda Zara.* Cambridge Texts and Studies, no. 8, 2 (1911) p. 24.

[121] Sot. 49a, pp. 265, 267 f.

"During the war with Vespasian [which ended in the destruction of the second temple] they [the rabbis] decreed against [the use of] crowns worn by bridegrooms and against [the use of] the drum. During the war of Quietus[122] they decreed against [the use of] crowns worn by brides . . . ." Sot. 49b discusses whether even if a crown of salt and brimstone were not permitted, would myrtle and rose be permitted. The answer was "No." The passages cited are similar to Tertullian's arguments in *De Cor.* 12:1, 2. Tertullian mentions myrtle but he also mentions the city of Jerusalem: this is apposite both because of the Fall of Jerusalem and because the crown worn by a Jewish bride was a miniature golden city in the form of Jerusalem.[123]

(7.)   *De Jejunia*

I have already discussed fasting in the Montanist system and indicated its possible connection with the Jewish precepts. Here I should like to make the following additional comments.

Tertullian supports the keeping of the Jewish fasts prescribed in Leviticus.[124] He also denies that *xerophagia* is a heathen practice and appears to be thinking of Jewish *xerophagia*, that is abstinence from certain foods, such as those from a pig.[125] One learns from *De Jejunia* that the Catholics accused the Montanists of being the heretics described in Galatians and in 1 Tim. 4. That is these heretics were apparently following Jewish practices. Tertullian himself defends the practices as long as they do not

[122] Apparently a Moorish prince appointed by Trajan (*ibid.*).
[123] See Sot. 49b, n. 4, p. 268.
[124] *De Jejun.*, 2.
[125] *Ibid.*, 4.

involve denying Christ.[126] Further Tertullian speaks of the possibility of St. Peter keeping a station day. This is not an anachronism if the thesis of Wieder[127] is correct. The Christian stations may have originated from the *ma'amad* (*ma-amodoth*) lit. station), a group of lay people (Israelites) who participated in the Temple service as representatives of the public. Tertullian may well have been acquainted with this practice. Further Tertullian accuses the Catholic of fasting on the Sabbath. This suggests that Tertullian still saw both the Sabbath and Sunday as days of re-joicing. Fasting was forbidden on the Sabbath.

Finally, just as in *De Anima*, Tertullian says that *divina doctrina* comes from Judaism not Hellenism, so in *De Jejun.* 12. 6 he meets the Catholics' charge that he is introducing novelty with the sentence, "*Aspice ad Judaicos fastos*[128] *et invenies nihil novum . . . .*" The Montanists seem, therefore, not only to follow the Jewish solar calendar, but also to claim precedence for their fasting regulations from the same source.[129]

Therefore, if both Phrygian Montanist and Tertullianism illustrate Jewish tendencies, this must be brought into consideration when one examines their attitudes toward marriage.

[126] *Ibid.*

[127] Wieder, *op. cit.*, pp. 116–118.

[128] I.e., feast days in general.

[129] There may be a Jewish reference also in c. 14: "With us at all events every day is celebrated with a special consecration" cf. Ber. 60b, 378 f.

CHAPTER 8

Tertullian on Celibacy

I JEWISH INFLUENCE ON TERTULLIAN'S TREATISES ON CELIBACY

Tertullian's works on chastity comprise the following: *Ad Uxorem* (two books) (c. 203 A.D.); *De Exhortatone Castitatis,* (before 207 A.D.); *De Monogamia* (c. 217); *De Pudicitia* (after 217 A.D.). It does not seem necessary to include *De virginibus velandis* (before 207 A.D.) or *De cultu feminarum* (two books, 197–201) within the actual works on chastity because they deal only generally with the behavior of women and young girls; there is no teaching about consecrated chastity in them. It is otherwise with the works listed above. Tertullian's teaching in these works is easily summarized. In the two books written to his wife, he stresses that marriage is good and permissible and re-marriage (after widowhood) is also permissible; however, he emphasises the value of continence and in 1 *Ad Ux.* 4, 16 cites the example of faithful widows:

Et adversus consilia haec eius adhibe sororum nostra-rum exampla, quarum nomina penes dominum, quae

190

nullam formae vel aetatis occasionem praemissis maritis sanctitati anteponunt. Malunt enim deo nubere. Deo speciosae, deo sunt puellae. Cum illo vivunt, cum illo sermocinantur, illum diebus et noctibus tractant, orationes suas velut dotes dómino assignant, ab eodum dignationem velut munera maritalia, quotienscumque desiderant, consequuntur. Sic aeternum sibi bonum, donum domini, occupaverunt, ac iam in terris non nubendo de familia angelica deputantur.[1]

He refers to 1 Corinthians to support his views about widowhood, but does not refer to it when he mentions virgins; further he terminates his first book by quoting pagan examples of continence and virginity, but he does not give any reference to Old Testament continents or to Christian ascetics. Book two is mainly devoted to enforcing the principle of marrying a Christian, not a pagan, partner. There is no mention of the "prohibition of remarriage" by St. Paul: the treatise ends with one of the most beautiful passages concerning partnership in Christian marriage.

---

[1] "But as for you, do you oppose against such specious arguments the example of those sisters of ours—their names are known to the Lord—who, having seen their husbands go to God, prefer chastity to the opportunities of marriage afforded them by their youth and beauty. They choose to be wedded to God. They are God's fair ones, God's beloved. With Him they live, with Him they converse, with Him they treat on intimate terms day and night. Prayers are the dowry they bring the Lord and for them they receive His favors as marriage gifts in return. Thus they have made their own a blessing for eternity, given them by the Lord; and remaining unmarried, they are reckoned, even their still on earth, as belonging to the household of the angels."
(Tertullian's *Treatise on Marriage and Remarriage*, trans. and annoted by William P. Le Saint, Ancient Christian Writers, vol. 13, London, 1951.) The sentiments expressed above were later applied to virgins, not widows.

De Exhortatione Castitatis is addressed to a man and urges him very forcibly to maintain widowhood after the death of his wife. Tertullian reduces the "permission" to remarry to an absolute minimum and declares that what is merely permitted is not really the will of God. In c. 9 he calls second marriage a kind of adultery. In c. 13 he refers to both Christian and pagan examples of continence; of the Christians he says, "*Quanti igitur et quantae in ecclesiasticis ordinibus de continentia censentur, qui deo nubere maluerunt, qui carnis suae honorem restituerunt . . . .*"[2] As one will see below, the Jewish influence on Tertullian is more pervasive in this work.

De Monogamia condemns second marriage completely and there is a sharp distinction in Tertullian's mind between the Catholic sensualists and the Montanist spiritual men. The arguments from *De Exhort. Cast.* are repeated with greater emphasis, and St. Paul's teaching on marriage and remarriage is adapted to support Tertullian's own views. A number of Old Testament and Christian examples of continence are cited.

De Pudicitia is the treatise in which Tertullian continues his condemnation of second marriage and repudiates absolution given to adulterers and fornicators.

This brief summary indicates the development of Tertullian's thought. It would now be advisable to consider in a more detailed study the increasing Jewish influence in the works and to indicate the sources of this influence. The main texts used are the Mishna, the Talmud, the Midrash Rabbah, *Legends of the Jews*, and the Pseudepigrapha. It

---

[2] "How many men and women there are whose chastity has obtained for them the honor of ecclesiastical orders! How many who have chosen to be wedded to God! How many who have restored to their flesh the honor it had lost!"

is difficult to date the material from Ginzberg's [3] work, but a reading of M. Simon,[4] Monceaux [5] and Frend [6] gives one reason for thinking that the legendary material collated by this scholar is certainly characteristic of the type of Judaism found in North Africa and that the ideas about continence which are expressed in it are consonant with the precepts of such groups as the Abelonians and the Caelicoles.[7]

(A.)

One notes firstly the Jewish influence—specifically illustrated by the literary form in which *Ad Uxorem* is written: it is the form of an ethical will; this form was popular among the Jews of ancient times and continued after the Middle Ages.[8] Biblical scholars are acquainted with those contained in the Pseudepigrapha, the Testaments of the Twelve Patriarchs.

(B.)

Secondly, Tertullian's arguments against successive polygamy are similar to those used by the Rabbis against concurrent polygamy.

(1.) In 1 *Ad Ux.* 2 he produces the argument that God took but one rib from Adam so that man should have but

[3] L. Ginzberg, *Legends of the Jews*, 7 vols., Philadelphia, 1909.

[4] Simon, *Recherches d'Histoire Judeo-Chretienne*, Paris, 1962.

[5] Monceaux, *Rev. des Etud. Juives*, 44 (1902) pp. 184–190.

[6] Frend, *art. cit.*

[7] *Vide supra*, pp. 32 f.

[8] Israel Abrahams, *Hebrew Ethical Wills*, Philadelphia, (The Jewish Publication Society of America, 5708) 1949, and also the *SJE* under "Ethical Wills."

one wife. A similar, but not identical,[9] argument is found in *Aboth Rabbi Nathan*, 2, 5a where Job bases his preference for monogamy on the fact that God gave only one wife to Adam. Ginzberg,[10] commenting on the monogamy of Adam and Job, says that Job " . . . had never had more than one wife at a time, for he was wont to say, 'If it had been intended that Adam should have ten wives, God would have given them to him. Only one wife was bestowed upon him and therefore one wife suffices for me, too.'" Tertullian's argument receives progressive expansion from 1 *Ad Ux.* 2 through *Exhort. Cast.* 5 to *De Mon.* 4. However the fullest argument appears in *De Mon.* 4, 2, 3:

> Quod pertineat ad antiquitatem, quae potest antiquior forma proferri quam ipse census generis humani? Unam feminam masculo Deus finxit, una costa eius decerpta, et utique ex pluribus. Sed et in praefatione ipsius operis: Non est. inquit, bonum homini solum eum esse, faciamus adiutorium illi. Adiutores enim dixisset, si pluribus eum uxoribus destinasset. Adiecit et legem de futuro, si quidem prophetice dictum est: "Et erunt duo in unam carnem: non tres, neque plures: ceterum ian non duo, si plures. Stetit lex.[11]

[9] The Fathers according to Rabbi Nathan, trans. by Judah Goldin, New Haven, 1956. See also D. J. Daube, *The New Testament and Rabbinic Judaism*, London, 1956, p. 77.

[10] Ginzberg, *op. cit.*, vol. 2, p. 241.

[11] "As regards the antiquity of the law, what form of marriage could be singled out which is older than one found at the very beginning of the human race? God fashioned one woman for man, taking only one of his ribs, even though he had many. And even before He did this, He said, 'It is not good for man to be alone, let us make him a helpmate.' He would have said helpmates, if He had intended him to have many wives." One notes in the last sentence the characteristic Jewish reverence for the Scripture whereby there is meaning in every letter.

(2.) In 1 *Ad Ux.* 3:1, there may be a reference to the idea of the androgynous man or, perhaps, to ideas such as that expressed by Simeon ben Johai, that is ". . . in marrying it is the man that seeks that which was lost—the rib,"[12]

> *Viderint qui inter cetera perversitatum suarum disiungere docent carnem in duobus unam, negantes eum, qui feminam de masculo mutuatus duo corpora ex eiusdem materiae consortio sumpta rursus in se matrimonii compactione compegit.*[13]

In this treatise the manuscripts vary (*compactione* N F R *computatione* A (Rig. Oehler) *coniugatione*. Hild).

Le Saint[14] prefers *computatione* and translates "in the mathematics of marriage"; if, however, the myth of the androgynous man is behind this passage then the better attested reading "*compactione*" is quite understandable. Marriage grafts the two together into one again. ("*Compingo*," to join several parts into one whole).[15]

(3.) The analogy taken between the unity of God and the unity in marriage is also essentially Jewish; one may compare *De Mon.* 1, 2 "*unum matrimonium novimus, sicut unum Deum*" with the statement found in *J.E.* (vol. 8 p. 657), "the monogamous ideal was illustrated by the prophetic use of marriage as typical of the revelation between God and Israel. In this monogamy became the corollary of the divine unity."[16]

[12] Daube, *op. cit.*, p. 82.

[13] "This is a charge they must be prepared to answer who, among other perversions of doctrine, teach their followers to divide those who are *two in one flesh*, opposing the will of Him who first subtracted woman from man and then, in the mathematics of marriage, added two together again who had originally been substantially one."

[14] Le Saint, *Marriage and Remarriage*.

[15] Cf. *Zohar* vol. I, pp. 177 ff.

[16] Cf. Ginzberg, *op. cit.*, vol. 3, p. 260 (on Osee and Yahweh) and *passim* in *Zohar*.

(4.) Throughout *De Pud.*, Tertullian associates idolatry, adultery and murder, all of which he regards as "unforgivable." "The rabbis . . . listed adultery with idolatry and murder as those cardinal sins which must not be committed even under pain of death."[17]

(C.)

Over and above the use of these Rabbinic arguments against polygamy, Tertullian produces examples of men renowned among Jews for their monogamy and continence.

(1.) There is, for example, Isaac, who is taken by the Rabbis as the example of monogamy, cf. *S.J.E.* " . . . the household of Isaac, regarded as the model in later Jewish tradition, was monogamous."[18]

Tertullian says in *De Mon.* 6, 4, "*Si ex libera es, ad Isaac pertinens, hic certe unum matrimonium pertulit*" (cf. *De Mon.* 17, 1 and 11, 4 "*Si vult nos iterare coniugia, quomodo semen nostrum in Isaac semel marito auctore defendit?*") Other examples are: (2.) Josue (*De Mon*, 6, 4) "*Secundus quoque Moyses populi secundi qui imaginem nostrum in promissionem Dei induxit in quo primo nomen Domini dedicatum est, non fuit digamus*";[19]

(3.) Noë, (*De Mon*: 4, 5) "*Iterum duo in unam carnem crescere et redundare suscipiunt, Noë et uxor filiique eorum*

[17] *SJE* under "Chastity." Cf. also G. F. Moore, *Judaism*, Cambridge, Mass., 1954, vol. 2, p. 58. These sins were expiated on *Yoma*.

[18] *SJE* under polygamy.

[19] "The second Moses, leader of the second people, was not a digamist. This is he who first bore the name of our Lord and who brought the prototype of the Christian people into the promised land." *Vide infra*, note 40, p. 200 on the principle of· exegesis in Tertullian and the principle, *Negat scriptura quod non notat et cetera.*

in unicis nuptiis." This is an argument from silence once again, but one may compare both the Pseudepigraphal literature [20] where Noë takes a wife with reluctance, which action shows a tendency toward asceticism and Ginzberg's account [21] of the Raven's argument with Noë in which he accuses Noë of wishing to send him away so that he may have the Raven's wife! Noë replies, "Wretch, I must live apart from my own wife in the ark. How much less would such a thought occur to my mind as thou imputest to me?" (4.) The example of Noë leads naturally to the example of the animals who are said to live monogamous lives in the ark (*De Mon.* 4, 5) "*Etiam in ipsis animalibus monogamia recognoscitur, ne vel bestiae de moechia nascerentur. Ex omnibus, inquit, bestiis ex omni carne duo induces in arcam, ut vivant tecum masculus et femina: quid amplius dicam? Immundis quoque alitibus cum binis feminis introire non licuit.*" [22] Similar ideas are expressed in Jewish thought; compare, for example, Ginzberg ". . . it was the raven who advised the animals not to obey Noë's command to lead a monogamous life and it was the eagle who was the first to slay a bird." [23]

(5.) However, the most notable examples from the Old Testament are Moses and Elijah. The case of Moses is complicated because of his apparent second marriage (Ex.

[20] R. H. Charles, *Pseudepigraphic*, Oxford, 1964, p. 131, and also Ginzberg, *op. cit.*, vol. I, p. 159 (Noë's marriage with Naamah at the bidding of the Lord) and vol. 5, note 31.

[21] Ginzberg, *op. cit.*, vol. I, p. 164.

[22] "Even among the animals monogamy can be observed: the very brute beasts were not to be born of adultery. For God said: 'Of every beast of all flesh, thou shalt. . . .' On the same principle, He orders groups of seven pairs to be chosen—one each, male and female. What more can I say. Not even unclean birds could enter in company with two females."

[23] *Ibid.*, vol. 5, note 51 on Noë.

2:21 and Num. 12).[24] Tertullian either chooses to ignore Num. 12 or he may have adhered to Jewish tradition which taught that Moses was continent during his first marriage[25] or his continence from the time of the revelation on Sinai.[26] The mysteries of the Holy Name were only entrusted to a few and for them strict purity was required. When God revealed Himself to Moses and to the People of Israel, they were enjoined to abstain from coitus, Israel for the time being, Moses for all time.[27] Those in hope of divine revelation abstained from coitus as well as from impurities.[28] I have already quoted from Sifre Num. 99 which records Zipporah's exclamation when she heard that Eldael and Medad had become prophets, "woe to the wives of these men!" (for this meant cessation from conjugal intercourse). The relationship between prophetism and continence for both Old Testament and New Testament prophets has also been pointed out.

This idea of the necessity of continence for prophecy and

[24] Rashi explains that Moses' wife had two different names.

[25] Ginzberg, *op. cit.*, vol. 2, p. 287 (under Moses as King of Ethiopia). He married the daughter of the King of Ethiopia but did not consummate the marriage remembering that Abraham and Isaac forbade their sons to take Canaanite wives.

[26] *JE*, vol. 3, p. 224. See also Ginzberg, *op. cit.*, vol. 2, p. 316 where the removal of Moses' shoes is interpreted as his abstinence from earthly things even from conjugal life. The passage continues: "Thereupon the angel... Michael spoke to God: 'O Lord of the world, can it be thy purpose to destroy mankind? Blessings prevail only if male and female are united, and yet Thou biddest Moses separate from his wife'. God answered saying, 'Moses has begot children, he has done his duty towards the world. I desire him to unite himself now with the Shekinah that she may descend upon the earth for his sake'." Cf. also vol. 8, p. 255, where Miriam and Aaron complain that Moses abstains from coitus through pride.

[27] Shab. 87a; Pes. 87b; Aboth R.N. 2. The basic scripture texts are Ex. 19:15 and Deut. 5:27.

[28] *JE*, vol. 5, p. 224 ff. and cf. Enoch 83:2.

revelation is very important when one is considering the background of the Montainist insistence on abstention from second marriage and also the importance of purity, and possible continence, among the Jewish sectarians.

Moses is associated with Elijah in *De Mon.* 8, 7 "... *cum in revelatione gloriae suae de tot sanctis et prophetis Moysen et Heliam secum mavult, alterum monogamum, alterum spadonem. Non enim aliud fuit Helias quam Joannes qui in virtute et spiritu venit Heliae....*"[29] The Aggada attributes perfect continence to Elijah and Elisha, and the Pseudo-Clementine Epistles[30] speak of them as in Ep. 1 c. 6 among the saints whose lives were "holy and blameless." Brock has kindly translated this for me from the Syriac and made some comparisons with the Coptic: there does not seem to be a clear opinion that they were virgins.[31]

Jewish tradition looked upon Elijah as an angel[32] and traditions concerning angels and prophets like Moses and Elijah are sometimes common to both, for example, both angels[33] and Moses[34] were born circumcised.[35] Adam was said to be circumcised in Paradise: to be born circumcised

[29] "... when, at the revelation of His glory, with so many saints and prophets to choose from, He preferred to appear with Moses and Elias, the one a monogamist, the other a celibate—for Elias was no different from John, who came *in the power and spirit of Elias....*"

[30] Ps. Clem., *Ep.* 2:5 and 6 (*Ep.* 2).

[31] Cf. Ginzberg, *op. cit.*, vol. 4, note 2, p. 316 where it is stated that Elias never married and therefore nothing is said in Scripture concerning his family. Elias is especially thought of in his role of judging the purity of families when the Messiah comes; however this is not "purity" in the ascetic sense but refers to those families which have not intermarried with foreign peoples.

[32] *JE* under Elijah. He is often thought of as Metatron.

[33] *Jub.* 15, 27.

[34] *JE* vol. 9 p. 47.

[35] *JE*, vol. 4, p. 93.

was regarded as the privilege of the saints, from Adam "who was made in the image of God and Moses to Zerubbabel."[36] This connection with angels may have led to the supposition that Elias was *virgo intactus*: one notes the connection between angels and continence at Qumran, in the New Testament and in the Midrashim.[37]

It is noticeable that all Tertullian's examples of monogamous men[38] (except the example of Adam) occur in *De Mon.*, a work thoroughly imbued with Montanism. In his earlier works on chastity, Tertullian is content to name pagan examples of monogamy,[39] but in *De Mon.* these are augmented with Jewish examples. This confirms the view that he seems to have become more deeply implicated in Judaism of a "non-conventional" type as he became more attracted toward Montanism.[40]

[36] See *A.R.N.*, ed. by Schecter, p. 153, Sotah 12a.

[37] T. H. Gaster, *The Dead Sea Scrolls*, rev. ed., New York, 1964, p. 269 (The War 7. 1–7). Luke 20:36.

[38] Judith is produced as the example of a monogamous woman (*De Mon.* 17, 1); this is fully in the Jewish tradition (Jud. 16. 26). It is surprising that Enoch is not mentioned, cf. Justin, *Dial.*, c. 19.

[39] 1 *Ad Ux.* 1, 6; *Exhort. Cast.* c. 13.

[40] I append this note with some hesitation as I have been unable to study Rabbinic exegesis in any detail; however I feel that the following suggestion is worth some consideration. Perhaps the most arresting trait in Tertullian's later works in his strange form of argument. William P. Le Saint (*Tertullian, Treatises on Penance*, A.C.W., London, 1959) comments, "His whole habit of thought and manner of expression, even his method of argumentation, are utterly foreign and strange to us..." (p. 7). Indeed Tertullian's style of exegesis does not harmonize, as in his earlier works, with his Alexandrian predecessors; neither does it present the straight logic of the Roman lawyer, yet it is consistent, systematic and very subtle. Could one find the explanation of this enigma in Tertullian's growing acquaintance with Rabbinic exegesis and his use of this method even though he may not have fully understood the difference between *halakah* and *haggadah*? Frend (*art. cit.*) comments, "It has also been recognised that the ethical code imposed by the rigorist element in the African

Church bore a striking resemblance to the Jewish *halaka* of the day.
Detailed comparisons can be made between Tertullian's prescriptions
for avoiding contact with pagan society, contained in the *De Idolatria*,
and those to be found in the Jewish *Aboda Zara* of the same date."
Using the brief, yet comprehensive, chapter on Hermeneutics of the
Talmud and Midrashim (c. XI pp. 93–98) by Hermann L. Strack
(*Introduction to the Talmud and Midrash*, New York, 1959) as a base,
I offer the following examples to show that Tertullian may have been
acquainted with Rabbinic exegesis.
(1) Tertullian is particularly fond of the type of argument which re-
sembles the principle, "From that contained in a negative statement
one may infer that which is the rule for the positive, and *vice versa*,"
(Strack, *op. cit.*, pp. 288–289). In Tertullian this occurs, for example,
in *Exhort. Cast.* 4, 1, 2.
". . . Praeceptum domini, inquit, non habeo, sed consilium do, quasi
misericordiam consecutus a domino fidelis esse. 2 Ceterum neque in
evangelio neque in ipsius Pauli epistolis ex praecepto dei invenias
permissam matrimonii ⟨ite⟩ rationem. Unde unum habendum con-
firmatur, quia quod a domino permissam non invenitur, id agno-
scitur interdictum."
The same Rabbinic principle may be in Tertullian's mind when he
quotes (*De Mon.* 4, 4): "*Negat scriptura quod non notat*," and *De
Mon.* 7, 4, "*. . . sepulta lege succedendi in matrimonium fratris,
contrarium eius obtinuit, non succedendi in matrimonium fratris.*" One
may also compare *De Mon.* 4, 2 quoted above pp. 9–10. All the above
arguments reflect the type of reasoning used, for example, in the
Midrash Rabbah on Genesis (R. A. Stewart, *The Earlier Rabbinic
Tradition*, London, 1949, pp. 25–26), which argues that "the appear-
ance of old age began with Abraham, physical suffering with Isaac,
illness before the death of Jacob and repeated sickness with Hezekiah
. . . The entire argument is that previous cases are not recorded in
Holy Writ and that, therefore, there were no previous cases" (Cf.
Philo, *Quod Deterius*, 177–178 and Heb. 7, 3).
(2.) Tertullian frequently uses arguments similar to the principles
expressed in the fifth and sixth *middoth* of Ishmael (Strack, *op. cit.*,
p. 96) namely "Explicit inference *a minori ad maius* and *vice versa*"
and "When such an inference is merely suggested." Examples of this
are:
(a.) *Ad Uxor.* 1, 3, 3, the argument of the whole chapter is summed up
in the sentence, ". . . *quod autem necessitas praestat, depretiat ipsa.*"
(b.) *Ad Uxor.* 1, 6, 1 "*Quodsi hi qui habent obliterare debent quod habent, quanto magis non habentes prohibentur repetere quod non habent?*"
(c.) *Exhort. Cast.* 3, 4, "*Nam ostendens quid magis velit, minorem
voluntatem maiore delevit . . .*"; cf. also *Exhort. Cast.* 10, 2.

Père Audet [41] has traced the affinity between the *Didache*, the Epistle of Barnabas and the *Shepherd of Hermas* and Jewish thought and literature, especially the Manual of

---

(3.) Tertullian uses the principle of *Middah* 19: "A statement is made with reference to one subject, but it is true just as well with reference to another" (Strack, *op. cit.*, p. 97). In *De Mon.* 6, Tertullian produces the following arguments: Abraham believed before he was circumcized. It is in this state that one regards him as our father. But at that time he was also monogamous. "*Si reicis circumcisum, ergo recusabis et digamum. Duas dispositiones eius binis inter se modis diversas miscere non poteris. Digamus cum circumcisione esse orsus est, monogamus cum praeputiatione. Recipis digamiam, admitte et circumcisionem....*"

(4.) In addition Tertullian seems to know *Middah* 18: "A specific case of type of occurrences is mentioned, although the whole type is meant." This principle may underlie *De Mon.* 7, 5, namely that one should not marry a brother, but we are all brethren (as Christians); therefore remarriage is wrong both for women and for men; and *De Mon.* 12, 4, namely that if in 1 Tim. 3:2–7 monogamy, sobriety, *et cetera* be required of a bishop, then all these things, including monogamy (by which Tertullian means abstaining from second marriage altogether), should be required of all Christians.

I note with extreme interest Tertullian's statement about the priesthood of all Christians (*De Mon.* 7, 7–9 above) and the argument that priestly observances are, therefore, incumbent on all believers, especially in view of Frend's thesis (*art. cit.*, p. 283); "Thus it is reasonable to look for parallels to the *seniores* (of the African Church) farther afield than Africa, perhaps in the organization of the most primitive Church in Palestine. It may be worth recalling that at Q'mran the highest direction of the Sect lay in the hands of a council of three priests and twelve laymen. These decided administrative and disciplinary matters.... If we are confronted by a similar oligarchy of lay and priestly officers in existence in the churches in North Africa, it may be that the explanation must be sought in a Jewish or Judaeo-Christian environment out of which the North African Church developed in the second century A.D. *The traditional 'legalism' of the African Church might be explained with reference to this background as well as to the secular professions of its first leaders, Tertullian and Cyprian*" (the italics are mine).

[41] "*Affinités Litteraires et Doctrinales du Manuel de Discipline,*" *RB* LIX (1952) pp. 219 ff. and in a later number, LX (1953) pp. 41–82.

Discipline. It would seem also that there may be a link between Tertullian's works on chastity and certain statements about marriage in the Dead Sea Scrolls, representing, as they do, a branch of Jewish sectarianism.

When one examines Tertullian's quotations from the Old Testament in his works on chastity, there are several quotations which are imprecisely given or impossible to locate. One of the most interesting occurs in *De Mon.* 7, 6, 7 where Tertullian states that the Law forbids priests to remarry: "... *Denique prohibet eadem sacerdotes denuo nubere ....*"

Oehler found this impossible to locate. D'Alès[42] refers to Lev. 21:14[43] which prohibits a high priest from marrying a widow or a divorcee. Le Saint[44] comments that the Talmud and later Rabbinic literature interpret the text as requiring the High Priest to be monogamous.

In the Damascus Document one reads: "Similarly, too, it is said concerning the *prince*: 'He shall not take more than one wife'" (Deut. 17:17).[45] The Hebrew word for "prince" in this text in *C.D.* is "Nasi" which was the title of the Chief of the Great Sanhedrin in Jerusalem and its successors;[46] from the second century A.D. the Nasi was

[42] Le Saint, *op. cit.*, p. 158, note 95.

[43] *Ibid.*

[44] Unfortunately Le Saint does not give the precise reference. In a personal communication with me he expressed doubt about his statement.

[45] *The Zadokite Documents*, edited and translated by Chaim Rabin, 2nd ed., Oxford, 1958, pp. 18–19.

[46] See Jastrow under נאשי and its cognates. See also Frend, *op. cit.*, p. 282 "... the 'sacerdotalism' of the African bishop has long been attributed to an Old Testament attitude towards priesthood, which would account for the bishop (or priest) being regarded as subject to the same taboos of purity as the Levite."

always a descendant of Hillel.[47] "Nasi" was also the name
of the priestly family. Some of the Rabbis who visited
Carthage were entitled "ha-Nasi,"[48] for example, Gamaliel Nasi. It is possible that they, as rulers and teachers,
chose to observe continence like Akiba and Ben Azzai and
that this eventually became an established practice. From
such an environment, first in Palestine and then in Carthage, may have arisen the regulation for monogamy of
presbyters which seems to be already established in the
New Testament[49] and which is emphasised by Tertullian.
A closer resemblance to the Damascus Document is found
in *De Mon.* 4, 2 and 5, 1, 6, 7. The *C.D.* refers to "the
whorish practice of taking two wives at the same time"[50];
then follow arguments from Genesis and from Leviticus.
There is some affinity but not verbal correspondance
between the two arguments.

Damascus Document. 4, 21	*De Mon.*
1 (*a*) an analogy with Adam and Eve: "the true basis of nature being the pairing of one male with one female, even as it is said (of Adam and Eve), 'A male and female created He them.'"	1 (*a*) cf. 4, 2 '... *Unam feminam masculo Deus finxit. una costa eius decerpta*' cf. also *De Mon* 5, 1.

(*b*) Both quote Gen. 1. 27

2 (*a*) Those that were in the ark, "in pairs they entered."	cf. *De Mon.* 4. 5. '*Etiam in ipsis animalibus monogamia recognoscitur . . . .*'.

[47] *SJE* under *Nasi*.
[48] Cf. Keth., 103a–b, p. 658. Hor. 13b.
[49] Titus 1:6.
[50] Rabin, *Zadokite Documents*, Oxford, 1954, p. 16 and 17.

(*b*) Both quote Gen. 7 omitted in the Gospel of Matthew.

Damascus Document. 5. 8–9a.	*De Mon. c. 7*
(3) A quotation (not precise) of Lev. 18. 13 "Moreover they marry their brothers and sisters, whereas Moses has said, 'Thou shalt not enter into intimate relations with the sisters of thy mother; she is thy mother's kin.'"	(3) Tertullian argues that we should not marry a brother or a sister "for we are all brothers," then he freely quotes Lev. 20, 21, "He that marrieth his brother's wife does a base and unclean thing; he will die without children."

C.D. and *De Mon.* refer to different texts of Leviticus; in both cases the text is imprecise, but the principle behind both is similar, namely the prohibition of affinity (of niece marriage in *C.D.* and of levirate in Tertullian).

(4) Both *C.D.* and Tertullian follow these quotations by similar statements:

C.D. 5, 9b–10a	*De Mon. c. 7*
"The Laws of forbidden degrees are written, *to be sure,* with reference to *males,* but they hold equally for females."	"Therefore, if a *man* is prohibited from marrying in these circumstances, *doubtless* a *woman* is also, for she has nobody to marry but a brother."

Tertullian's statement in this respect is strange in that the beginning of para. 6 (c7) of *De Mon.* refers indeed to males but para. 5 has argued from the side of the woman.

Rabin's[51] comment is very interesting: ". . . in contrast to Philo the Rabbis take *zonah* of Lev. 21:7 as a woman who has broken the incest laws. . . . Our sect thus sides with the Rabbis particularly on Ginzberg's view that our law is really derived by combination of Lev. 18:17 and Lev. 18:16 . . . thus placing it among the incest laws, while Gen. 1:27 is adduced as *asmakhata*, Midrashic support." The "whorish practice of taking two wives in (her) his (or their) lifetime" appears to be a ruling arising from discussion of principles such as those expressed in T.B. Yeb. c. 2 p. 94 ff., namely the prohibition of marrying "the wife of his brother who was not his contemporary"[52]; but this prohibition covers even one who was contemporary (in his or their lifetime).

In all four treatises on continence, Tertullian's whole purpose is to dissuade from second marriage, and the reasons which he asserts against remarriage are those relating to affinity as an incestuous union,[53] that is that remarriage between Christian brothers and sisters is incestuous.[54] Consequently, Tertullian explains away St. Paul's permission to remerry by saying that this permission is given only when the previous partner has been a pagan.

[51] Rabin, *op. cit.*, p. 17, note 3.

[52] Cf. Yeb., c. 2., p. 94 ff. Cf. also Athenagoras, *Suppl.* 33 where successive polygamy is called "cloaked adultery" and Hermas, *Mand.* 4, 4 who dissents from this opinion. For a fuller discussion see Joyce, *Christian Marriage*, New York, 1933, pp. 584–600.

[53] This appears to be the main reason behind Tertullian's argument, but one must still remember Tertullian's idea of the lasting contract of marriage, lasting even after death (*Exhort. Cast.* c. 11). Cf. the frequent Jewish expressions of grief on the death of a first wife, C. G. Montefiore and H. Loewe, *A Rabbinic Anthology*, London, 1938, pp. 509 and 511 (Git. 90b and San. 22a).

[54] This is not dissimilar to the principle whereby a godparent may not marry his or her godchild because of the spiritual affinity contracted.

There is some analogy here to the Jewish idea of *porneia* in the sense of forbidden degrees, but *porneia* does not apply in the case of a proselyte whose former relationships are sometimes annulled when he becomes a Jew so that he can marry whomsoever he wishes.[55] For Tertullian, baptism like circumcision or Jewish baptism (for the woman) sets up a similar new relationship.[56]

A comparable idea may exist behind the Qumran idea of continence for a sacerdotal community with a closely knit brotherhood; furthermore, this may have been influenced by the principles of priestly monogamy and a more scrupulous application of the laws of "incest."

I have already made some comparison between the theories and practices of the Karaites and the Montanists. In an article Monceaux treats a work by Anan[57] entitled *Fadhatika*. This deals with Lev. 18:18 and the laws of incest. The karaites interpreted this text differently than the Rabbinites: *"D'après ceux-ci, le législateur veut dire seulement qu'il n'est permis à aucune condition d'éspouser la soeur de sa femme, tant que celle-ci vit."*[58] The word "sister" was variously interpreted, "... *ils vont jusqu'a l'expliquer, les uns par 'soeur de lait'* (אחיות ביניקה), *les autres par 'coreligionnaire,' et ils disent qu'un homme ne doit pas éspouser, outre sa femme, une autre femme et 'opprimer' celle-là* (רארור). *C'est-à-dire reporter son affection sur la seconde et négliger la première."*

[55] See Daube, *op. cit.*, on 1 Cor. 6:1 and also Acts 15:20.
[56] This may be behind the edict of "Callistus" concerning second marriage and the dissenting views of Hippolytus (*ANF*, vol. 6., p. 342); Justin Martyr, *Apoc.* 15., "So that all who, by human law, are twice married, are in the eye of our Master sinners" *et cetera*. The argument is that of *tertia concarnatio* (*De Mon.* 9, 7).
[57] Monceaux, *art. cit.*
[58] *Ibid.*, p. 185.

These are two points which Tertullian emphasizes: firstly, one may not remarry a Christian (*De Mon.* 7) and secondly, that one may not replace affection for one's first wife (even after her death) with affection for another (*De Exhort. Cast.* c. 11). This may also be the meaning of the "whorish practice of taking two wives in (her, his or their lifetime," (cf. Monceaux *op cit. p.* 187, *"Tu ne prendras pas une femme avec sa soeur, pour l'opprimer, pour découvrir sa nudité aupres d'elle pendant la vie de celle-là")*.

Anan ben David dates from the second half of the eighth century and was the oldest son of the Babylonian exilarch and learned in the Jewish law. The main feature of the sect which he founded was its opposition to Talmudic law, interdiction on wine and meat and the introduction of numerous fasts.[59] These are the features which appear in Montanism.

It would seem, therefore, that there are affinities between Montanist, Jewish-Christianity and sectarian Judaism. The influence seems to come through such media as Qumran[60] and through the Asiatic Babylonian exiles, through Jewish-Christianity and the Pseudo-Clementine type of literature to Montanism.[61]

II   TERTULLIAN'S EXEGESIS OF 1 COR. 7

Some preliminary remarks may be made about Tertullian's exegesis of 1 Cor. 7. Firstly, it should be noted that Ter-

[59] *SJE* under Anan.

[60] Ideas such as one finds at Qumran may be fairly widespread rather than confined to one area, the Judaean desert.

[61] See the diagram (p. 116) in *A Guide to the Scrolls* (A. R. C. Leaney, J. Posen and R. P. C. Hanson, London, 1958). To the vertical line in this diagram I should add "Montanism."

tullian recognizes the state of consecrated virginity, for example in *Exhort. Cast.* 9:4. *"Ideo optimum est homini mulierem non attingere, et ideo virginis principalis est sanctitas, quia caret stupri affinitate. Et cum haec etiam de primis et unis nuptiis praetendi ad causam continentiae possint, quanto magis secundo matrimonio recusando praeiudicabunt?..."*[62] (cf. 1 *Ad. Ux.* 8; *Exhort Cast.* 1 and 9, 5); but secondly, Tertullian does not admit celibacy as a general practice, *De Mon.* 3, 1 *"... Illud enim amplius dicimus, etiamsi totam et solidam virginitam sive continentiam Paracletus hodie determinasset, ut ne unis quidem nuptiis fervorem carnis despumare permitteret, sic quoque nihil novi indicere videretur, ipso Domino spadonibus aperiente regna caelorum ut et ipso spadone...."*[63]

Thirdly, Tertullian employs Matt. 19:12 in support of virginity, but he uses 1 Cor. 7 in an entirely different way. This difference is patent when one reflects that, while recognizing the voluntary practice of virginity for a selected few, Tertullian's principle purpose in his four treatises on continence is to oppose second marriage as something absolutely forbidden to all Christians: in his apology he uses 1 Cor. 7. This being so, one must examine

---

[62] "Therefore, *it is best for a man not to touch a woman.* So, too, the most perfect sanctity is that of the virgin, because it has nothing in common with fornication. Furthermore, since arguments of this kind can be used to urge abstention from even a first and second marriage, how much more valid are they against contracting a second!" (Cf. 1 *Ad. Ux.* 8; *Exhort. Cast.* 1 and 9:5.)

[63] "Actually, I shall go beyond this and assert that even if the Paraclete had in our day required complete and absolute virginity or continence, so that the hot passion of lust would not have been permitted gratification, in even monogamous marriage, not even such legislation could be considered an innovation, for the Lord Himself opened the kingdom of Heaven to eunuchs and He Himself lived as a eunuch."

what use Tertullian makes of 1 Cor. 7:25, 36–38. There are several references to *v.* 25.

In *Exhort. Cast.* 4:1, *v.* 25 is quoted, but it is related to second marriage and there is no mention of virgins.

> Ceterum de secundo matrimonio scimus plane apostolum pronuntiasse: Solutus es ab uxore, ne quaesieris uxorem, sed et si duxeris, non derelinquis. Perinde tamen et huius sermonis ordinem de consilio sue, non de divino praecepto introducit. Multum autem interest inter dei praeceptum et consilium hominis.[64] Praeceptum domini, inquit, non habeo sed consilium do, quasi misericordiam consecutus a domino fidelis esse.[65]

Then still commenting on "commandment of the Lord," Tertullian continues, "*Ceterum neque in evangelio neque in ipsius Pauli epistolis ex praecepto dei invenias permissam matrimonii ([ite]rationem).*"[66] Following this, Tertullian

---

[64] Patristic sources later than Tertullian make a distinction between a command from the Lord and a counsel from the Lord, but this does not seem to be a distinction which is supported from the Greek ἐπιταγή. Cf. for example, *De Virginibus* I, 5, 23 and *Exhort. Virg.* III. 17 of Ambrose. He quotes 1 Cor. 7:25 and explains that it is the Apostle's counsel, not command, concerning virgins. The last reference is interesting, for it read: "*Unde et Apostolus dicit: De virginibus praeceptum Domini non habeo, consilium autem do, tamquam misericordiam consecutus a Domino. Legerat enim dixisse Dominum spadonibus. . .*" then Ambrose quoted Is. 56:4–5 and Matt. 19:11–12. This is probably the first time that all these texts have been brought together on the subject of virginity.

[65] "As we know, the Apostle, when he speaks of second marriage, says plainly: *Art thou loosed from a wife? Seek not a wife. But if thou take a wife, thou doest not sin.* However, this statement also is introduced as a matter of personal opinion and is not based on any divine precept. There is a big difference between a commandment given by God and a counsel given by man. I have no commandment of the Lord, he says; but I give counsel, as having obtained mercy of the Lord, to be faithful."

[66] "Neither in the Gospel nor in the epistles of Paul himself will you find any permission for second marriage based on a commandment

quotes part of *v.* 28 and *v.* 29 ("*Verum tamen huiusmodi pressuram carnis habebunt*" and "*tempus in collecto*") without apparently seeing any anacoluthon between *v.* 25a and the following verses 26 ff.

This passage shows clearly

(a) that Tertullian when referring to ἐπιτάγη does not make a distinction between a mandatory command from God and an advisory counsel from God but between a counsel from God and a counsel from man (but see note 64 *supra*).

(b) that either he does not believe St. Paul knew what is now written in Matt. 19:11, 12 or that he thinks St. Paul is speaking about a different subject altogether, namely second marriage.

The same approach is found in *De Mon.* 11:9 where *v.* 25a is followed immediately by *v.* 27 ff. and the juxtaposition suggests that "*parthenos*" in *v.* 25a is regarded as masculine, although Tertullian uses "*homo*" not "*vir*"; again there is no reference to "virginity": "*Quaerebant et de virginibus consilium (praeceptum enim Domini non erat), bonum esse homini si sic permaneat, utique quomodo a fide fuerit inventus. Vinctus es uxori, ne quaesieris solutionem. . . .*"[67] Tertullian completely omits any reference to verses 36b and 37a and there is only a very enigmatic and brief reference to *vv.* 37b and 38 in *De Pud.* 16, 20. Here

---

of God's. This fact, then, confirms the conclusion that marriage is to be contracted only once, since we must acknowledge that a thing is forbidden by God when there is no evidence that he permits it."
[67] "*Concerning virgins* they had also made inquiry: his *counsel* was (for there was no *commandment of the Lord*), that *it is good for a man so to remain*, that is, to remain as he was at the time of his conversion; *Art thou bound to a wife?* Seek not to be loosed. *Art thou loosed from a wife? Seek not a wife. But if thou take a wife, thou hast not sinned.*"

Tertullian speaks of *v.* 32 (the unmarried caring for the things of the Lord) and then states "*Sic melius facere pronuniat* (*Paulus*) *virginis* (B. reads *virginem*) *conservatorem quam erogatorem.*" I suggest that *conservator* is used in the sense of one who maintains, while *conservare* is used of *res familiaris*, that is to maintain or keep property. This would give the same sense as τηρεῖν (*vide supra* p. 97). *Erogator* means one who pays out money which could be used of one who pays the *kethubah* for a bride, (it could not, however, be used of a father, who does not pay the *kethubah*). The case under discussion by Tertullian seems to be one of a widow, formerly married to a non-Christian, who is to remarry. That "*virginis*" (B *virginem*) means widow is suggested by the fact that Tertullian links *vv.* 37–38 very closely with *v.* 40 (*De Pud.* 16, 21). After speaking of the man concerned, Tertullian turns to the woman, "*Sic et illam beatiorem discernit quae amisso viro fidem ingressa amaverit occasionem viduitatis. Sic haec omnia continentiae consilia ut divina commendat: puto, inquit, et ego spiritum Dei habeo.*"[68]

One notes

(a) that the *et* seems to quality *illam* and thus to make a correlation between *conservatorem* (presumably masculine) and *illam* without any reference to another woman except the "virgin" (presumably feminine) in *De Pud.* 16, 20b;

(b) that "*haec omnia continentia consilia*" seems to point to the passage as a harmonious whole and to attribute the counsel to continence, not virginity;

[68] "So, also, he judges that a Christian woman is more blessed who, after losing her husband, embraces the opportunity of remaining a widow. And he proposes all these counsels of continence as coming from God. *I think*, he says, *that I also have the Spirit of God.*"

(c) that Tertullian does not use the possessive pronoun with virgin.

Clearly one cannot state unequivocally that Tertullian interprets these verses as a question of levirate marriage, but it is important to notice that he does introduce this very subject when he discusses 1 Cor. 7 in *De Mon.* 7:1. Tertullian explains that some burdens of the Law have been alleviated but others "*quae vero ad iustitiam spectant, non tantum reservata permaneant, verum et amplicata, ut scilicet redundare possit iustitia nostra super scribarum et pharisaeorum iustitiam. Si iustitia, utique et pudicitia.*"[69] Immediately after this paragraph, Tertullian discusses the *levirate law saying that some people have used* it as an argument for multiple marriages.[70] Tertullian gives reasons for this law being superseded (both the Karaites and the Samaritans considerably limited the levirate practice almost out of existence) and then states (para. 4)

At ubi et Crescite et redundate evacuavit extremitas temporum (cf. 1 Cor. 7:29) inducente apostolo: Superest ut et qui habent uxores sic sint ac si non habeant, quia tempus in collecto est . . . sepulta lege succedendi in matrimonium fratris, contrarium eius obtinuit, non succedendi in matrimonium fratris . . . Ergo non nubet defuncto viro uxor, fratri utique nuptura, si nupersit. Omnes enim nos fratres sumus . . .[71] (cf. *Matt.* 23:9, 8

[69] "However, such of its precepts as have to do with righteousness not only continue in force but have even been extended, so that *our justice may abound more than that of the Scribes and Pharisees.* If this holds true of justice, it also holds true of chastity."

[70] It would be interesting to know whether they quoted 1 Cor. 7 in their arguments.

[71] "But now that the last days which are upon us have abrogated the precept, *Increase and multiply,* the Apostle introduces a new precept: *It remaineth that they also who have wives be as if they had none, for the time is short....* Therefore, the law which required a

and Yeb. c. 2 p. 94 ff.). The Karaites take "brother" in the sense of "kinsman" (Epstein, *Marriage Laws* p. 144). Further, in *De Mon.* 11, 3 ff., Tertullian explains that the abrogation of the levirate law is consistent with St. Paul's teaching in 1 Cor. 7:39, 40 (which verses he had previously connected with *vv.* 37b and 38), for in every case where St. Paul gives a clear indication that successive polygamy is permissible, Tertullian asserts that the Apostle is speaking to the newly converted to whom the prohibition of remarriage does not apply since their first marriage is not a marriage in the true sense.[72]

Tertullian even suggests that 1 *Tim.* 3, 2–7 refers to those who had previously had pagan partners.[73] There seems to be no warrant whatsoever for this in the scripture texts except for 1 Cor. 7: *vv.* 8–24.

I can come to no decisive conclusion about Tertullian's exegesis of 1 Cor. 7. If he did realize that the question behind 1 Cor. 7:25–40 was that of levirate marriage, then this explains why he introduced the subject in his exegesis; but his conclusion is consonant with his exegesis of the rest of the chapter, that is in both cases he asserts that St. Paul forbade a practice (second marriage and levirate)

---

man to marry his brother's wife has been suppressed, and a contrary law has taken its place, that is, the law which forbids him to marry his brother's wife. ...Accordingly, a wife is not to remarry if her husband dies, since she will have to marry a brother if she does. For we are all brethren. Moreover, if she is going to remarry, she must *marry in the Lord*, that is, she must not marry a pagan, but one of the brethren, since the Old Law forbade marriage with those of other stock."

[72] Cf. Origen who does not regard non-Christian alliance as true marriage; Crouzel, *Virginité et Mariage selon Origène*, Paris, 1962, p. 145 f.

[73] *De Mon.* 13.

instead of leaving the matter to the free choice of the individual concerned. Unfortunately, Tertullian's method of exegesis does not make it impossible that characteristically he omitted to mention the very verses which were not compatible with this thesis, that is which allow levirate marriage, namely *vv.* 36b and 37a. If *vv.* 36–38 deal with the levirate, then he glosses over these verses as he glosses over St. Paul's emphasis on the free choice of abstinence or remarriage. Tertullian's exegesis is profoundly different from either Clement's or Origen's; however, it is singularly important to notice that the writer who seems to have been most intimately acquainted with Jewish law [74] is the only one who (a) does not connect *v.* 25 with virginity but treats *parthenos* in the sense of widow; (b) introduces the levirate question into his exegesis of 1 Cor. 7.

[74] I do not deny that other fathers were acquainted with Jewish law and exegesis, for example, Origen, who consulted Rabbis, G. Bardy, "Les Traditions Juives dans 'oeuvre d'Origène," *RB* (1925) pp. 149 ff., but Tertullian seems to show a greater knowledge.

CHAPTER 9

Epilogue

This thesis has, as it were, presented a trilogy on celibacy.[1] I have examined the subject in different geographical areas, different cultures and different epochs: it is the task of an "Epilogue" to draw together the various threads and to seek for a common conclusion if possible. This thesis has challenged four assumptions and, perhaps, has gone some way in proving that these were false. Firstly, the terms *bethulah, parthenos* and *virgo* in the first two centuries of the Christian era are seen to have wider connotations than generally believed, and the contexts in which they appear must be scrutinized to discover whether they should bear the meaning of "youthfulness"

[1] It is called a "trilogy", for the discussion has been centered upon three different cultures, the Jewish, the Jewish-Christian and the Alexandrian. It is difficult to relate the ideas of all three and therefore I have made the conclusions a reflection of the general principles underlying all three rather than forcing a direct contrast between any of them.

or "celibacy." Secondly, linguistic evidence suggests that the word *parthenos* was used as frequently for men as for women and that the word *eunuchos* was the most common word to denote a celibate: this denoted men, not women. Thirdly, the only group of "consecrated virgins" has retired from the pages of the New Testament and in their place are left young widows and widowers living in a Jewish-Christian community which clings rather tenaciously to traditional social patterns, class distinctions and questions that exercised Jewish teachers both before and after St. Paul. Fourthly, St. Paul and the Christians contemporary with Christ and those living in the sub-apostolic age do not seem to have embraced absolute celibacy.

The first strong drive toward a fairly widespread practice of a life of continence is found among schismatics from the orthodox Church, namely Montanists, and appears to have derived from prophetic chastity and forbidden relationships. This type of continence was never accepted by the orthodox Church but from the beginning was condemned by papal authority;[2] moreover it was never rescinded even though the practice of second marriage was frowned upon in the East and to some extent in the West. What then was the true source of the practice of celibacy in the orthodox Church? Although one must deny any organized or widespread practice of celibacy in the first two centuries of the Christian era, one notes that beginning from 1 Corinthians through 1 Timothy, St. Matthew 19:11, 12, through Minucius Felix, Hermas, Ignatius, Polycarp, 1 Clement, Justin Martyr, Athenagoras and the pagan Galen, there is always fragmentary yet decisive

[2] The Edict of "Callistus."

evidence that a few outstanding people did keep "their flesh pure" or practice continence and some even embraced virginity. The impetus for this was possibly the eschatological expectation of an imminent *parousia* which encouraged men to cut earthly ties and to be ready for death and the future life. The corollary of this is found in the Wars of the Maccabees. One has no means of checking whether, as the expectation of an imminent *parousia* grew less, this manner of life became less frequent. Yet as the eschatological hope was projected more into the future, when the Temple and the City were razed to the ground, the Christians like their Jewish contemporaries revised their notion of Torah.

Animal sacrifice for Jews and Christians was now impossible and the Jews under the leadership of St. Paul's contemporary, Rabbi Johanan ben Zaccai,[3] established their academy at Jamnia and began to accomodate Torah to the changed circumstances of their lives. The Rabbis, like R. Akiba and R. ben Azzai, became increasingly absorbed in the Law and increasingly detached from earthly and family ties. To such an extent did they accomplish this that they were able to sublimate their natural physical instincts and to substitute natural marriage duties for spiritual. The *Canticle of Canticles* has always been regarded as the love song of Yahweh and his people.[4] The Torah is the bride which God gave to his people and the students and teachers of Torah are either compared to "brides"[5] because of their association with Torah or regarded as "bridegrooms" when they are re-

[3] See J. Neusner, *The Life of Rabban Yohanan ben Zaccai*, Leiden, 1962.
[4] Hag. 76, p. 76, note 4.
[5] *Vide supra*, pp. 109 ff.

garded as individual recipients of Torah.[6] The Rabbis
were considered living Torahs and perhaps in a sense,
"brides" of God. This is what happened among the
Palestinian Jews. A similar, but more imaginative, process
had taken place on Alexandrian soil. Philo allegorized
marriage out of legitimate existence, and principally in
his treatise *De Congressione*, but also elsewhere in his
writings, had used nuptial imagery with reference to the
attainment of true knowledge. To some extent Philo's
ideas were based on irrational misogyny and therefore
were antagonistic to true Jewish thought, yet one element
in his teaching could be accepted, namely the association
of wisdom and continence. This in practice was accepted
by the Rabbis. For the love of Torah-Wisdom, the Rabbis
sacrificed a greater part of their conjugal life.

This climate of thought could not but affect the Christians.[7] They devoted themselves to the Living and New
Torah, Jesus. Hence one finds Ps. Ignatius describing the
purpose of virginity" . . . for the sake of meditating on
the law. . . ."[8] The continent Rabbis followed the example
of their masters who abstained within marriage but the
Christian followed the example of Jesus who, apparently,
never married. There appears to be no evidence for Jesus
as a married man throughout history; moreover there is
frequent reference to His virginity.

---

[6] See the *JE* under "Bridegroom of the Law." The term *Chathan*
probably originated from the Midrash *Shir ha-Shirim*. The title
"bridegroom of the Law" and "bridegroom of Genesis" are titles
given to persons who read the chapters ending and beginning the
Pentateuch respectively.

[7] Until 132 A.D., one cannot really separate Jews and Christians,
and I am becoming increasingly aware of evidence for Jewish-
Christianity as late as the fourth century C.E. in Northern Palestine.

[8] *Vide supra*, pp. 141 f.

The concept and practice of "Torah-celibacy" did not finish with mere imitation of master by disciples. Already in Origen, one sees the details of Torah, particularly the sacrificial system, allegorized and accommodated to chastity and celibacy. Even before, this sacrificial terminology had been attributed to widows.[9] In Christianity continence and virginity appear to some extent to be a substitute for animal sacrifice, or, perhaps one should say, the fulfilment of the sacrificial system, a holocaust of one's complete person.

Did the Christians borrow the nuptial imagery, which they used with regard to celibacy, from the Rabbis? One cannot be dogmatic about this. Yet it is important to note that Tertullian, who was so much influenced by Jewish legal thought, was the first to use the title *sponsa Christi* of those who lived in continence: he applied it to widows, not to *virgines intactae*.[10]

Over and above this influence, however, the controversy over Is. 7:14 and the heretical views concerning the Virgin Mary made Christians turn more attention to the Mother of God. So it was that women as well as men began to live lives of celibacy: the example of Mary made up for the lack of dominical teaching on celibacy for women. The insistence on the meaning *virgo intacta* for *parthenos* in Is. 7:14 probably caused readers to use the same meaning for other contexts including 1 Cor. 7. This would explain why teaching on virginity was attributed to St. Paul in the third century but not before.

By this time, too, the social conditions of the Roman Empire and its Christian subjects had changed. The Emperor had become Christian; the laws against childless-

[9] *Vide supra*, pp. 140 f.
[10] Cf. p. 190 *supra*.

ness[11] had been rescinded; women had gained greater emancipation; the receiving of the status of "person"[12] enabled them to make an offering of themselves to God. The individual sanctity and consecration of Christians became popular and resulted in the monastic movement. The statement in *Ep. Barnabas*,[13] "That the Black One may find no means of entrance, let us flee from every vanity, let us utterly hate the word of the way of wickedness. Do not, *by retiring apart, live a solitary life, as if you were already (fully) justified*" was no longer the opinion of the majority of Christians.

Celibacy became feasible because certain heresies concerning marriage had become divorced from orthodox teaching and because the individual had become emancipated from the community and its social obligations regarding marriage and childbearing. Thus celibacy evolved, not from the influence of pagan superstitions concerning marriage, coition and women or from heretical Gnostic

[11] The reign of Constantine, *Cod. Theod.* 8, 16, 1 of March 31, 320.

[12] Crehan has pointed out to me that until the time of Callistus there was uncertainty about the concept of person, but that he seems to have said some thing about it which provoked the wrath of Hippolytus. The two references are both in the *Refutatio haeresium* of Hippolytus 9, 12, 19 (*GCS* 26, 249) and 10, 26, 3 (*GCS* 26, 283). From these it appears that Callistus "was unwilling to say that the Father had suffered and was one Person (with the Son)" and that God was "one Person, divided indeed in name but not in substance." These two charges do not make complete sense, but if one thinks of Callistus groping for a distinction between person and substance, that will probably be near the truth. In Origen's *Dialektos* there is another bishop at about the same time doing exactly that, but in his case the word used is *dynamis*.

I have applied "this groping" for the concept of "person" to the theory and practice of celibacy. When "Callistus" declared that right of slaves and women to choose marriage partners, he was, in effect, treating them as "persons."

[13] *Ep. Barn.* 4:9 (Trans. Apostolic Fathers, Loeb edition).

teaching, but rather from a love and pursuit after wisdom
that was now hypostatized in Jesus Christ, the Living
Torah. By the mid-third century, virgins comprise a
notable section of the Christian community:

> ...Virgins whose glory, as it is more eminent, excites
> the greater interest. This is the flower of the ecclesias-
> tical seed, the grace and ornament of Spiritual endow-
> ment... the more illustrious portion of Christ's
> flock...? (Cyprian, *De Hab. Virg. 3,* trans. *ANF*).

It has been deemed appropriate to terminate this study at
the period when continence gives place to virginity,
namely the transition from Tertullian's writings to
Cyprian's. Yet since this work has concentrated on the
"Jewish influence on continence," it might be of interest
to readers to catch of glimpse of the progress of "Jewish
continence" as it is portrayed in the mystical writings falling outside the scope of this book but bearing marks of
early influence and certainly wholly consonant with the
ideas of the Rabbis quoted in this Trilogy.

The Jewish mystic did not feel the necessity of embracing
a celibate life; indeed, the reverse was true. In the *Zohar* [14]
the *Shekinah* appears as the feminine element in the deity [15]
and, far from depreciating woman and marriage, the
mystic relationship between God and the community of
Israel is seen as a harmony between male and female. The

[14] The *Zohar*, 5 vols., trans. by Harry Sperling and Maurice Simon
with an Introduction by J. Abelson, Soncino Press, New York, 1933.
The *Zohar* is of extremely uncertain date, but G. Scholem, *Major
Trends in Jewish Mysticism*, New York, 1941, pp. 40–43, has argued
for an earlier date for some works on Jewish mysticism, portions
of which are contained in the *Zohar*. The present writer is in full
agreement with this thesis. See also G. Scholem, *Jewish Gnosticism,
Merkabah Mysticism and Talmudic Tradition*, New York, 1960, pp. 3 f.
[15] G. Scholem, *On the Kabbalah and its Symbolism*, trans. by Ralph
Manheim, New York, 1965, pp. 104 ff.

Shekinah was the feminine aspect of the deity itself but was also identified with the "mystical Ecclesia of Israel"[16] and through Her Israel was united to Yahweh. This, of course, was not wholly dissimilar to the Christian concept of the Church as the Bride of Christ and indeed may have influenced Pauline thinking.

But the importance of introducing these concepts here is to demonstrate that within Judaism there existed this mystical element which achieved considerable importance among the masses of the Jewish people[17] but which was directly opposed to such writings as the Gospel of Thomas[18] that looks toward the cessation of the work of the female and of Philo for whom the female must become male before any salvific operation could become effective. For the writers of the *Zohar*, it was human sin which caused, as it were, a breach in the feminine and masculine aspects of the deity and resulted in the "exile" of the Shekinah.[19] Redemption is seen precisely as the reunion of God and His Shekinah and the restoration of the male and the female to their original unity. Hence in inter-

---

[16] *Ibid.*, p. 106.
[17] *Ibid.*, p. 105.
[18] Cf., for example, the *Gospel of Thomas*, Logion, 114.
"Simon Peter said to them:
'Let Mary depart from us,
For women are not worthy of life.'
Jesus said:
'See, I shall lead her,
So that I make her a man,
That she too may become a living spirit,
Who is like you men.
For every woman who makes herself a man
Shall enter the kingdom of heaven.'"
Quoted in B. Gartner, *The Theology of the Gospel of Thomas*, London, 1961, p. 253; see also pp. 250–256.
[19] Scholem, ... *Kabbalah* ... *Symbolism*, *op. cit.*, pp. 108 ff.

preting[20] " . . . Male and female he created them" (Gen. 1:27) the *Zohar* comments:

> From this we learn that every figure which does not comprise male and female elements is not a true and proper figure, and so we have laid down in the esoteric teaching of our Mishnah. Observe this. God does not place His abode in any place where male and female are not found together, nor are blessings found save in such a place, as it is written, *and He blessed them and called their name man on the day* that they were created: note that it says *them* and *their* name, and not *him* and *his* name. The male is not even called man till he is united with the female.[21]

This forms a distinct contrast to Philo, for example, in his exegesis of Gen. 2:24:

> "*For this cause shall a man leave . . . .*" For the sake of sense perception of the Mind, when it has become her slave, *abandons God and the Father of the universe, and God's excellence and wisdom*, the Mother of all things, and cleaves to and becomes one with sense-perception . . ." and " . . . resolves itself into the *order of flesh which is inferior*, into sense-perception, the moving cause of the passions" (*Leg. All.* 2; cf. also *Spec. Leg.* 1:81 and 171).

The *Zohar*, however, demonstrates how the perfect man is both male and female:

> It is incumbent on a man to be ever "male and female", in order that his faith may be firm, and that the Shekinah may never depart from him.

This statement is followed by one of the most tender and beautiful passages in mystical literature. It describes the

[20] *Ibid.*, p. 108; see also pp. 130 f.
[21] *Zohar*, vol. 1, pp. 177 f.

conduct of a man, obliged to go on a journey, who must leave his wife behind and therefore risk making himself deficient without the woman. He is told to pray to God for the gift of the *Shekinah* who will take the place of his wife and accompany him on his travels and enable him to remain both male and female. When he returns to his home he must give his wife pleasure "because it is she who procured for him this heavenly partner . . . ." Then the writer meets an obvious objection:

> You may object that, according to what has been said, a man enjoys greater dignity when he is on a journey than when he is at home, on account of the heavenly partner who is then associated with him. This is not so. For when a man is at home, the foundation of his house is the wife, for it is on account of her that the Shekinah departs not from the house. So our teachers have understood the verse, "and he brought her to the tent of his mother Sarah" (Gen. 24:67), to indicate that with Rebecca the Shekinah came to Isaac's house. Esoterically speaking, the supernal Mother is found in company with the male only at the time when the house is prepared, and the male and female are joined. Then the supernal Mother pours forth blessings for them.[22]

But these ideas did not mean that abstention was not practised. This is seen from the mystics' interpretation of Isaiah 56:4 (cf. Matt. 19:11–12):

> The "eunuchs" are, in fact, students of the Torah, who make themselves "eunuchs" during the six days of the week for the Torah's sake, and on the Sabbath nights have their conjugal union, because they apprehend the supernal mystery of the right moment when the Matrona

[22] *Ibid.*, pp. 158 ff.
[23] *Zohar*, vol. 3, pp. 272–275.

(*Shekinah*) is united with the King. Such adepts of the mystic lore concentrate their hearts on the Divine union, on the Faith of their Lord, and are blessed in their own union ....[23]

In fact the Sabbath itself both for Rabbinic Judaism and for the mystics was regarded as the Queen and Bride.[24] Hence the rabbis cohabited on the eve of the Sabbath and saw in the earthly union of man and woman the potent symbol of the union of heaven and earth and of God with the *Shekinah*.[25]

The liturgical occasion *par excellence* that celebrated the marriage of the *Shekinah* was the Feast of Weeks,[26] the commemoration of the giving of the Torah.

> Thus one reads that R. Simeon was sitting and studying the Torah during the night when the bride was to be joined to her husband. For we have been taught that all members of the bridal palace, during the night preceding her epousals, are in duty bound to keep her company and to rejoice with her in her final preparations for the great day: to study all branches of the Torah, proceeding from the Law to the Prophets, from the Prophets to the Holy Writings, and then to the deeper interpretations of Scripture and to the mysteries of Wisdom, as all these represent her preparations and her adornments. The bride, indeed, with her bridesmaids, comes up and remains with them, adorning herself at their hands and rejoicing with them all that night. And on the following day she does not enter under the canopy except in their company, they being called the canopy attendants. And when she steps under the

[24] Scholem, ... *Kabbalah* ... *Symbolism, op. cit.,* pp. 140 ff.
[25] *Ibid.,* p. 155. *Vide supra,* pp. 223 f.
[26] *Ibid.,* p. 138 ff.

canopy the Holy One, blessed be He, enquires after them and blesses them and crowns them with the bridal crown: happy is their portion.[27]

At midnight the nuptials were consummated (cf. Matt. 25:1–12).[28] The ceremony became very elaborate in some places and on occasion was even accompanied by the reading of a marriage contract.[29]

Thus for these Jewish mystics, coition and marital life in its legitimate sphere was a sacred act and a means to union with the deity. The misuse of generative powers on the other hand was regarded as demonic.[30] This, indeed, led to a cult of extreme chastity and among the Kabbalists a disregard for woman; but among the old mystics of the *Merkabah* period, there was a perfect balance with regard to marital life.[31]

This delicate balance between the state of the "eunuch" for the love of Torah with a restrained and loving use of coition is possibly the atmosphere in which the texts of the New Testament, namely Matt. 19:11, 12; 1 Cor. 7 (possibly 14:4) and especially the Parable of the Foolish Virgins (Matt. 25:1–13)[32] were written down and in which the practices of "academic continence" possibly obtained until about the mid-third century. However, the increasing reverence for the virginity of Christ and the desire to imitate His life as closely as possible as well as the increasing veneration of the Virgin Mary led to a development from temporary continence to perpetual virginity. This development was a purely Christian ideal and wholly

[27] *Zohar*, vol. 1, pp. 32 f. *Vide supra*, pp. 117.

[28] Scholem, . . . *Kabbalah and Symbolism*, *op. cit.*, pp. 148 f.

[29] *Ibid.*, p. 139.

[30] *Ibid.*, p. 154 f.

[31] Scholem, *Major* . . . *Mysticism*, *op. cit.*, p. 37 f.

[32] *Vide supra*, pp. 102 ff.

consonant with Gospel teaching, but the extraneous addition of middle-Platonic and Philonic elements marred the intrinsic value of the celibate state and lessened it in the eyes of many: unfortunately these misogynist tendencies were read back even into the teaching of St. Paul. Nothing, however, could be more alien to his thought.

If this Trilogy has enabled the reader to see that the origin of celibacy is not associated with Gnostic heresies and disparagement of woman but rather with wisdom and love of Torah, then the author is satisfied. It remains to observe that had celibacy remained wedded to its Jewish inheritance certain aspects of the Church's life might have reflected more radiantly the glory of the *Shekinah*.

Table to show the increasing

popularity of virginity

Table to show the increasing popularity of virginity

Author	Date	References to I Cor. 7	References to I Cor. 7 25, 36–8
1 Clement	C 1	—	—
Barnabas	C 1–C 2	—	—
Ignatius	C 2	—	—
Polycarp	C 2	—	—
Didache	C 1–C 3	—	—
Diognetus	C 2 or C 3	—	—
Hermas	C 2	1	—
Justin Martyr	C 2	—	—
Pseudo-Justin	—	—	—
Athenagoras	C 2	—	—
Tatian	C 2	—	—
Theophilus	C 2	—	—
Clement (Recogn.)	Probably C 3	—	—
(Homilies and epistles)	—	7, 32, 34 (only once)	1
Irenaeus	C 2–C 3	7, 5, 12, 14, 31	1 reference to *v.* 25
Minucius Felix	C 2 or C 3	—	—
Hippolytus	C 2–C 3	—	—
Clement of Alexandria	C 2–C 3	26	1 reference to 36–38, none to 25
Tertullian	C 2–C 3	94	25 (3 times), 35 (once), 38 (2 times

Complete sections or works on either continence or virginity	Remarks
—	—
—	—
—	Only 1 reference (Ad Pol. 5, 2) to a man remaining ἐν ἁγνείᾳ
—	—
—	I suggest that the lack of references to "virginity" might be an argument in favor of an early date
—	—
—	Mention of "allegorical virgins." No sin is committed if one receives back an adulterous wife or if one remarries
One sentence in *Apol.* c 15. Some remain pure up to 70 years of age	Second marriage is a sin; castration is permissible
One sentence *De Resurr.* c 3	The reference is to male virginity
One sentence	Remarriage is "decent adultery" (*Suppl.* c. 33)
Encratic	He does not seem to have used I Cor. 7 to support his encratic ideas
—	—
—	Much about chastity but not virginity
Mention of chastity	—
—	Much about St. Mary, nothing about celibacy, *v.* 25 in context of divorce
1 sentence, many grow old in purity	—
—	Disagrees with digamist priests and marriage between slave and free
1 lost work on continence and one extant section on continence	—
5 works on continence (not including *De Virg. Vel.* or *De Cult. Fem.*)	—

Table to show the increasing popularity of virginity (cont'd)

Author	Date	References to I Cor. 7	References to I Cor. 7 25, 36–8
Origen	C 2–3	*	*
Cyprian and pseudo-Cyprian	C 3	22	—
Athanasius	C 3–C 4	*	*
Basil of Caesarea	C 4	*	*
Ambrose	C 4	*	*
Jerome	C 4–C 5	*	*

Note. Readers should take this table as a general guide. *, Uncounted.

Complete sections or works on either continence or virginity	Remarks
No complete work on continence or virginity	Advocates asceticism
Cyprian 1, pseudo-Cyprian 3 (all on virginity)	No significant use of 1 Cor. 7 in *De Habitu Virg.*
5 on virginity	—
1 complete work on virginity and many other references	—
7 works on virginity	—
2 complete works on virginity (excluding work on the Virgin Mary) and many references	—

SELECTED BIBLIOGRAPHY

ABRAHAMS, I., *Hebrew Ethical Wills*, 2 vols., Philadelphia, 1949.

ACHELIS, H., *Virginea Subintroductae, Ein Beitrag zu 1 Cor. 7*, Leipzig, 1902.

ADAM, *Roman Antiquities*, London, 1835.

ADAMS, M. A., *The Latinity of the Letters of St. Ambrose*, Washington, 1927.

ALLEGRO, J. M., *The Dead Sea Scrolls*, London, 1961.

ALLEN, W. C., *A Critical and Exegetical Commentary on the Gospel According to St. Matthew*, I.C.C., Edinburgh, 1907.

ALTANER, B., *Patrology*, Edinburgh, 1960.

ALTMANN, A., ed., *Biblical Motifs, Studies & Texts*, vol. III, Cambridge, Mass., 1966.

ARMSTRONG, A. H. and MARKUS, R. A., *Christian Faith and Greek Philosophy*, London, 1960.

ARNDT, W. F. and GINGRICH, R. W., *A Greek-English Lexicon of the New Testament and other early Christian Literature*, trans. from W. Bauer's *Griechisch-deutsches Wörterbuch zu den Schriften des Neuen Testaments und der übrigen Urchristlichen Literatur*, 4th ed., Chicago, 1949–1952.

234

ARNOLD, E. V., *Roman Stoicism*, London, 1958.
AUDET, J. P., *La Didache*, Paris, 1958.

BAER, R. A., *Philo's Use of the Categories Male & Female*, Harvard University Dissertation, 1965 (unpublished).
BARDY, G., *La Théologie de l'Eglise de saint Clement de Rome à saint Irenee*, Paris, 1945.
——, *La Vie Spirituelle d'après les pères trois premiers siècles*, Paris, 1935.
BARKER, E., *Greek Political Theory, Plato and his Predecessors*, London, 1918.
BARRETT, C. K., *The Holy Spirit in the Gospel Tradition*, New York, 1947.
——, *The Pastoral Epistles*, Oxford, 1963.
BEASLEY, S. R., *Jesus & the Future*, London, 1956.
BENOIT, P., *Exegèse et Théologie*, 2 vols., Paris, 1961.
BENSON, E. W., *Cyprian, Life and Times*, London, 1897.
BETZ, O., *Der Paraklet*, Leiden, The Netherlands, 1963.
BLACK, M., *An Aramaic Approach to the Gospels & Acts*, London, 1957.
——, *The Scrolls and Christian Origins*, London, 1961.
BLOND, G., *L'hérésie encratite vers la fin du C 4, Science Religieuse Travaux et Recherches*, Paris, 1944 (published during the War as a substitute for *Recherches de Science Religieuse*) pp. 157–210. (This article is an extract from Etudes sur Encratisme heterodoxe pendant les 4 premiers siècles de l'Eglise.)
BONSIRVEN, J., *Les Enseignments de Jesus-Christ*, Paris, 1946.
——, *Le Judaisme Palestinien*, 2 vols., Paris, 1934–1935.
——, *Textes rabbiniques des deux premiers siècles chrétiennes pour servir à l'intelligence du Nouveau Testament*, Rome, 1954.
——, *Théologie de Nouveau Testament*, Paris, 1950.
BRANDON, S. G. F., *The Fall of Jerusalem and the Christian Church*, London, 1957.
BRIGHTMAN, F. E., *Liturgies Eastern and Western*, Oxford, 1896.

BROWNE, L., *The Wisdom of Israel*, London, 1960.

BROWNLEE, W. H., *The Meaning of the Qumran Scrolls for the Bible*, New York, 1964.

BRUCE, F. F., *Biblical Exegesis in the Qumran Texts*, London, 1959.

———, ed., *A New Bible Dictionary*, London, 1962.

———, *Second Thoughts on the Dead Sea Scrolls*, London, 1956.

———, *The Spreading Flame*, London, 1961.

BULTMANN, R., *Primitive Christianity*, trans. by R. H. Fuller, Edinburgh, 1960.

———, *Theology of the New Testament*, Eng. trans. by K. Grobel in 2 vols., New York, 1951–1955.

CAMELOT, T. H., *Virgines Christi*, Paris, 1944.

CARMELITAINES, LES ETUDES. *Mystique et Continence*, Paris, n.d.

CARRINGTON, P., *According to Mark*, Cambridge, 1960.

———, *The Early Church*, vols. I, II, Cambridge, 1957.

———, *The Primitive Christian Calendar*, Cambridge, 1940.

CERFAUX, L., *Christ in the Theology of St. Paul*, Eng. trans. by G. Webb and A. Walker, New York, 1959.

CHADWICK, H., trans. from Origen, *Contra Celsum*, with introduction and notes by Henry Chadwick, Cambridge, 1953.

CHADWICK, H. and OULTON, J. E. I., eds., *Alexandrian Christianity*, London, 1954.

CHARLES, R. H., *Pseudepigrapha*, Oxford, 1964.

COHEN, A., *Everyman's Talmud*, London, 1961.

COURTONNE, Y., *Saint Basil and Hellenism*, Paris, 1934.

CROSS, F. L., *The Ancient Library of Qumran and Modern Biblical Studies*, London, 1958.

———, *The Ancient Library of Qumran*, the Haskell Lectures 1956–1957, London, 1958.

———, ed., *The Jung Codex*, *Three Studies* by H. G. Puech, G. Quispel and W. C. van Unnik, London, 1955.

———, *The Oxford Dictionary of the Early Christian Church*, London, 1958.

CROUZEL, H., *Virginité et Mariage selon Origène*, Paris, 1962.

CRUDEN, A., *Concordance of the Old and New Testaments*, rev. ed., London, 1863.

CULLMAN, O., *Die Neuentdeckten Qumran texte, Neutestamentliche Studien für Rudolf Bultmann*, Berlin, 1954 (Beihefte zur Zeitschrift für die Neutestamentliche Wissenschaft, pp. 35–51).

———, *The Early Church*, trans. by A. J. Higgins, London, 1956.

DANIÉLOU, J., *The Angels and their Mission*, trans. by D. Heimann, Westminster, 1957.

———, *Origène*, Paris, 1948.

———, *Philon d'Alexandrie*, Paris, 1958.

———, *Sacramentum Futuri*, Paris, 1950.

———, *Théologie du Judeo-Christianisme*, Tournai, 1958.

DAUBE, D., *Exodus Pattern in the Bible*, All Souls Studies, Oxford, 1963.

———, *The New Testament and Rabbinic Judaism*, London, 1956.

DAVIDSON, A. B., *Hebrew Syntax*, Edinburgh, 1954.

DAVIES, J. G., *Daily Life in the Early Church*, London, 1952.

DAVIES, W. D. and DAUBE, D., *The Background of the New Testament and its Eschatology* (Studies in Honor of C. H. Dodd), Cambridge, 1956.

DAVIES, W. D., *Christian Origins and Judaism*, London, 1962.

———, *Paul and Rabbinic Judaism*, London, 1962.

———, *The Setting of the Sermon on the Mount*, Cambridge, 1964.

DENZINGER, *Enchiridion Symbolorum*, Barcelona, 1948.

DE VAUX, R., *Ancient Israel*, trans. by J. McHugh, London, 1961.

DIBELIUS, M., *Der Hirt des Hermas*, Tubingen, 1923.

———, *From Tradition to Gospel*, London, 1934.

DILL, S., *Roman Society from Nero to Marcus Aurelius*, New York, 1958.

238   *A Trilogy on Wisdom and Celibacy*

——, *Roman Society in the Last Century of the Western Empire*, New York, 1958.

DODD, C. H., *The Parables of the Kingdom*, rev.ed., New York, 1961.

DORESSE, J., *Les livres secretes des gnostique d'Egypte*, Paris, 1958; also E.T. *The Secret Books of the Egyptian Gnostics*, London, 1960.

DUCHESNE, L., *Early History of the Christian Church*, vol. I–III, Paris, 1924.

DUDDEN, F. H., *Life and Times of Ambrose*, 2 vols., Oxford, 1935.

EHRLICH, E. L., *Die Kultsymbolik im alten Testament und in Nachbiblischen Judentum*, Stuttgart, 1959.

ELMSLIE, W. A. L., *the Mishna on Idolatria, Aboda Zara*, Cambridge Texts and Studies, vol. 8, no. 2, Cambridge, 1911.

ELTESTER, W., ed., *Neutestamentliche Studien für Rudolf Bultmann*, Berlin, 1957.

EPSTEIN, I. M., *Marriage Laws in the Bible and Talmud*, New York, 1942.

——, *Sex Laws and Customs in Judaism*, New York, 1948.

EVANS, E., *Tertullian's Treatise, Adversus Praxean*, London, 1948.

——, *Tertullian's Treatise, De Resurrectione*, London, n.d.

FAGGIOTTO, A., *La diaspora catafrigia*, Rome, 1924.

——, *L'eresia dei Frigi*, Rome, 1924.

FARRER, A., *A Rebirth of Images*, Glasgow, 1949.

——, *The Revelation of St. John the Divine*, Oxford, 1964.

FEHRLE, E., *Kultische Keuscheit im Alterum*, Giessen, 1910.

FINEGAN, J., *Light from the Ancient Past*, Oxford, 1959.

FINKELSTEIN, I., *Akiba, Scholar, Saint and Martyr*, New York, 1936.

——, *The Pharisees*, 2 vols., The Jewish Publication Society, Philadelphia, 1962.

FUNK, R. W., *A Greek Grammar of the New Testament and*

Other Early Christian Literature, rev. by F. Blass and A. Debrunner, Cambridge, 1961.

GARTNER, B., *The Temple and the Community in Qumran and the New Testament*, Cambridge, 1965.

————, *The Theology of the Gospel of Thomas*, London, 1961.

GASTER, T. H., *The Dead Sea Scrolls*, rev. ed., New York, 1964.

GEORGI, D., *Die Gegner des Paulos im 2. Korintherbrief*, Neirkirchen-Vluyn, 1964.

GERHARDSSON, B., *Memory and Manuscript*, Uppsala, Sweden, 1961.

GINZBERG, I., *Legends of the Jews*, Eng. trans. by H. Szold in 7 vols., Philadelphia, 1942 (these volumes were consulted for me by two colleagues while they were on leave in Britain).

GLASSON, T. F., *Greek Influence in Jewish Eschatology*, London, 1961.

GOESSLER, L., *Plutarchs Gedanken über Die Ehe*, Zurich, 1966.

GOODSPEED, E. J., *Index Patristicum sive clavis patrum apostolicorum operum*, Leipzig, 1907.

GRANT, R. M., *Gnosticism and Early Christianity*, Columbia, 1959.

————, *The Secret Sayings of Jesus According to the Gospel of St. Thomas*, London, 1960.

GROLLENBERG, L. H., *Atlas of the Bible*, Edinburgh, 1957.

GUILDING, A., *The Fourth Gospel and Jewish Worship*, Oxford, 1960.

GUILLAUMONT, PUECH and QUISPEL, *The Gospel According to St. Thomas*, trans. from the Coptic, London, 1959.

HALDAR, A., *Association of Cult Prophets among the Ancient Semites*, 1945.

HANDFORD, S. A., *The Latin Subjunctive*, London, 1947.

HANSON, R. P. C., *Allegory and Event*, London, 1959.

————, *Tradition in the Early Church*, Philadelphia, 1962.

HARRIS, W. B., *The First Epistles of St. Paul to the Corinthians*, Mysore City, India, 1958.

HASTINGS, J., ed., *Dictionary of the Bible*, 5 vols., Edinburgh, 1898–1902.

HEDLAND, M. F. and ROWLEY, H. H., *Atlas of the Early Christian World*, London, 1958.

HERFORD, R. T., *The Pharisees*, Boston, 1962.

HERING, J., *The First Epistle of St. Paul to the Corinthians*, London, 1962.

ISAKSSON, A., *Marriage and Ministry in the New Temple*, Lund, 1965.

JASTROW, M., *Dictionary of Talmud Babli, Jerusahalmi Midrashic Literature and Tarqumin*, New York, 1950.

JEREMIAS, J., *Infant Baptism in the First Four Centuries*, trans. by D. Cairns, London, 1960.

———, *The Parables of Jesus*, trans. by S. H. Hooke, New York, 1963.

JACKSON-FOAKES and LAKE-KIRSOPP, *The Beginnings of Christianity*, vols. I–V, London, 1922.

JOHNSON, A. R., *The Cultic Prophet in Ancient Israel*, Cardiff, 1944.

JOYCE, G. H., *Christian Marriage*, New York, 1933.

KANIECHKA, M. S., *Vita Sancti Ambrosii, Mediolanensis Episcopi, a Paulino eius notario ad beatum Augustinum conscripta*, Washington, 1928.

KIEFER, O., *Sexual Life in Ancient Rome*, London, 1963.

KILPATRICK, G. D., *The Origins of the Gospel According to St. Matthew*, Oxford, 1946.

KITTEL, G., *Theologisches Wörterbuch zum Neuen Testament*, Stuttgart, 1957.

KLASSEN, W. and SMYDER, G. F., *Current Issues in New Testament Interpretation*, London, 1962.

KLAUSNER, J., *From Jesus to Paul*, New York, 1943.

————, *The Messianic Idea in Israel*, London, 1956.

KOCH, H., *Cyprianische Untersuchungen*, Bonn, 1926.

KOSCHAKER, *Marriage among the Indo-Germans*, n.d.

KOSMALA, H., *Hebraer-Essener-Christen-Studien zur vorge-schichte der frühchristlichen verkundigung*, Leiden, 1959.

KRAUSS, S., *Talmudische Archaologie*, reprint, Berlin, 1966.

KUHN, C., *The Prophets of Israel*, Edinburgh, 1960.

LABRIOLLE, P. de, *La Crise Montaniste*, Paris, 1913.

————, *Les Sources de l'histoire du Montanisme*, Paris, 1913.

LAGRANGE, M. J., *L'Evangile de Jesus Christ*, Paris, 1954.

————, *L'Evangile selon St. Matthieu*, Paris, 1948.

LAMPE and WOOLCOMBE, *Essays in Typology*, London, 1956.

LAWSON, H. J. and OULTON, J. E., *Eusebius of Caesarea*, trans. with introduction and notes, vols. I and II, London, 1954.

LAWSON, J., *The Biblical Theology of St. Irenaeus*, London, 1948.

LEANEY, A. R. C., *Rule of the Community*, London, 1966.

LEANEY, A. R. C., POSEN, J., HANSON, R. P. C., *A Guide to the Scrolls*, London, 1958.

LEANEY, A. R. C., *From the Judaean Caves*, Wallington, Eng., 1961.

————, *The Rule of the Community*, London, 1965.

LEBRETON, J. and ZEILLER, J., *The History of the Primitive Church*, 4 vols., London, 1942–1947.

LEGRAND, L., *The Biblical Doctrine of Virginity*, London, 1963.

LEON, H., *The Jews of Ancient Rome*, Philadelphia, 1960.

LE SAINT, W. P., trans., Tertullian, *Treatises on Penance*, A. C. W., London, 1959.

————, trans., Tertullian's *Treatise on Marriage and Remarriage*, Ancient Christian Writers, London, 1951.

LEWIS, C. T. and CHARLES SHORT, *A Latin Dictionary*, Oxford, 1890.

LICHT, H., *Sexual Life in Ancient Greece*, London, 1956.

LIDDELL, H. G. and ROBERT SCOTT, *A Greek-English Lexicon*, a new ed. rev. and augmented by Henry S. Jones, reprint, Oxford, 1953.

LIGHTFOOT, J. B., *The Apostolic Fathers*, vols. I–III, London, 1889.

MCNEILE, A. H., *The Gospel According to St. Matthew*, London, 1961.

MALONE, E., *The Monk and the Martyr*, Washington, 1950.

MANNIX, S., *S. Ambrosii, De Obitu Theodosii*, Washington, 1925.

MANSON, T. W., *Ethics and the Gospel*, Bristol, Eng., 1962.

——, *The Sayings of Jesus*, London, 1961.

——, *Studies in the Gospels and Epistles*, Manchester, Eng., 1962.

MARTINEZ, F., *L'Asceticisme Chrétien pendant les trois premiers siècles de l'église*, Paris, 1913 (*Etudes de Théologie Historique*).

MESSENGER, E. C., *The Mystery of Sex and Marriage*, 3 vols., London, 1938.

MILLAR-BURROWS, *Light on the Dead Sea Scrolls*, London, 1956.

——, *More Light on the Dead Sea Scrolls, New Scrolls and New Interpretations*, London, 1958.

MINGANA, A., Woodbrooke·Studies, *Editions and Translations of Christian Documents in Syriac and Garshumi*, with introduction by Rendel Harris, Fasc. 2, (i) *A New Jeremiah Apocryphon*, pp. 329–398; (ii) *A New Life of John the Baptist*.

MONTEFIORE, C. G. and LOEWE, H., eds., *A Rabbinic Anthology*, London, 1938.

MOORE, G. F., *Judaism of the First Centuries of the Christian Era*, 3 vols., Cambridge, Mass., 1954.

MOWRY, L., *The Dead Sea Scrolls and the Early Church*, Chicago, 1961.

MUNCK, J., *Paul and the Salvation of Mankind*, London, 1959.

NEMECEK, O., *Virginity, Pre-Nuptial Rites and Rituals*, New York, 1958.

NETTLESHIP, R. L., *Lectures on the Republic of Plato*, London, 1920.

NEUSNER, J., *A Life of Rabban Yohanan ben Zaccai*, Leiden, the Netherlands, 1962.

NOVECK, S., ed., *Great Jewish Personalities*, London, 1962.

NUGENT, M. R., *Portrait of the Consecrated Woman in Greek Christian Literature of the First Four Centuries*, Washington, 1941.

OESTERLEY, W. O. E. and BOX, G. H., *A Short Survey of the Literature of Rabbinical and Mediaeval Judaism*, London, 1920.

PARRY, R. St. JOHN, *The First Epistle to the Corinthians*, Cambridge, 1957.

PAULY, A., *Real-Encyclopedia der classischen Alterthumwissenschaft*, ed. by G. Wissowa, Stuttgart, 1893.

PETERSON, E., *Frühkirche, Judentum und Gnosis*, Freiburg, 1959.

PFEIFFER, R. H., *Introduction to the Old Testament*, London, 1959.

PHILONENKO, M., *Le Testament de Job et les Therapeutes*, Semitica, viii, Paris, 1958.

PLOEG, J. van den, *The Excavations at Qumran*, trans. by Kevin Smyth, S. J., London, 1958.

PLUMPE, J. C., *Mater Ecclesia*, Washington, 1943.

RABIN, C., *Qumran Studies*, Oxford, 1957.

——, *The Zadokite Documents*, 2 nd. ed. Oxford, 1958.

RAMSAY, W. M., *Cities and Bishoprics of Phrygia*, Oxford, 1899.

RICHARDSON, A., *A Theological Word Book of the Bible*, London, 1957.

RIESENFELD, H., *The Gospel Tradition and its Beginnings*, London, 1941.

ROBERTS, A. and J. DONALDSON, *Ante-Nicene Fathers*, New York, 1890.

ROBERTSON and PLUMMER, *First Corinthians*, I.C.C., Edinburgh, 1958.

ROTH, C., *The Historical Background of the Dead Sea Scrolls*, Oxford, 1958.

ROTH, C., ed., *Jewish Art*, London, 1961.

ROWLEY, H. H., *Jewish Apocalyptic and the Dead Sea Sect*, London, 1957.

————, ed., *The Old Testament in Modern Study*, Oxford, 1951.

————, *The Zadokite Fragments and the Dead Sea Scrolls*, Oxford, 1952.

SCHEPELERN, W., *Der Montanism und die Phrygienne Kulte*, Tubingen, 1929.

SCHOLEM, G., *Jewish Gnosticism Merkabab Mysticism and Tulmudic Tradition*, New York, 1960.

————, *Major Trends in Jewish Mysticism*, New York, 1941.

————, *On the Kabbalah and its Symbolism*, trans. by R. Manheim, New York, 1965.

SELWYN, E. G., *The First Epistle of St. Peter*, London, 1958.

SIMON, M., *Recherches d'Histoire Judeo-Chretienne*, Paris, 1962.

SKINNER, J., *Commentary on Genesis*, I.C.C., Edinburgh, 1961.

SPANNEUT, M., *Le Stoicisme des Pères de l'église*, Paris, 1957.

STENDAHL, K., *The School of St. Matthew and its use of the Old Testament*, Uppsala, Sweden, 1954.

————, ed., *The Scrolls and the New Testament*, New York, 1957.

STRACK, H. L., *Introduction to the Talmud and the Midrash*, New York, 1959.

STREETER, B. H., *The Four Gospels*, London, 1926.

SUTCLIFFE, E. F., *The Monks of Qumran*, London, 1960.

VAN GOUDOEVER, J., *Biblical Calendars*, 2nd. ed., Leiden, the Netherlands, 1961.

VERMES, G., *The Dead Sea Scrolls in English*, London, 1962.

————, "Essenes, Therapeutai, Qumran," *Durham University Journal*, vol. 52, no. 3, ns. vol. 21 (June 3, 1960).

————, *Scripture and Tradition in Judaism*, Leiden, the Netherlands, 1961.

VIZMANOS, B., *Las virgenes christianas de la iglesia primitiva*, Madrid, 1949.

WASZINK, J. H., *De Anima* with trans. and commentary, Amsterdam, 1933.

WEBER, M., *Ancient Judaism*, London, 1952.

WENGER, A. A. A., *Archives de l'Orient Chretien*, 5, L'Assomption de la T.S. Vierge dans la tradition Byzantine du 6 au 10 siècle, Etudes et Documents. Publié avec le concours du Centre National de la Recherche Scientifique, Institut Française d'Etudes Byzantines, Paris, 1955.

WHITTAKER, M., ed., *The Shepherd of Hermas*, Berlin, 1957.

WIEDER, N., *The Judean Scrolls and Karaism*, London, 1962.

WIKENHAUSER, A., *New Testament Introduction*, Edinburgh, 1958.

WILCOX, V., *The Image of God in Sex*, London, 1953.

WILLIAMS, N. P., *The Ideas of Original Sin*, London, 1927.

WILSON, R., *The Gnostic Problem*, London, 1958.

YADIN, Y., *Art of Warfare in Biblical Lands*, London, 1964.

———, *The Scroll of the War of the Sons of Light against the Sons of Darkness*, Oxford, 1962.

YOUNG, R., *Analytical Concordance to the Holy Bible*, London, 1953.

ZIMMERLI, W. and JEREMIAS, J., *The Servant of God*, London, 1957.

SUBJECT INDEX*

* The indices were compiled by Piero L. Frattin, Department of Theology, University of Notre Dame.

NAME INDEX

SCRIPTURE INDEX

254   *A Trilogy on Wisdom and Celibacy*